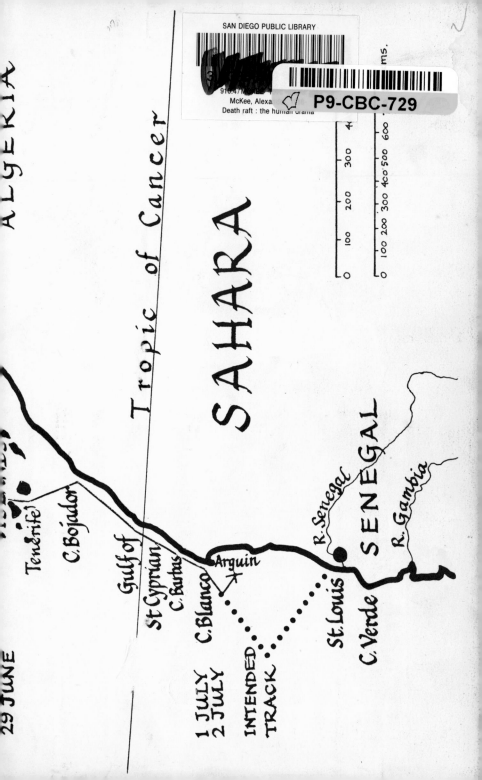

ALGERIA

Tropic of Cancer

SAHARA

SENEGAL

Tenérife)

C. Bojador

Gulf of

St Cyprian
C. Barbas

C. Blanco

Arguin

St. Louis

C. Verde

R. Senegal

R. Gambia

29 JUNE

1 JULY
2 JULY

INTENDED
TRACK

100    200    300    4
0    100    200    300   400  500  600

# DEATH
# RAFT

## Other books by Alexander McKee

Caen: Anvil of Victory
Vimy Ridge
Strike from the Sky
The Friendless Sky
From Merciless Invaders
The Golden Wreck
Black Saturday
The Coal-Scuttle Brigade
The Race for the Rhine Bridges
King Henry VIII's Mary Rose

*The Raft of the Medusa* by Géricault, Louvre, Paris

# DEATH RAFT

The Human Drama of
the *Medusa* Shipwreck

ALEXANDER McKEE

Charles Scribner's Sons
New York

Library of Congress Cataloging in Publication Data

McKee, Alexander, 1918-
 Death raft.

 Includes index.
  1. Méduse (Frigate)   2. Shipwrecks—Senegal.
 I. Title.
 G530.M5M32 1976       966'.1       76-40932
 ISBN 0-684-14809-9

1 3 5 7 9 11 13 15 17 19  V/C  20 18 16 14 12 10 8 6 4 2

PRINTED IN THE UNITED STATES OF AMERICA

# CONTENTS

# 1

# Landlocked

## *(June 1816)*

The girl who ran impulsively into the fields to gather blooms was saying good-bye to France. Picking a few of the red poppies and the blue cornflowers, she hurried back to join her family on the road, overcome by a feeling of sadness. Perhaps it was only a brief homesickness, but afterwards she thought it might have been a premonition. Like many others making their way toward Rochefort that day, she was destined to witness the most horrible sea tragedy of the century, possibly the most terrible that has ever taken place.

It was June 12, 1816, less than a year after the downfall of Napoleon Bonaparte at Waterloo. The fate of the *Medusa*, both her original mission and her terrible end, flowed as a direct consequence of that critical moment when Napoleon's Guard recoiled and the British bayonets began to move forward, the flanking Prussians driving deep into the ruined French army. French power, which had dominated Europe for twenty years, had been humbled. Monarchy, which France had twice rejected, was once more imposed upon her victorious foes.

The French colony of Senegal in West Africa was to be handed back by its English captors as part of the peace settlement. The *Medusa* was to lead a mission to reestablish a French garrison and a French administration on that fly-blown fever coast, still largely unexplored. Charlotte-Adélaïde Picard, the girl who had so impulsively picked the flowers, was one of the 365 passengers to embark in a four-ship convoy consisting of the frigate *Medusa*, the corvette *Echo*, the transport *Loire* and the brig *Argus*. Soldiers of a low-grade battalion under an elderly lieutenant-colonel formed the bulk of the passengers, but there were also engineers, accountants, hospital staff, explorers, bakers, schoolmasters and a solitary gardener. Some had been able to bring their families with them, so that there were twenty-one women and eight children among a largely male throng.

Charlotte was one of about 240 people taking passage in the *Medusa*, the flagship of the little fleet. With her crew of 160, a total of 400 men, women and children were crammed into her wooden hull. One hundred and forty-nine of them were destined never to reach Africa. Of those who did, some did not long survive the terrible ordeal they had undergone.

The girl was the eldest daughter of the official intended to become the new public notary of Saint-Louis, the capital of the colony. She loved him dearly, although he was inclined to be outspokenly critical. M. Picard had great responsibilities already, for he had married a second time. Apart from the two grown-up daughters from his earlier marriage, he was accompanied by his second wife and their much younger children, Laura, Charles and Gustavus. Laura was six years old, and the youngest child was still a baby. He had taken under his care as well a five-year-old boy, Alphonse Fleury, who was Charlotte's cousin and now an orphan. In any emergency this large family would be peculiarly vulnerable.

The family's journey to Rochefort was leisurely, almost a seaside holiday for the children. The town lay on the river Charente, four leagues* from the wide roadstead off the isle of Aix where the ships were waiting. First they had to board a boat to take them down the winding river toward the sea. Contrary winds delayed this craft so much that it was not until the next day that they approached the *Medusa*, which was to be their home for the next few weeks. The journey might take a month, they thought. It was exciting for the children, who had never seen a ship this close. Only their father, an old colonial "hand" who had been working a plantation in Senegal when the English took over, had been to sea before.

Charlotte-Adélaïde, a girl of good education steeped in the mystique of fashionable Paris, found provincial Rochefort monotonous and boring. It was an important naval arsenal, but the *Medusa* herself conveyed no warlike impression. To her, the frigate was just a great hulk of wood.

The *Medusa* was built at Saint Nazaire in 1810. She had been a warship until recently and had carried a battery of forty-four (mostly eighteen-pounder) guns almost entirely on one deck. But she was far from being a battleship, for they had superimposed tiers of guns on two, three or even four decks, and most of those guns were of much heavier metal than the *Medusa* could mount. She was a long, low ship, lightly built—in modern terms a cruiser, designed for scouting, message-carrying, patrol and convoy duties.

She no longer ranked as a warship because, in order

*A league is usually taken to equal 3 miles. But a nautical mile (6,080 feet) is longer than a land mile and a marine league correspondingly so. Most of the witnesses appear to use the French marine league of 5,556 meters because they are referring to distances shown on charts.

to turn a frigate into a troop transport, thirty of her forty-four guns had been removed. What had been the gundeck, running almost the full length of the ship, had been converted into a makeshift accommodation deck for hundreds of passengers, and the real accommodation deck below was too near the waterline to mount guns. A frigate had far more space per man than any other warship of the time, which was the reason they were so often temporarily converted into fast transports.

It was true also that the *Medusa* did appear clumsy when seen close by, with her bluff bows and wide, square stern and hull with its oddly inward-sloping sides. Contemporary pictures by marine artists hardly hint at this aspect of the "wooden walls," but a frigate contemporary with and almost identical to the *Medusa* is still afloat to show what Mlle. Picard meant. This vessel surprised everyone when in 1972 she had to be towed away for repairs; in spite of her apparent clumsiness, "she slipped through the water like a racing yacht." Below the surface, her lines were as fine as her upperworks were crude. The Parisian girl could not appreciate what a fast ship the *Medusa* really was, but that part which she could see she described with admirably blunt honesty.

The first impressions which the Picard family received when they boarded were disconcerting; nothing was ready and no preparations had been made to receive them. Including the baby, they all had to find places for the night on the bare planks, surrounded by their luggage like refugees. Not until next day was a berth made available "near the main deck." Probably temporary cabins were erected. There was so little headroom that only the children could move about freely without fear of cracking their skulls on the deck beams above. The centers of the decks were crowded with all sorts of interesting objects, such as capstans, bitts for running rigging and riding bitts for the anchor cables, and were cut by hatchways and companionways (one for cargo, the other for people) which were a standing temptation to the more daring children. Even with the gunports and hatches open, the sunlight was subdued and uneven, lending an air of shadowy mystery to the ladders which led farther down to the darkness of the hold below the waterline, where the powder magazines were placed. There was treasure down there—three barrels full of gold coins amounting to 90,000 francs and destined for the treasury of the colony.

The Picard family had plenty of time to get used to their new floating home, to the constant movement of the deck underfoot, the sounds of wind and water against the hull, a continual background of noise, now subdued, now insistent. Day after day the *Medusa* and her consorts swung at their anchors within sight of the green fields of France, for the great roadstead between the isles of Oleron and Ré is almost land-locked, and contrary winds penned the ships as if in a trap.

A trap it was in truth. It was late in the year for a voyage to West Africa, even had all been well with the little expedition. On June 15, one officer was sufficiently worried to make an entry in his ship's log "for the record." He was the commander of the cor-vette *Echo*, Frigate-Captain François-Marie Cornette de Vénancourt. He noted: "We have already wasted too much time . . . we shall arrive in a season very much advanced. I shall be able to serve on that coast for only a short while. This will be inefficient, espe-cially in view of the unique nautical description with which I have been supplied by the Minister of Marine! As for the charts enclosed with the Hydrographie

Française, they are so imperfect that it is hardly possible to use them. Further, the chronometer No. 131, issued to me at Rochefort, is decidedly erratic.* However, with such poor means and in such an unsuitable season, I shall do my very best."

Although he had emigrated after the Revolution, de Vénancourt was an experienced seaman, as his contemptuously critical assessment of the navigational and hydrographic information shows. But he had a black mark against him in the French navy and had had to wait twelve years before obtaining a worthwhile position. And now he had been passed over for command of the whole convoy in favor of an officer who, although of equal rank, was far less suited to command a single ship, let alone a squadron.

The reason for the black mark on his record went to the heart of the trouble with the entire expedition, which in turn reflected the divisions within France herself. While in exile, de Vénancourt had served as interpreter on the British battleship *Queen Charlotte*, Lord Howe's flagship in the first major sea clash of the Revolutionary Wars, which the English refer to as "The Glorious First of June," 1784. The French know it as "the Fight on the Thirteenth of Prairial" and remember the engagement chiefly for the heroic revolutionary legend of the battleship *Le Venguer du Peuple*, which fought until she sank, supposedly with all hands, supposedly after sinking three British ships. She did fight well but there were many survivors, and one of them was now commanding another ship of the Senegal convoy. He was Lieutenant Auguste-Marie Gicquel des Touches, captain of the transport *Loire*. Now aged thirty-three, des Touches had served in the French navy from the time that he was ten years old.

*Roughly, an error of four seconds in the watch may result in a miscalculation of one mile in a ship's position.

Six of those years had been spent in an English prison, following the battle of Trafalgar in 1805. He had been awarded the Legion of Honor for bravery.

The naval command of the expedition had been given to Frigate-Captain Hugues Duroy de Chaumareys, who was also the captain of the *Medusa*. At the time of the Revolution he had been a lieutenant and had faced the same choice as de Vénancourt—exile or execution. He had chosen to emigrate and had joined the Royalist forces fighting with the English against the Revolution. In 1795 he had taken part in the landing at Quiberon in support of a Royalist insurrection which ended in failure and massacre. He had become something of a hero by escaping after capture and getting safely back to England, where he wrote a book about it.

Genuinely proud of his family name, he affected a dandified air of gallantry, particularly toward women, which was fashionable then among young aristocrats and the gentry. He had good reasons for not wanting to return to France under Robespierre and did not go back until 1804, whether from homesickness or because he thought that the Bourbons had lost their chance is not known. He applied for the quiet post of customs officer at Bellac, where he waited out the tumultuous last years of the Napoleonic Empire. His dislike of the upstart Corsican artilleryman was known to the secret police, who kept him under routine surveillance, but without result.

As soon as Napoleon abdicated in 1814, de Chaumareys moved. On May 3, Louis XVIII was king again, and on May 12 de Chaumareys obtained an audience with the monarch's brother. He produced the records of his naval service and asked for an appointment. It was the greatest mistake he ever made. He was now fifty-three and had not been to sea for twenty-five years. Then he had been only a lieutenant. He had never commanded a ship, let alone a squadron of ships. But he yearned to make a name for himself and an inordinate vanity blinded de Chaumareys to the reality of his position, which would have been difficult enough even had he, like de Vénancourt, possessed all the necessary qualifications and experience.

Veterans of the Nile and Trafalgar were not likely to take too kindly to a customs officer being set in command over them, even had there been no suppressed hostility between the largely Republican officers and the émigré aristocrats. But still, de Chaumareys would probably have managed well enough had he enlisted their aid. However, that was not the way of the new captain. Lieutenant des Touches of the *Loire* recalled his first meeting with de Chaumareys: "He was a courteous gentleman, but not very serious-minded and he seemed to find it natural that I would be his obedient servant. First I made him understand that I was myself as true a gentleman as he was, and that I did not think that I had done wrong in serving my country during the time he had chosen to go into exile. Then, he changed his attitude toward me. This was quite characteristic of him. Was it just a gentlemanly reflex or did it show a basic lack of character? The latter, I think, for it seems that in spite of his 'show-off' manner de Chaumareys was easily manipulated, like all cocksure fellows."

He was also sensitive and hesitant below the debonair surface assurance and, after he had read his instructions from the Ministry, deeply worried. There would be no opportunity for heroic deeds with the Senegal convoy, but rather a fair chance of making a disastrous error and being wrecked. He was warned that the coast of West Africa ranked as one of the least known and most imperfectly charted areas in the world. In 1816 that was saying a good deal. The technical means of establishing an accurate position for any feature on the globe's surface were poor, particularly when the observation point was a ship. Little survey work had been done by governments, and real hydrographic departments had only just begun to emerge from the old chart and map depots. Their charts were often based on early and erratic observations taken from commercial charts, which were not to be relied on for distant waters.

The principal chart given to de Chaumareys was just such a one. It had been compiled by Jacques Nicolas Bellin (1703–1772), the first hydrographer of the French navy. The Ministry warned de Chaumareys to navigate with caution and not to be surprised if he found himself well to the north or south of a cape which, from his own calculations, ought to be abeam. The positions were wrong and so were the distances given. It was vital that he use the sounding lead often, noting depths and types of seabed, in order to avoid running into shallow water unexpectedly. In particular, he was warned to be careful of the Arguin Bank, a vast uncharted sandbank stretching many miles out from the coast north of Senegal. In this area he should start to sound while still in water too deep for the sounding lead to reach and then, when the sounding lead did touch bottom, immediately alter course out to sea away from the hazard.

To the inexperienced de Chaumareys this frank admission of the deficiencies of his charts was unnerving. It had to be added to the hazards presented by the inaccuracies of the only navigational instruments available at the time, augmented by the fact that no ship, let along a wall-sided sailing vessel, actually goes in the direction it is steered. Almost always, it is offset to one side or the other by the forces of wind and current, whose combined effect is hard to estimate with precision. The cumulative errors that were possible horrified de Chaumareys. Already, he could see himself aground on that notorious sandbank. Its fatal reputation began to exert a hypnotic lure on him. Its terror was that of the unknown, for the bank was not outlined on any chart. Whereas in other areas the chart was busy with figures and symbols which meant that someone had been there before him, the section for the Arguin Bank was blank. There the soundings ceased. No one knew where that bank ended and deep sea began.

When the worried captain discussed the matter with des Touches, a Breton who had been to sea since he was ten, the veteran laughed at his fears. Anyone who took a big ship anywhere near it would be a fool, des Touches told de Chaumareys. Just give it a wide berth, leave it off your route altogether. He even offered to take over the navigation at that point. This would be easy to do, for the four ships were ordered to keep together in convoy and as the *Loire* was by far the slowest of the four, the others would have no difficulty in following the course she set.

Mellowed by their rapid reversal of roles, the lieutenant wrote down for the captain a summary of his navigational advice. It was pleasing to have his genuine superiority so quickly recognized. De Chaumareys could have used this human trait with most of his officers, and if he had done so no one would ever have heard of the *Medusa* or, for that matter, of de Chaumareys.

From the conflicting advice and instructions received at Rochefort, de Chaumareys chose the worst possible route to Senegal. He claimed that it was in accordance with instructions from the Ministry. All the practical seamen, like des Touches and de Vénan-court, understood that it is not the sea which is a danger to ships, it is the shore. The safe route to Senegal was out of sight of land from beginning to end. That is, the ships would sail westward past Cape Finisterre until they were far out in the Atlantic and then turn south on a track which would keep them well clear of, successively, the Gibraltar current, the islands of Madeira and Porto Santo, the dangerous Ca-nary Island group and the barren Sahara coast with its shallows and sandbanks extending well offshore. A final turn when opposite the estimated position of Saint-Louis in Senegal would then bring them straight in to a gently shelving coast, so that even if there was an error it was likely to be perceived in time.

The route decided on by de Chaumareys required hardly any navigation; it was little more than glori-fied map-reading. It included a close approach to all the hazards which could possibly be encountered. All that could be said for this procedure was that it would give plenty of navigational "fixes" from recog-nized landmarks. There was no danger of actually getting lost, provided it was understood that the land-marks might not be exactly where they were thought to be and that the position of the ship itself would be merely an estimate. The hazards lay in an approach at night or in bad visibility from one inaccurate position to another inaccurate position, and, above all, in the fact that the West African coast for much of the time would be a lee shore. For a vessel dependent entirely on the wind, this route involved quite unnecessary risks. Although a competent and cautious seaman could manage it well enough, given good weather, even so he would be well advised to allow a very great margin for error when off the Arguin Bank.

Left to himself, de Chaumareys might have listened

to the experienced seaman and taken the longer but much safer route far out to sea. But he was not really the leader of the expedition, for he had a V.I.P. aboard the *Medusa*. This was Colonel Julien-Désiré Schmaltz, designated commander-in-chief and governor of Senegal, a mysterious personality who soon had de Chaumareys under his thumb. He was of German origin but his mother was half-Irish. He had been to the Military Academy but after the Revolution had gone into business most successfully. The business involved shipping and in 1811 he was called up for the navy. He was taken prisoner almost at once, when a British expedition beat a French expedition to Batavia by a short head. Oddly, he had his first glimpse of the *Medusa* then, for she was with the French squadron when it turned back off Surabaja.

The English summarily returned him two years later as unfit for active service, and he vanished from sight until the return of the Bourbons, when suddenly honors, rank and rewards were lavished on him. He was garrison commander, under Admiral Linois, of a town in Guadeloupe when Napoleon returned from Elba, and as Guadeloupe declared for the emperor, Schmaltz again had his career interrupted by an English seaborne invasion. Linois was accused of treason but Schmaltz courageously wrote a memoir in his defense. He was now a governor himself (when the English would be pleased to allow it) on an extremely high scale of salary and expenses. He was taking his wife and daughter out with him and one suspects that his colonial and business experience fitted him for his new post.

But he was a colonel who was no real colonel and may have been a Royalist all along, even when serving Napoleon. His nature was devious and complex, but his self-confidence—amounting to tactlessness—was absolute, unlike that of the apparently cocksure de Chaumareys. He was a very strong-willed, dominant personality and difficult for de Chaumareys to argue with, for part of what he said, even if amounting only to 20 percent, was undoubtedly true. He gave the overwhelming impression of being gifted less with real intelligence than with a remarkable flair for promoting his own interests.

During the long days while the convoy lay idling in the roadstead for want of a favorable wind, Schmaltz was pushing, pushing, pushing for speed. The route was for de Chaumareys to decide, but his uncertainty could not withstand this continual driving demand for efficiency. The safe and easy route was also apparently the longest. Against it, Schmaltz could argue the minister's warning concerning their late start and the dangers of being caught by the storm season. De Chaumareys could not deny this, but he must have felt uneasy as he acquiesced, feeling perhaps that Schmaltz himself was driving the *Medusa* toward the Arguin Bank. Schmaltz was in an excellent position to "needle" everyone, for he had had access to the personal files of all the officers while he had been visiting the Ministry of Marine. Perhaps this was how he prevailed at last over de Chaumareys. Not only would they take the shortest route but they would disregard the Ministry's instructions to proceed in convoy, given partly for safety reasons but also in order to arrive together at Senegal as an imposing squadron rather than as four straggling ships appearing separately.

De Chaumareys could not deny that convoy was laggard. They would be tied to the speed of des Touches's transport, the *Loire*, a slow ship made slower by her aging canvas. The minister had ordered them to keep together but no doubt Schmaltz could argue speciously that this instruction contradicted the equal warning concerning the lateness of the season and the necessity for speed. In any event, de Chaumareys now openly declared, as if he had thought of it for himself, that he had no intention of waiting for any ship which lagged behind. So the die was cast. The ships would risk the hazards of the short route and hug the unknown and dangerous coast of Africa right down to the Arguin Bank. And they would risk it separately and alone, not as a united squadron able to aid each other.

That was the plan. But des Touches was too wily a seaman to take foolish risks. He took the *Loire* well out on the route they all should have taken and arrived safely, although his vessel was a very poor sailer. De Vénancourt, with the fast corvette *Echo*, stayed with the *Medusa* as long as he dared and then escaped under the cover of darkness at the critical moment. Lieutenant Léon Henry de Parnajon, commanding the little brig *Argus*, which had a much shallower draught than the *Medusa*, nevertheless also kept well clear of that notorious coast where the furnace of the desert sucked in the sea winds and the ships that sought to use them.

# 2

# A Passage to Senegal
## *(June 17 to July 2)*

At last, on June 17, the winds blew favorably for the
small squadron waiting in the roadstead. The passengers, few of whom had been to sea before, watched the
men laboring at the capstans to haul in the wet,
slimy anchor cables while others aloft prepared to set
the sails. As the huge bow anchors rose dripping from
the water the canvas was sheeted home and the
vessels began to move slowly. This takes a long time
and a large sailing ship covers many miles before all
the sails are out and drawing properly. And all these
ships were of different types with varying perform-
ances and handling characteristics. It was also the start
of a voyage, when crews are not fully worked up. They
had not yet settled down into a routine which soon
would become almost automatic, requiring a minimum of commands.

Once the ships did begin to move they were steadier
than a modern powered vessel because of the balanc-
ing effect of the wind on the sails; they had a more
natural motion. Nor could they be brutally bashed
into a head sea, with resulting jarring shocks to the
hull and the passengers' stomachs. This was also their
weakness, as was demonstrated almost at once. Before the squadron could escape from the wind trap of

the roadstead they were brought almost to a standstill because the ebbing current which was slowly helping them out died away and the flood tide began to pour in.

Then the wind shifted again and the ships were now in danger of being forced down onto a notorious reef called Les Roches Bonnes. They had to tack across the wind to avoid destruction, thus losing still more time. The weather was breaking up and there was a gale on the way.

At midnight Charlotte Picard was still awake, listening to the shock of the waves smashing against the timbers of the *Medusa*. Above the roar of broken water and the creaking of straining woodwork sounded the high-pitched howling of the gusts through the rigging mixed with the clatter of blocks and spars. Unable to sleep because of an uneasy presentiment of misfortune for the frigate and now thoroughly alarmed, believing that the moment had come, the girl ran up on deck. There she paused in horror at the scene.

The laboring vessel was almost broadside to the gale. Out of the night came marching rank on rank of great combers. They burst in fury over the bulwarks, white water washing along the cambered deck and roaring out of the scuppers back into the sea. One moment the vessel was lifted half up to the lowering sky and the next she was wallowing down in the trough. Each shock seemed to split open her side while high above, the sails bellied and cracked and protested noisily.

Gazing around in desperate hope of succor, the girl noticed the other three ships of the squadron, sometimes half hidden by water, sometimes rising lazily on the crests of the combers. *Echo, Loire, Argus*—they were all there and all bearing sail. Evidently, there was no danger at all, as long as there was no land near. Much comforted, Charlotte went below again to rest.

June 18, 1816 was the first anniversary of the Battle of Waterloo. A year ago this morning two great armies had faced each other across half a dozen fields in Belgium and the day's end had riven French society. Those who had been up went down, and those who had been down had climbed up again, uneasily. The lines of division, the stresses, still showed, not only in France but in that part of French society which was afloat in the *Medusa*.

It seems that a number of officers were hostile to de Chaumareys from the first moment he came aboard; indeed it would be remarkable if they had not resented his appointment and the cocksure manner in which he assumed it. Either from original prejudice or because he sensed hostility, de Chaumareys did not trust his second-in-command and, ignoring him, turned elsewhere for advice. The first lieutenant of the *Medusa*, Joseph Pierre André Reynaud, had been a zealous and efficient officer in Napoleon's fleet. His "big ship" experience included service in the seventy-four-gun *Duguay-Trouin*, but Reynaud's real flair was for small commands where initiative was valuable. He could certainly have run the *Medusa* efficiently if de Chaumareys had let him. Instead, de Chaumareys rejected Reynaud—his official second-in-command and a tried and tested officer—in favor, not of another officer, but of a passenger. Indeed, he made a crony of this man, M. Richefort, who had never served in the navy and was not now a member of the crew but who claimed vast seagoing experience. Richefort was a member of the so-called Philanthropic Society of Cape Verde; he was to be employed by the exploration team in Senegal. He had no official status on board the frigate.

While Governor Schmaltz had slight justification for

interesting himself in some aspects of the expedition which were not strictly his concern, his interference was understood if not approved. But for de Chaumareys to degrade his second-in-command, the officer who would take over the ship if anything happened to the captain, by in effect promoting the poser Richefort to that position was to alienate Reynaud irrevocably and to set most of the other officers on the side of the first lieutenant, against their captain. The command structure of the *Medusa* was riven even before the squadron left France. But this situation did not become apparent to everyone on board until several weeks had passed.

The passengers were still settling down to their unaccustomed life. After a disturbed first night in a rough sea, which seemed to them a howling, dangerous storm, their nerves received another shock at ten o'clock the next morning. A chilling cry rang out from the upper deck, followed by the rush and thud of madly stampeding feet overhead. Charlotte Picard ran up on deck to find the whole crew in motion. They were scrambling up the rigging, pouring into the tops and inching out along the yards. Some began to bellow in unison as various teams pulled at various ropes, while others swore or whistled, the officers of the deck roared out above and below and the helmsman roared back. Charlotte detected some actual words, although she could not recall their exact order. Starboard! Larboard! Hoist! Luff! Tack! were among them.

The yards turned, creaking in their pivots, the sails were reset and the ropes tightened, then the raw crew came rushing down on deck faster than they had ascended. The motion of the vessel was now much easier and the noise of wind and sea less violent. The frigate had changed course and the canvas had been trimmed to follow a shift in the direction of the wind. That was all.

Within a week the *Medusa* was clear of the Bay of Biscay and passing Cape Finisterre on the northwest coast of Spain. But only the *Echo* was with her, white with canvas in the attempt to keep up. The clumsy *Loire* and the little *Argus* were out of sight, left clean behind, although the *Medusa* was not carrying her topsails or studding sails. Even so she was making nine knots, or more than two hundred miles a day. De Chaumareys was not waiting for the remainder of his squadron. Bows slicing the water, the frigate raced on among a school of porpoises which plunged and surfaced in their play, the gray blue bodies diving in succession with effortless precision to reappear a minute later still in formation.

Charlotte Picard was by now enjoying sea travel almost as much as she loved journeys by land. But she did not describe, perhaps did not witness, the first tragedy of the voyage. Shouting with excitement and pleasure, passengers and crew alike had crowded to the poop, the bulwarks and the ports to watch the dolphins. Amid the hubbub a cry of distress went largely unheard. A fifteen-year-old sailor lad, leaning too far out of a port to watch the shining display, had fallen overboard and was now clinging to a rope, buffeted by the foaming torrent of the wash, spray silvering his head. For a few moments he hung on, then was plucked from his hold and swept astern into the bubbling wake.

If there had been three ships astern of the *Medusa*, keeping close station, his chances of being picked up would have been better. But only the *Echo* was in sight far-off. A flag signal was run up to the *Medusa*'s masthead and a gun was ordered to be fired to draw the distant corvette's attention. Then it was found that none of the frigate's fourteen guns were loaded. However, the large marker buoy was ready and this was pushed overboard. About a yard (one meter) across, it was topped by a small mast and flag. It would be much easier for the searchers to locate than the head of a swimmer.

De Chaumareys did not stop his ship by immediately coming up into the wind but had the sails laboriously clewed up. Then he launched a rescue boat. Although the boat was intended to be rowed by six men, only three were ordered into it. The strong breeze drove it sideways and as a rescue attempt it was hopeless. Both the frigate and her boat drifted to leeward with the wind for such a distance that not even the buoy was sighted again, let alone the seaman, who had been swimming strongly when lost to view in the wake. When the *Echo* at last caught up with the *Medusa* she reported that her lookouts had not seen anything either. De Vénancourt had lost a man overboard from the *Echo* the previous day, but he was a nonswimmer so almost any measures would have been too late.

All the *Medusa*'s logs and charts were to be suspiciously "lost" later on, so all occurrences on board were subject to the vagaries of individual memory. This particular incident was recorded in the joint narrative of two survivors who became friends. They were J. B. Henry Savigny, junior surgeon of the frigate, and Alexander Corréard, a geographical engineer in charge of a party of twenty workmen intended for exploration work in the interior of the colony. They were careful to check technical points with some of the surviving naval officers and the detail they gave in their account is probably based on that. Their story reveals a lack of preparation and precision in an emergency which is not entirely unexpected in a ship still in the "working-up" stage, particularly if the officers are fighting among themselves instead of getting down to the main task.

Leaving the boy somewhere in the middle of the ocean, de Chaumareys hoisted sail and the *Medusa* again began to draw ahead. It seems that he was anxious to make his next landfall at the islands of Madeira off the coast of Africa and would not wait for his squadron, although there was a navigational hazard ahead, a cluster of rocks extending about five leagues, which would have to be passed in darkness. His instructions from the Ministry were quite precise on this point. All ships were to keep together and not to separate. If for any reason they did become separated, de Chaumareys was to indicate rallying points where they would meet. Contrary to what he had decided (under pressure from Schmaltz) while still off Rochefort, de Chaumareys initially ordered this normal procedure to be carried out. Then, seeing its difficulty and the delays which resulted, he changed his mind again (or had it changed for him) and charged on, regardless, in the *Medusa*. Neither Savigny nor Corréard knew of these instructions in fact, but they correctly assumed their existence because there was no point in forming a squadron unless the ships were to keep in company. They did not know of the hesitations and vacillations to which de Chaumareys was subject (although their officer advisers did) and assumed their incompetent captain guilty of a thoughtless and headlong rush to destruction.

The situation the next morning certainly reinforced that view. Madeira should have been in sight already but there was no sign of the islands, only empty sea. When the approximate position of the ship was calculated by observation of the sun at midday, it indicated that the frigate was thirty leagues to one side of her intended track. Some thought this was conservative and that the real error was larger—in excess of one hundred miles. Therefore, the *Medusa* had to make an embarrassingly large turn to bring her bows onto the right heading, or what was thought to be the right heading, because it was assumed that the Gibraltar current had been the main factor in offsetting the ship and possibly was still affecting her. In any event, there must have been some very red faces aft on the quarterdeck that morning.

It was not until sunset that the masthead lookout sighted land on the far horizon. That meant that the navigational error amounted to the best part of a good day's sailing. It should have been a sobering thought for anyone contemplating a run down the coast of Africa toward a vast and poorly charted hazard. Possibly it was this which pushed the hesitant de Chaumareys toward his final, desperate decision.

On the morning of June 28, as the *Medusa* neared Madeira, the situation was clear even to the passengers. De Chaumareys and Richefort were happily paired. While de Chaumareys had last sailed as a lieutenant twenty-five years before and was really a customs officer, M. Richefort was fresh from an English prison, where he had spent the last ten years. He could speak at great length of his profound knowledge of the waters off the coasts of Africa but even assuming that he was not indulging in a little compensatory self-importance, ten prison years in wartime must have taken their toll. It is known that the Philanthropic Society of Cape Verde was engaged in an ill-fated attempt to colonize the interior. There is also a note to suggest that he was intended to serve as a port captain, that is, as a harbor master. One of the boats aboard the frigate had been shipped expressly for the use of the port, an eloquent testimony to its importance, for what little trade it did was in slaves.

Having previously declared his intention to put in to the town of Funchal in Madeira for a boatload of supplies, de Chaumareys turned to M. Richefort as the man with local knowledge for advice as to how to enter the bay. Richefort bloomed like a shriveled flower upon which the soft rain has suddenly fallen, and from that moment he began to take over the command of the *Medusa*.

Not even the decision to call at Funchal was really made by the captain, for the *Medusa* was not short of supplies. The decision was made by Governor Schmaltz, or Mme. Schmaltz or Mlle. Schmaltz. All urgency to arrive quickly at Senegal vanished if it was a question of satisfying their whims for fresh fruit or other delicacies.

With the wind behind her the frigate was making nine knots as she ran along the coast of the island, close enough for the passengers to take in the comfortable air of the place, with its tended vineyards and groves of orange and lemon trees. The strength of the wind was due in part to its flowing around the hills of the island, but as soon as the *Medusa* tried to enter the Bay of Funchal she entered an area of calm where the breeze was blocked by the hills. The frigate's sails ceased to belly in the wind and her bow-wave dropped away to a gentle ripple. But she did not stop moving. Caught by a current which was setting onshore, the *Medusa* was no longer under control; not even the most knowing asides by M. Richefort could remedy matters. After three hours spent drifting outside the entrance to the Bay of Funchal, the responsible officers took advantage of a faint breeze to move farther out to sea and, de Chaumareys declaring that he would not now bother to send in a boat, they at last entered the area of the offshore wind and were soon speeding away again at eight knots.

It was still possible, as the officers advised, for de Chaumareys to escape his fate by sailing far out to the west, but the captain had put his trust in the certainties of M. Richefort. There were also the whims of the Schmaltz family to be considered. So their next landfall was to be the Canary Islands, another unnecessary hazard at night or in poor visibility. However, so clear was the air that the great peak which crowns Tenerife was visible on the horizon the next morning, although it took them until sunset to reach the island. In that red light the summit of the volcanic mass, rising more than ten thousand feet from the sea, seemed to be crowned with fire.

They stood off during the night and in the morning followed the coastline toward the port of Saint Croix at a distance of a few hundred yards. The black sterile rocks, gigantic in size and piled in fantastic confusion, rose steeply out of the sea, and the more nervous passengers began to imagine that any stirring of the volcano would bring the very mountain down upon them. But the summit was quiet that morning and it was plain that the old travelers' tales of a crater continually pouring forth lava of molten metal into a surrounding field of snow could not be entirely true.

It was the sight of a small fort, the mouths of cannon still pointing from its embrasures, which raised the most emotion. One passenger was literally leaping for joy as he recognized it and remembered.

"We raised it in haste," he cried. "Just a few of us! That was when the English under Admiral Nelson attempted to take possession of the colony. It was there, just there, that a great fleet, commanded by one of the bravest admirals of the English navy, failed before a mere handful of French! They covered themselves with glory. They saved Tenerife. We made Admiral Nelson take flight, and it was there he lost an arm!* Oh, yes, the conflict was long and obstinate, my friends!"

This was delicate ground indeed, recalling the military glories of the recent past and the hatreds bred by more than twenty years of war against the hereditary foe. But it was also a reminder that de Chaumareys had fought for a time on the other side, had actually landed in France from English ships. It must have sounded ill in the ears of his new friend, M. Richefort, whose ten years as an English prisoner did not constitute a conqueror's record.

The *Medusa* put into the bay opposite Saint Croix and sent a boat ashore to get wine, fruit and fresh vegetables for the Schmaltz family. Richefort stepped forward, saying darkly that it was very dangerous for the ship to remain where she was. Purpling with importance, he added that he was well acquainted with these rocky islands, indeed he had navigated in all these latitudes. The resentment of the ship's officers came to the boil and they protested to de Chaumareys, saying that it was shameful of him to put such confidence in a stranger and to ignore the advice of his own officers. They would not obey Richefort; he had no worth as a commander. The tense, raised voices were the first indication Charlotte Picard had of the unpleasant situation which had arisen. She distinctly heard the captain refer to Richefort as "a good and

---

*Nelson was shot down on the shore at Saint Croix by Spanish troops, among whom were a few French. His "great fleet" consisted of four battleships, three frigates and a cutter; they carried no soldiers, only seamen and marines. The attack was Nelson's own idea and he proved to be a very poor hand at managing amphibious operations, which require more skill than simple land or sea battles. The basic causes of the defeat were the wind and current factors, which were the same as those which had baffled the *Medusa* off Funchal, plus heavy surf over rocky shallows.

able seaman." The words stuck in her memory.

De Chaumareys, in turn inflamed at the threat to his authority, ordered all the officers and crew to obey Richefort as pilot and to do it because he, the captain, said so. Since he was captain by the orders of the king, they should obey him.

Nothing could hold Richefort after that. The vain but amiable man suddenly began to bluster and shout, volleying a string of orders; putting the frigate first on one tack, then on the other; then charging the reefs, then going about—all to demonstrate his mastery of the ship and of them, while the sailors snarled aloud that the old fool was a vile imposter. At length, beaming with satisfaction and declaring that he had saved the *Medusa* from certain shipwreck, Richefort assured de Chaumareys that he had often been employed to explore the shores of Africa and none knew better than he how to avoid the perils of the Arguin Bank which was now only a few days' sail away.

It may be that Charlotte Picard, whose account this is, was confusing the arrival at Funchal with the arrival at Saint Croix, but her narrative reads at certain points as though it has been constructed from a diary. In any event, she has correctly and vividly depicted the situation which by this time had arisen among the officers.

During the day the *Echo* came into the anchorage, having caught up once more, and in the late afternoon Savigny and Corréard recalled that the *Medusa*'s boat returned from shore and that there was tension among the officers who had gone in it to buy fruit for the Schmaltz family and to post their own letters. The Canaries were Spanish and when Spain had changed sides the French soldiers there had become prisoners. Now that they were free to go home they had pleaded to be allowed on board the *Medusa*, which would be returning to France after she had carried out her mission to Senegal. This had been refused by one of the officers, although another had pleaded the case of the ex-POWs. The harsh decision was a fortunate one for the men concerned.

Another tidbit for shipboard gossip was the reportedly depraved morals of the Spanish women of Saint Croix. No sooner had they learned that some Frenchmen had landed from the frigate than they stood in their doorways and made inviting gestures, in spite of the fact that in many cases their husbands were at home. Nor was this all. The husbands were actually forbidden to show their jealousy by the Holy Inquisition. It was shocking, but it seemed that the local monks had told the husbands that their feelings were mere "conjugal mania" sent by Satan to torment them and that only offerings to the Church could deliver them from it.

The French whispered among themselves that abuses were of course inevitable in such a burning climate where passion was often bound to be stronger than reason. Others, of the anticlerical party, took the view that these abuses were typical of the actual effects of a religion claiming to be sublime. One of the officers who actually went ashore, Midshipman Charles Alexandre Léonard Rang, saw the Palace of the Inquisition and made some biting comments concerning the effect of superstition on the human mind. This was yet another division in France which was reflected in microcosm aboard the *Medusa*.

Already, as the *Medusa* and the *Echo* slipped away from Tenerife and left the chain of islands behind, the hot winds off the coast of Africa could be felt, and at noon the sun blazed down from directly overhead. On the last two nights of June the frigate twice caught fire between decks, both times in the kitchen where the master baker had been at work. Neither fire proved serious, being discovered before it could spread from the brick-lined area of the oven. On the first day of July, Cape Bojador was in sight, as were the edges of the Sahara, a wilderness of great sand dunes shimmering white in the heat. The ladies aboard, including Governor Schmaltz's wife and daughter, as well as M. Picard's eldest daughters, who had struck up a friendship with them, thrilled at the sight. This was the legendary and romantic great sand sea stretching right across the Dark Continent from west to east, the abode of lions and all sorts of strange wild beasts, peopled only by Moors accustomed to the fierce heat.

At ten o'clock that morning the ceremony of "crossing the line" into the tropics was performed, some of the passengers remarking sourly that the sole nautical purpose of it was to procure the sailors some money. But the crude slapstick was amusing at first and the appearance of high ceremonial was well carried off, with de Chaumareys in great good humor, quite the old sailor, presiding over the baptism of the neophytes. Charlotte Picard much enjoyed it. Meanwhile M. Richefort strode the deck and guided the vessel as calmly as if the surrounding sea had been the Bay of the Seine instead of the Gulf of Saint Cyprian.

This part of the coasting route to Senegal was certainly not recommended by the Ministry of Marine and was notorious locally for being almost impassable at low water except for small craft because of the numerous reefs. With an almost theatrical indifference M. Richefort gazed at the waves breaking on the black fangs of the higher rocks already exposed by the falling tide and with equal disdain at the ominous swellings of the sea over still-hidden obstructions, at the current running inshore and at the distinct change in the color of the water itself, which was no longer clean and clear and deep blue.

For most of the passage the frigate had been sailing in blue ocean water a thousand or more fathoms deep and, even after leaving the Canaries and unwisely heading in toward the coast of Africa, had always had at least a hundred fathoms under the keel. The sudden change from deep, clear water to the sediment-filled shallows was obvious to crew and passengers alike. The officer of the watch, knowing that a submerged reef extended one and a half leagues out to sea from the next headland, took emergency action. The frigate tacked away just in time to clear the danger. De Chaumareys went into a rage and reprimanded him for acting without orders, but it seems that the captain and his crony had mistaken a dangerous cape which juts out into the middle of the Gulf of Saint Cyprian for Cape Barbas, the headland which marks the end of the gulf. Recognition sketches of such landmarks, as seen from various angles to seaward, are part of a navigator's equipment.

The last great shoremark before the Arguin Bank was the long, southward-stretching promontory of Cape Blanc (the White Cape). De Chaumareys had declared his intention of sighting and then positively identifying this distinctive headland. It was to be his final "fix" before turning out to sea to steer a dogleg around the Arguin Bank, which lay a short distance south of Cape Blanc and extended a great distance out into the Atlantic. His instructions were to turn on to west-southwest and make good that track for a minimum distance of twenty-two leagues. Then he should be safely past the bank and could turn southeast for a direct run to Saint-Louis. Providing no onshore gale was encountered, this was not too risky; if correctly carried out, the procedure would nullify any position error on the charts. If the ship was by direct observation five miles due west of the actual cape, then it did not matter in the slightest where that headland was located on a piece of paper. The notorious bank must be to the south, and a track west-southwest from that point, if continued for a sufficient distance, would take the vessel clear of the hazard.

It was an enormous, uncharted area of shallow banks and weedy gulleys, of warm water and bright light, both a haven and a feeding ground for multitudes of fish. It was reputed to stretch thirty leagues out into the Atlantic and to have an uncertain but steep slope. It had not been surveyed then, and it has not been surveyed now; it was known only to the fishermen who went there in small boats at certain seasons of the year. For a ship it was deadly. She would be bound to strike many miles out from shore and that shore would be almost uninhabitable desert known then only to the natives, for the nearest European settlements were hundreds of miles distant.

All day the *Medusa* and the *Echo* coasted southward along the African shore. De Chaumareys repeatedly told his officers that he had a mind to anchor a cable's length from Cape Blanc because the minister had ordered him to make certain of its position. The southern extremity of the cape was distinctive, resembling a ship with a ram bow, like a Roman galley or a modern oil tanker, when seen from due west. A cable's length is one-tenth of a nautical mile or some six hundred feet and according to the modern charts, this would bring the frigate in among a maze of shoals and currents to an area where the low water depth varies between six and sixteen feet. The *Medusa* probably drew about twelve feet, but that is not the measure of the matter. The depths given on charts are correct only for flat calm; they take no account of the crests and troughs of waves, which increase and decrease the depth alternately according to their height. Apart from that, the motion of a ship in very shallow water is affected by the interaction between the seabed and the water displaced by the hull immediately above it.

Given their inshore route, to anchor off the cape was a good idea; not only would this provide an accurate "fix" but if they were prepared to wait until noon the next day, there would be the positive value to themselves and others of taking observations to establish more accurately the real position of this headland. The distance of six hundred feet is astounding, particularly in view of the contemporary lack of knowledge of the area and the fact that the vessel was powered only by whatever wind happened to blow.

This was the pattern of the navigation since the moment M. Richefort took over off Madeira. Risks were taken for no good reason from then on. The sending in of a boat at Tenerife, happily without incident, was an example. De Vénancourt of the *Echo* noted in his log, "A stiff breeze was blowing and I did not find it suitable for sending anyone ashore." The place was notorious; indeed, most of Nelson's boats had been smashed or come to grief in the surf during the British landings. Then there had been the pointless risking of the reefs in the Gulf of Saint Cyprian, possibly fatal if the wind had dropped or changed direction. And now this.

In wartime, such chances may have to be taken, the risks weighed and accepted. But there was no emergency in any of these cases, nor does one have the impression that the hazards were recognized, let alone calculated. It was rather as if Richefort were playing with a toy boat in the bath.

An even more incredible occurrence followed. By evening, there was still no sign of Cape Blanc and, notwithstanding what de Chaumareys had been saying all day, the course was altered out to sea, to west-southwest. An officer quoted by Savigny and Corréard wrote: "He continually repeated that the minister had ordered him to make Cape Blanc; he talked of it till the evening, but on going to bed he thought no more about it." Perhaps de Chaumareys had become inwardly unnerved by the nightmare of the Arguin Bank looming somewhere dead ahead and on impulse shied away from it, away too from any chance to get an accurate "fix" before turning onto the first course of the dogleg designed to take the frigate around the bank at a safe distance. Perhaps he merely gave in to the hostility of his officers toward him, a hostility which now increased perceptibly in step with the rapidly closing distance between the frigate and the obstacle in her path.

As darkness fell on July 1, the *Echo* was still keeping company with the *Medusa* and both ships were headed west-southwest, going away from the coast of Africa very nearly at a right angle. This was the recommended course, but de Vénancourt was clearly not happy about their general situation and began to signal to de Chaumareys. Henry Savigny, the junior surgeon of the *Medusa*, was pacing the deck at the time and saw the corvette start signaling. She burned several charges of powder and hung a lantern at her mizzenmast. The only acknowledgment given by the *Medusa* was to hang a lantern from the foremast, where it gleamed for only a minute or two before going out. It was not replaced and Reynaud, the officer on duty, did not bother to inform de Chaumareys. Savigny suggests that Reynaud knew well enough that de Chaumareys intended a fast passage and that every time the *Medusa* had outrun the *Echo* and put her down the horizon, de Chaumareys had rejoiced at the fact. Why wake him now?

At eleven o'clock the *Echo* was ahead and to the left of the *Medusa*. Her signals being unanswered, Savigny saw the *Echo*'s silhouette alter. She was steering an intersecting course with the frigate and was about to pass her bows. She merged for a minute or so with the bowsprit and then Savigny saw her clearly off to the right, on the other side of the *Medusa*, and steering farther away from the presumed position of the Arguin Bank.

In his log, de Vénancourt wrote: "No answer was had from the frigate nor was a signal given by her regarding the night course. Therefore I continued to steer west-southwest, which had been her route up to now, and a wise one, as it would take us safely clear of the Arguin Bank which spreads in a southwesterly direction from Cape Blanc and for a very great distance out from the land." He also noted that the bank was actually situated much more to the west than was shown on the chart and that the *Medusa* had deflected from the safe course of west-southwest.

Conceivably, de Vénancourt may have meant that and nothing more. Or, he may have meant merely that the winds and African current would drive both ships sideways toward the bank, so that a compass course of west-southwest would not in fact mean that the track of the ships was west-southwest, but pointed more to the south, into the danger zone. Just possibly, he may have known of the unholy trio in command of the frigate—Governor Schmaltz nagging for more speed, Captain de Chaumareys making decisions and failing to see them carried out, M. Richefort radiating glib self-confidence—opposed by almost all the officers, led by Reynaud, the second-in-command. The sane course, considering the known hazards to the southwest, the vagueness and inaccuracy with which the charts depicted them and the pointless risks taken by the frigate for the past week, was for the corvette to use the cover of night to part company with the suicide and to get well clear of the danger zone. In any event, in the morning the *Echo* was no longer with them, not even as a speck on the horizon.

During the night the *Medusa* had sounded every half hour while still on the move and had stopped every two hours to obtain a more accurate measurement. Each time the sounding line showed shallow water, and so the course was continually altered a little more out to sea and toward safety, in the general direction which the *Echo* must have taken. The other two ships of the squadron, the *Loire* and the *Argus,* had of course been lost sight of many days before. They were well to seaward, taking the safe route which did not approach the African coast at all until opposite Saint-Louis in Senegal. De Chaumareys and his frigate were now quite alone.

The captain came up on deck at about five or six o'clock on the morning of July 2 and asked a remarkable question: Had Cape Blanc been seen yet? Someone said that the White Cape had been sighted the previous evening and most of the officers wanted de Chaumareys to believe this. Otherwise, he might turn due south directly onto the Arguin Bank in an endeavor to find Cape Blanc. Several officers pointed to a distant white shape over on the African coast behind them and said it was Cape Blanc still in sight.

One of the passengers then on deck knew better. This was Alexander Corréard, a geographical engineer who had been born in the Alps and knew the difference between a mountain covered in snow and a distant cloud gleaming in the sun. He told the officers, privately, that what they were looking at was only a cape of vapor. They laughed and agreed. But its position was not too far off that of the real Cape Blanc and, as they were probably ten leagues or so on the wrong side of it already, the most urgent question of the hour was to get their captain to believe that if he stood away from the shores of Africa he would be obeying strictly those instructions which he said he had had from the Ministry.

De Chaumareys wanted to believe and was easily convinced, which was success of a sort. Unfortunately, this meant that the final "fix" for the first leg of the seaward zigzag, as officially calculated, consisted of a movable cloud rather than a cape of rock. Even so, the frigate had not yet wrecked. The weather was kind and the wind not unfavorable. By steering well out to sea for a longer distance than that recommended by the Ministry, by leaving a wide margin for error to the south and by sounding carefully, the frigate should be able to skirt the bank.*

By six o'clock that morning they had escaped from the shallows and were obtaining soundings of one hundred fathoms.† That is, they were over the lower part of the Continental Shelf of Africa, where the seabed rises steeply toward the land on the east and on the west slopes steeply down to the abyss. On learning that there were now more than five hundred feet of water under the *Medusa,* Richefort made the grand and knowing gesture of altering course to south-

*On modern charts a course of west-southwest from Cape Blanc gives a series of soundings, showing the steep slope to safety: 50 to 200 fathoms, then 700 to 800 fathoms, finally 1,200 to 1,700 fathoms (more than 10,000 feet), with a few submerged peaks coming up to 17 and 18 fathoms from generally much greater depths. These are English fathoms of 6 English feet.

†French fathoms (brasses) of 5 French feet, equaling just under 5 feet 4 inches English. None of these measurements would be at all exact, because a fathom is really just a rough and ready way of measuring lengths of rope by using the outstretched arms.

southeast, an alteration of nearly a right angle from their previous course of west-southwest. The course was right but the timing was wrong. This was the second stroke of the dogleg which should, if made at the right moment from the right position, have led the frigate directly to Saint-Louis. Made far, far too early, it could have only one result. From a point just clear of danger they were now heading right into it and, regardless of where Cape Blanc really was, they were bound to hit the coast well north of Saint-Louis, exactly in the area of the notorious shallows of Arguin.

Speculation is probably pointless. Momentary mental aberrations affect most of us at one time or another, when we are tired or distracted or upset. When they affect admirals or captains they have not infrequently resulted in terrible disaster. A tidy mind would try to find a logical cause for so large an error and seek to identify the flaw in the navigator's reasoning. The only cause which suggests itself is the Bellin chart. The frigate, observably, had not covered a sufficient distance to round the Arguin Bank, regardless of whether it extended twenty leagues or thirty leagues offshore. They were turning much too soon. But if at the back of some cloudy mind there was an idea that the western extremity of the bank lay at such-and-such a position, and that the ship from yesterday's sun sights was actually at a position almost clear of the (false) chart position for the bank, then that mind, suppressing the vital factor of the distance which must actually be run out from the actual coast to round the actual bank, might have momentarily slipped into a false conclusion. Even so, ordinary caution would advise waiting until noon before changing course, so that a sun "fix" could be obtained, for the real position of the frigate was as cloudy as the cape which was supposed to have been sighted. As it was now about ten in the morning, with only two hours until noon, the delay would not be considerable. But still Richefort ordered the course changed.

At once there were angry scenes, centered around M. Richefort. An officer who called him an imposter was put under arrest by the captain, whose faith in his good friend was utterly unshaken. They were safe enough, declared de Chaumareys, as Cape Blanc had been passed the previous evening and the good Richefort knew what he was doing. When someone questioned the accuracy of the sighting, de Chaumareys flushed and denied furiously that any doubt was possible. Voices called for a return to the westerly course, but Richefort was unmoved; like a wise and patient father surrounded by silly children, he seemed only amused.

After three of the more experienced officers—Lieutenants Reynaud and Espiaux and Ensign Maudet— had vehemently argued for a westerly course, and been brushed aside in the most infuriating manner, M. Picard had had enough. It was not merely his own life which was at stake, but the lives of his wife, his teenage daughters and the four younger children, two of them little more than helpless babies.

Aroused, the French family man advanced on Richefort and told him that they were about to strike on the Arguin Bank. Raising his voice over the man's deprecating tones, he said that he at least *did* know the Arguin Bank. He had twice been past it during a previous visit to Senegal and had once been aground on it, eight years ago, because the captain had stood in too close. Richefort merely smiled.

"My dear sir," he said, "we know our business. Attend to yours, and be quiet. I have already twice passed the Arguin Bank; I have sailed upon the Red Sea, and you see I am not drowned."

*45*

The fatuousness of the man was more effective than any righteous rage. The protests were stilled. M. Picard went below and flung himself on his bunk, exhausted with fury.

Ensign Maudet, the officer of the watch, repeatedly ordered soundings to be taken at ever shorter intervals. The sailors cried out with delight, for the fishing lines which were hung over the side in the faint hope of a catch all of a sudden became alive. Fish after fish was hauled in, all of the cod species. The officers gloomily noted the dulling color of the water, the masses of floating river grasses typical of the Senegal and Gambia rivers and of the occasional whiplike length of *Zostera*, a seaweed which flourishes in coastal shallows. Even Midshipman Rang, who knew nothing of the African coast, had only to listen to the talk around him to become alarmed. He wrote: "The usual remarks from the seamen made us believe that, if we were not yet on the Arguin Bank, we certainly were on its abrupt slope." It was now about half past eleven.

After the noon sighting had been taken, Charlotte Picard saw Ensign Maudet sitting on a chicken coop, which he was using as a table for working out the ship's position from this up-to-the-minute and more accurate evidence. It seemed to her that he appeared melancholy. The officer got up and formally reported to the "good and able seaman" Richefort that the frigate was on the edge of the Arguin Bank.

"Never mind!" beamed the unofficial navigator. "We are in eighty fathoms."

De Chaumareys nodded his approval, in spite of the lessening depth, from one hundred to eighty fathoms. "No cause for alarm," he told the officer of the watch. Then, raising his voice so that all nearby could hear it, he repeated, "No cause for alarm!"

The *Medusa* was in fact seaward of the bank and closing on it, not directly but at an angle, so that there was still time to turn away into deeper water. Until three in the afternoon the frigate coasted along, with a steadily rising wind and steadily flooding tide drifting her even farther in toward the shallows. The ladies, bewildered by the mysterious male technicalities of rough seamanship, had hardly known what to believe. Now even they remarked aloud upon the noticeable change in the color of the sea and could guess what it meant.

A kind of stupor pervaded everyone on deck, except the captain and his appointed navigator. All eyes but theirs were gazing in melancholy and resigned fashion at the water just alongside. Then a cry of horror went up from all. Just under the surface, rolling in the waves, they could make out tiny specks of sand.

Maudet ordered another sounding to be taken and instantly reported the result to the captain.

"Eighteen fathoms!"

Early in the morning 533 feet; at noon 425 feet; and now, 96 feet.

De Chaumareys nodded imperturbably and ordered the ship to be put a little more toward the wind, slightly away from the coast. At the moment of the order the frigate had the wind directly behind her and the studding sails set on the shoreward side. These sails were on booms extending beyond the normal reach of the yards and gave extra pulling power and speed. De Chaumareys now ordered them to be taken in. Everything was to be done in an orderly and seamanlike fashion.

The officer of the watch almost instantly ordered another sounding to be made. There was an anxious wait, not nearly so long as before.

"Six fathoms!"

Still uncertain whether or not he was dealing with an actual yet unimaginable emergency, de Chaumareys hesitated. Then he ordered the ship to be hauled around as close to the wind as she would lie. It was now 3:13 P.M., July 2, 1816 and that last sounding had shown thirty-two feet. There could be little more than fifteen to twenty feet of water below the keel.

Two minutes later, the *Medusa* gave a slight shudder. She sped on, bumped again, came free and moved on through the water. She grounded a third time with a thump which resounded through the fabric of her timbers, began to shake and this time heeled over noticeably.

The sails still bellied out in the wind, the rudder was hard over, the waves still dashed at her side. But there was no longer any wake astern. Instead around the bow, there were eddies and swirls of water which spun ahead of the *Medusa* and steadily lengthened toward the shore. The frigate was not moving through the water; the water was moving past her.

Savigny and Corréard noticed a most extraordinary change come over familiar faces, so that they became hardly recognizable. For a moment, not a word was spoken. But one man's features seemed to shrink in, so that he seemed hideous with horror. Another's face actually changed color, becoming yellow and finally green, as shock clutched his heart.

Gaspard Théodore Mollien, a young explorer on the governor's staff, read on the faces of de Chaumareys and his staff "a silent fever . . . a great anxiety."

Almost everyone was trembling, though some tried to suppress it. The officers were still for a moment and then volleyed orders in voices high with agitation.

The captain was speechless, and M. Richefort was the recipient of brutally direct insults and was very nearly assaulted. Some responsible officers were totally disoriented. M. Poinsignon, commanding some of the native troops, struck Charlotte Picard's sister Caroline a sharp blow, apparently under the impression that she was one of his recalcitrant soldiers.

While men who had known twenty years and more of war were profoundly affected by the grounding of the frigate, the wife and daughter of M. Schmaltz appeared not to take in the event at all. They gazed with unconcerned placidity across the heeling deck at the frightened passengers pouring up the companion ladders from below. It was as though these scenes could not possibly concern the family of so grand an official as a governor and commander-in-chief. Someone would take care of it. Someone always had—although up to now the worst that had been likely to happen to them was the wheel of a coach working loose.

# 3

# Stranded Off the Sahara
## *(Afternoon, July 2, to morning, July 5)*

Seen from a distance the *Medusa* looked gaunt and strange. Her sails were down, her top gallant masts were down, her topmasts had been lowered. Only truncated bare poles protruded from her decks, although her lower yards still spanned out over the water. The frigate's boats were out around her, the men heaving and struggling in the swell against a powerful current in their efforts to take anchors and cables out to a sufficient distance to be of use. It was the morning of July 3, the day after the ship had stranded.

The instant of striking had produced first a shocked silence and then uproar. It had awoken M. Picard and catapulted him on deck where he had flayed de Chaumareys and Richefort with what his eldest daughter described as "a thousand reproaches." M. Richefort had very nearly been thrown to the sharks. Then, as it was realized gradually that the frigate was in fact not wrecked but was merely aground, the tumult died down. Two energetic officers began to have everything in sight which was movable thrown overboard, in order to lighten the ship and get her off. It may be that they knew that the stranding had occurred at the worst possible time of the worst possible period—on high water of spring tides. From now on, every high water would be a little lower than the last for nearly a week. The chance to refloat the *Medusa* was only a fleeting one.

But no sooner had these officers begun to organize correct and decisive action than they were forced to stop. De Chaumareys seemed reluctant to take any desperately final measures which would eventually prove his incompetence. He sanctioned only those half remedies which would not show on the inventory of the *Medusa*, which would not indicate the near-disaster to which he had brought the ship under his command. And so the process of lowering the upper masts and yards and then floating them alongside the stranded hull was begun, but in halfhearted and haphazard fashion. The sailors worked hard, but not under any real direction; their efforts were not co-ordinated. They paid little attention to the orders of the officers in any case, for they had lost confidence in the men set over them.

The following day, July 3, matters became worse. Crew and passengers were milling about to little purpose. There were four distinct tasks to be undertaken. Relays of men had to work at the pumps, to lighten the hull of water leaking in through strained seams; seamen had to lower the masts and yards, swing them overboard and secure them alongside, to relieve the frigate of more unnecessary weight; large anchors had to be swung out into boats, and the boats had to carry the anchors out to a distance and set them in the ground; other men had to labor at the capstans which would haul at these anchors to move the lightened frigate. A good deal of organizing skill was needed for all these tasks to go smoothly, without interfering with each other; and the taking out of the anchors required, in addition, calm weather and slow or slack water. The passengers took their turns with the physically exhausting labor at the pumps and capstans, to spare the seamen for the skilled tasks. But almost all their hard work was wasted.

Because it was the period of the spring tides, the currents were strong and the seas very rough. The tasks set for the boats' crews were hard to carry out and de Chaumareys was too easily satisfied. He had had a small anchor taken astern the previous night, but to an insufficient distance. As soon as the capstan began to turn, it was the anchor which moved and not the ship. So another, heavier anchor had to be taken out and to a much greater distance in a very rough sea. This anchor proved to be too big for the boat and had to be floated out in tow; this meant fastening empty barrels to it as a means of flotation. After this long task had been completed the boat's crew labored to take the anchor out to a very great distance where the water was still shallow; indeed they could go no farther, because the anchor itself grounded while the upper end was still above the water, but in such an awkward position that neither of the flukes would bite. When the men put their weight to the capstan bars and the cable began to come dripping in, the *Medusa* did not move. All that happened was that the anchor came slithering back toward them through the soft sand and gray mud. All their efforts of the previous evening, and all their labors this day, had been to no purpose.

The efforts to lighten the ship showed a similar lack of thoroughness. The upper masts and yards and the booms were taken down and secured alongside, so that they could be recovered, but the heavy main yards were left in place, spanning out over the water; this was a precaution against the unlikely possibility of the *Medusa* heeling right over. However, the loglike appearance of the lashed timbers floating alongside did suggest another use for them, in case the ship really was immovable, and it was M. Schmaltz, the new governor of Senegal, who suggested it.

Leaning on the main capstan and using the top of it as a desk he sketched out the plan of a raft which could be made by lashing together this collection of masts, yards and booms. Gathered around him were the captain and officers and some of the passengers. There were four hundred people on board the *Medusa* and only six boats. They were of varied types and some were in poor condition. They certainly could not take four hundred people simultaneously to the African coast. But, M. Schmaltz explained, a raft could be made from these timbers which would support two hundred people, plus all the provisions for the entire party, those in the boats and those on the raft. The boats would tow the raft toward the shore in a regular convoy and be provisioned from it. Once ashore, weapons and ammunition would be handed out, and the whole party of more than four hundred persons would march along the beach until they reached Saint-Louis, their numbers being a deterrent against attack.

Others suggested a similar but less cumbersome plan: simply to use the boats to ferry everyone ashore in relays, plus provisions and weapons. However, the captain and his close advisers decided against this sensible solution in favor of the raft. Its construction was ordered to be begun at once.

Neither plan was impractical, although the details had not been calculated but merely guessed at; but both were defeatist. The best lifeboat is usually the ship itself, and this should not be abandoned, except in extreme circumstances. There was no lack of people to point this out and to urge that the really decisive measures usual in such circumstances should be taken. There were on board fourteen twenty-four-pounder guns, each weighing several tons; to jettison these would make a considerable difference. De Chaumareys shrank back in muddled horror from the suggestion. Throw the king's cannon overboard? He would do no such thing! Charlotte Picard heard someone mutter that the frigate was also the king's and would be sacrificed if the guns were not. Another pointed out that the guns could be taken out to a distance by the boats and would make admirable anchors for hauling the frigate off the bank.

Yet other voices urged that the bulk of the stores be jettisoned, particularly the many barrels of flour down in the hold. They protested that up to now the officers had been merely playing with the problem, lightening the frigate by a minute amount, twenty or thirty centimeters at the most, a matter of a foot or less. She would never come out of her bed that way. This time it was M. Schmaltz who squashed the suggestion with heavy-handed righteousness. Did they not know, he declared, that the greatest scarcity of flour prevailed in the European settlements of the province? To do such a thing was unthinkable.

Surgeon Savigny pointed out that they did not necessarily have to lose all the flour if they put the barrels in the water, for the moisture would form with it to make a thick crust on the outside, preserving the bulk of the contents. If the barrels were all roped together, they could be recovered on board once the frigate was afloat again. Grudgingly, it was agreed to give this method a trial and some barrels were pushed overboard; but the task of fastening them together proved difficult, and the whole project of jettisoning the heavy stores was abandoned. The guns also remained aboard.

That evening yet another anchor was taken a very considerable distance, in spite of strong winds and a heavy swell over the shallows. But when attempts were made to work the capstan, still the frigate did not move. Embarkation lists for the boats and the raft were made out. One of those who found himself put down for a boat was M. Bredif, the mining engineer. "Our mode of living, during all this time, was extremely singular," he wrote later in a letter to his sister. "We all worked either at the pump or at the capstan. There was no fixed time for meals, we ate just as we could snatch an opportunity. The greatest confusion prevailed, the sailors already attempting to plunder the passengers' luggage." All these exertions took place in the heat of the tropics, in weather which steadily grew worse and on tides which became lower and lower and thus less favorable.

On July 4, some of the stores were thrown overboard, a few barrels of flour and some barrels of powder; some of the water casks were staved as well. The guns and the bulk of the stores still remained aboard. Most of the effort this day was devoted to the construction of the raft and the repair of the boats, some of which were in poor condition. Just before high water that evening the working parties began to labor at the capstans again, hauling in on a stern anchor, designed to pull the frigate off, and a side anchor near the bow, which was intended to swing the ship so that she would be headed toward deeper water. After only a few minutes the hull began to move, swinging slowly to the left.

Seeing success at last, the men worked with fury, full of hope. The first few slight tremors were followed by a definite swinging movement of the hull. The laborers doubled their exertions. Reluctantly, the bows of the *Medusa* veered around until she was headed into the open sea, held only at the stern and very nearly afloat even there. At that point they had to stop, for they had hauled the ship around until she was almost over one of the anchors. The heavy sea and swell prevented the boats from taking out a really long warp, right out into the open sea, which was what was needed now. Had it been possible to do that, the frigate would have come afloat that evening. She might still have come afloat, had she been lightened of her guns and stores even as late as this, the third day aground.

As it was, all that had happened was that the heavily laden hull had been got out of the bed which it had dug for itself in the soft soil of the bank and had moved about two hundred meters away, before the falling tide grounded her again. It was an omen that sent many people wild with joy, a token that another day or two of similar effort would see the frigate not only completely refloated but under sail once more. That might have come to pass, had nothing changed. But after dark the sky clouded over ominously and the wind began to howl in from seaward, driving great waves before it which began to beat the insecurely moored frigate farther onto the bank. It was now too late to regret the wasted days and all the specious reasons for ineffective action.

There were plaintive and confused cries from the passengers who had been so joyful only a few hours before; so many sheep led in so many directions by uncertain shepherds, their despair held undertones of rage and suspicion. Others for the first time felt real fear, certain at last that the frigate was doomed and that her frames would split and her planks open at any moment. But the *Medusa* had been soundly built. She lasted intact until halfway through the night, when in rapid succession came a series of blows which spelled catastrophe. The hull was breached and the water began to pour in; unheard on deck, it sounded like a torrent down below. Then the great keel snapped and the broken-backed frigate began to work horribly in the waves. The seas could now rage at the stern with greater effect and smash it up and down on the sand with shuddering concussion. The great mass of interlocked timbers which formed the rudder was driven up and out of its securing pintles and, held now only by the side chains, began to act as a giant ram, flailing against the stern with every sea that struck. In a few minutes the captain's cabin was completely beaten in and the roaring breakers began to drive right into the ship itself.

Charlotte Picard, watching the mountains of water riding out of the black night and seeming to engulf the broken hulk of the *Medusa,* and fearing for the helpless children of her family, began to regret the spirit of adventure which had made them all eager to go out and see new lands and peoples. Surely they had been mad to forsake France at all! What on earth could Senegal hold for them that would make the risks of a perilous ocean journey worthwhile? She began to pray for her family, then for all the people aboard.

All work at the pumps was abandoned and a young sailor urged his comrades to take to the boats and at least save themselves. Some of the soldiers heard this and passed the word. They began to arm themselves and in a short time were in control of the deck, guarding every gangway and allowing no one up. They were determined that if the ship was to be lost, the sailors would be lost with it, as well as the soldiers.

Down below, another passenger came up to M. Picard and asked if he and his family were ready to go. This was the first they had heard of it, but they were soon convinced that a large part of the crew and some of the passengers were secretly preparing to leave immediately in the boats. Governor Schmaltz went on deck to quell what he thought of as "mutiny," to find the soldiers in control above. He assured them that there was no intention of abandoning any- body. Everyone would depart in orderly fashion at dawn. He was told roughly that that had better be the case, because anyone who tried to leave the frigate in a hurry was going to be shot. The governor descended, considerably chastened, certain coarse ex- pressions having been used which left no doubt in any listener's mind that the governor himself was regarded as the coward most likely to be fired upon. As the news spread that the soldiers were guarding the deck against illicit escapes, certain other passengers seemed confused and shamefaced.

In the midst of this mutual suspicion and anger came a tumult of shouting from above. The raft itself, supposedly destined to save two hundred people, had broken loose from the cable which fastened it to the frigate and was being driven off before the waves. A boat was manned and, despite the difficult conditions, the raft was brought back and resecured.

M. Schmaltz then called a council of all the officers and passengers and swore on the French flag that he would not abandon anyone. The boats would stay with the raft and tow it to shore, where they would all form a proper caravan and march as a body across the desert to Saint-Louis. That solemn declaration satisfied almost everyone, including the Picard family and started a new train of thought. What should they take with them in the morning?

As the black seas broke over the gaunt, broken and half-submerged hulk of the frigate, four hundred people reacted in their individual ways, many of them ludicrous, all understandable. Some of them had all their wealth in merchandise; without it they were penniless in a foreign land. But how to take it with them? Others had their fortunes in more portable form, in actual gold. These, of course, tried to secrete the heavy bullion in their clothing, in obvious places, such as the lining, or by sewing it into the waistbands of their trousers. The sharp operators were in a rage: the contraband which they had so successfully smuggled through customs, and on which they had confidently looked to yield 200 or even 300 percent profit, was in chests too bulky to move. There were even a few who fell into a wild and significant self-pity. In a destructive fury they hurled their money overboard, set fire to their belongings and, laughing like maniacs, surrendered to what tomorrow would bring. These people were the happiest when it was learned that no luggage of any kind could be taken.

The passengers who had been busily picking over their belongings in order to decide what to take with them were dismayed. The Picards would lose their trunks, their linen and their store of merchandise, but this seemed less important to them than the various manuscripts on which M. Picard had been laboring for a long time. They never thought to preserve part of their wardrobe by wearing two of everything, and an officer who had opened his sea chest to offer clothing to anyone who wanted it had few takers.

The ship's boys had got at the officers' wines and liqueurs and were making merry with the best. Thieves were on the prowl, in both the cabins and the hold, for tempting personal possessions or stores to be had for nothing. The sailors and the soldiers, people who had nothing very much to begin with and no hope of being able to carry much with them, generally made for the spirit room. They broached the casks and lapped at the brandy like thirsty dogs. Some, more impatient, staved a cask in their hurry so that the spirits flowed out over the planks. So they were all roaring, reeking drunk; serious drunk, knitting their brows and mouthing oaths; friendly drunk, eventually collapsing hazily into a corner; aggressive and assertive drunk, reeling along the decks in search of bother. Charlotte Picard was to declare primly that "the tumult of the inebriated made us forget the roaring of the sea which threatened to engulf us." As the sky lightened with the dawn, she heard piercing cries mixed with doleful groans. The frigate was being abandoned.

# 4

# "We Abandon Them!"
## (Morning, July 5)

There was no shore in sight, the waves were steep, the means of escape fragile and insufficient. There was not room enough for all; some would be left behind. Those who went in a good boat might survive; those who took to the raft were probably doomed. A great unease swept the crowds of people on the heeled deck of the frigate. There existed lists meticulously detailing the place to be taken by every man, woman and child, but these were still kept secret—with good reason.

The raft would have seemed a godsend only to a lone swimmer who had all but spent his strength. Viewed from the waterlogged hulk of the *Medusa*, the construction was horrifying, although on paper the dimensions might appear large. The outside timbers spanned a space some twenty meters long by seven meters wide, roughly sixty feet by twenty feet. There was no form of flotation, merely the negligible buoyancy of the topmasts, yards, fishes and booms of which it was framed, to which were lashed cross timbers and crudely nailed planks. The space was less than it seemed, for at one end the affair had been sharply angled to form a kind of bow. This was weak, as was the flat "stern" of the craft. Only at the center was the contraption at all strong.

The "bow" and "stern" were illusionary. Below the surface, the raft was simply an enormous sea anchor, a drag in the water. A further critical defect was that solid timbers have little buoyancy and float low. As a means of actual support for two hundred people plus stores of food and fresh water for over four hundred, it was a cruel joke.

There were six boats in all. The best was a fourteen-oared barge designated to take Governor Schmaltz, his family and their luggage. Thirty-eight people embarked in it; as it had once carried seventy fully armed and equipped soldiers, it was by no means overloaded on this occasion. The second-in-command, Lieutenant Reynaud, was appointed to command the barge. Equally capable of an ocean journey was the captain's barge in which de Chaumareys intended to embark with one of his cronies and no fewer than twenty-six sailors chosen for their fitness at rowing; he could hardly avoid survival. Next was a fourteen-oared pinnace commanded by Ensign Lapeyrère in which the Picard family was supposed to embark. It appears to have carried forty-two persons. The largest but weakest craft was the longboat commanded by Lieutenant Jean Espiaux. The forty-five persons originally appointed to it included Captain Beinière and his detachment of thirty-six soldiers. It had no oars at all, merely sails, and was therefore not so easy to maneuver. But because Lieutenant Espiaux would not abandon anyone on the frigate, eventually no fewer than eighty-eight persons were crammed into its thirty-foot length. Yet it was only a few feet longer than the twenty-seven-and-one-half-foot boats of the governor and Lapeyrère, both of which carried less than half that number. Ensign Maudet was given command of an eight-oared port boat intended for use in Senegal which had been damaged in collision with the raft the previous day and hastily repaired; even so, twenty-five people were taken off in it. Both this weak boat and the captain's excellent barge were twenty-four feet long. Finally, there was a twenty-foot yawl which had fifteen persons on board.

The small matter of who was to command the raft appeared to have been overlooked. The identity of this unfortunate individual was not at once announced because that would make it too clear that the people who had written out the lists had taken the best places for themselves. It seems to have been by convenient design that the senior naval officer discovered on board the crude raft turned out to be a twenty-three-year-old midshipman, Jean Daniel Coudein, in great pain from a leg injury sustained earlier. He also happened to be a Bonapartist not trusted by de Chaumareys.

The fact that the raft sank completely below the waves as soon as a mere 50 people got onto it, and that there seemed hardly any space for them to stand, let alone for any person to sit, was not helpful to the injured officer who was to command it. Eventually, when an estimated 149 persons got onto the raft and it sank so much beneath the weight that they were up to their waists in the sea, it was grasped that the governor's aim of embarking 200 men on it together with a mass of stores was totally impractical.

The last man to get on was an army officer, Lieutenant d'Anglas de Praviel, and he was most unwilling. He recalled: "I was the 150th to get down. I did not move. Then the captain, seeing me still standing on deck, spoke abruptly: 'For heaven's sake, sir, do get down!'

'I would rather die on board the frigate, for then

I shall be able to choose my own way of dying,' I replied."

This officer was not so brave as his words suggested and at length he obeyed the order. "I tied myself to the rope and with a tremendous effort succeeded in getting down. But the raft was already crowded. All the officers had occupied its center which was the safest part of it, being less exposed to the waves. From this privileged position, an impregnable fortress, they were pushing back those who wanted to escape from the edges of the raft. I got onto it, but in spite of my assistance earlier, I found no better place than the last planks of the raft, where the water covered half my body and the waves went over my head. This bitter situation forced me to take a desperate resolution. I threw myself into the waves and struggled back to the frigate, with no hope of salvation but intending only to leave an undeserved position."

The officers had in fact grouped themselves in the center, where they had better control of the struggling mass of humanity. At least two of them had no right to be on the raft at all, as they had been put down for a place in the boats. Surgeon Savigny did not record what his reason was, but he does say that his friend Corréard, the geographical engineer, felt it his duty to go because about ten men from his engineering detachment had been ordered on board and he felt that he could not separate his fate from theirs.

The bulk of the persons allocated to the raft consisted of soldiers, about 120 of them including officers. There was also a cantinière, the wife of a sergeant. There was a small group of some ten sailors, so that the most unseaworthy craft of all was shorthanded in the most important respect. Further, the construction lacked a mast to which a sail might have been attached. There were six wine casks and two water barrels, but no food, no tools, no watertight chests for arms and ammunition, not even a compass and chart for consolation.

But this was true also of most of the boats. Barrels of wine, water and biscuit had indeed been brought up from the storerooms and placed on the decks of the *Medusa*, ready for loading into the boats and the raft, but the embarkation took place in a rush and resounded with cries (from those in authority) of "Every man for himself!" Consequently, casks were thrown over rather than lowered, and most fell into the sea. The movement of the broken-backed frigate in the waves, together with the marked heel of the deck down to the port side, apparently convinced de Chaumareys that the *Medusa* was about to overset and that little time was left. As the frigate was firmly aground, with her keel deeply buried in the mud and sand, this was a highly imaginative conception. Nevertheless, the fright he communicated was sufficient to produce a frenzy on the ladder down which people were scrambling to get into the boats as they came alongside and to urge others to throw ropes over the side and try to climb down that way. A number lost their hold and fell into the sea and were recovered; surprisingly, no bones were broken by those who arrived prematurely in the boats.

By about seven o'clock four of the boats had been loaded and were standing off. The captain's barge was waiting ahead under the bowsprit, while the governor's barge and the raft were still alongside. Men were still struggling for positions on the raft and in their desperation to find room knocked over or threw off some of the flour barrels which had now been added to its load. These, washing in the waves which swept the timbers to a depth of several feet, struck the tightly grouped men feeling through the water under them for some insecure footing and with nothing to hold on to, for there were no rails or breastwork. They were so packed that it was almost impossible to move, and Alexander Corréard roared out for the captain. De Chaumareys immediately came to the bulwarks above.

"Are we in a condition to depart?" he shouted. "Have we instruments and charts?"

"Yes, yes, I have provided you with everything you need," the captain called back.

"What naval officer is to come and command us?"

"It is I!" cried de Chaumareys. "In a moment I shall be with you."

He disappeared at once, heading in fact for his own barge lying ahead by the bow. This was soon joined by the fourteen-oared barge into which, quite unobtrusively, Madame and Mademoiselle Schmaltz had slipped together with three trunksful of luggage. The purpose of the move was to embark the governor himself who, rather than climb daringly down a side ladder, required to be lowered down in an armchair suspended by a rope from the overhanging bowsprit. Once the commander-in-chief was aboard, his barge was then rowed around the side to the raft and a tow-rope thrown out from its stern to the raft.

While this was being secured to the angled "bow" of the raft, two sails were at last thrown over from the *Medusa* to the unwieldy contraption and then a bag of biscuit, which missed and hit the water but was caught with difficulty. The ropes which should have accompanied the sails were not thrown over. By now the first towrope, that linking the raft directly with the stern of the governor's barge, was firmly tied at both ends.

As the governor's barge drew away, oars beating the water, two of the other boats came in and also passed towropes, not directly to the raft but to each other, so that a line of three boats labored to move the raft slowly away from the broken, dismasted hulk of the once swift *Medusa.*

At this moment there were still about eighty people on board the frigate, including the numerous Picard family. It was then they realized that they were to be abandoned. Charlotte Picard had already wasted several minutes calling out to the officers in charge of various boats, and when the governor's barge came close alongside to take up the tow of the raft, she tried to catch the eyes of his wife and daughter. These two ladies promptly looked the other way. Charlotte even made a motion to descend the side of the frigate above their boat, but they ignored her. She had become very friendly with them during the last few weeks, but this friendship, it seemed, was as easily wrecked as the frigate.

Pleas to the captain were useless. Charlotte intercepted him on his way forward, but he told her that the Picard family positively would not be allowed into the governor's barge; it would do no good to hail it. According to the embarkation list the Picards had been allotted places in the pinnace, but so secret was the list that they were unaware of the fact. They did, however, see the pinnace moving away from the frigate rather lightly loaded, so they called out to the officer in command, Ensign Lapeyrère, but he also chose not to hear them.

A few minutes after they noticed a very small boat, the twenty-foot yawl, clawing its way close to the hull of the *Medusa.* As soon as it was near enough, M. Picard shouted for help. He asked the sailors just to take himself and his family over to the pinnace, so they could board it. The yawl held only thirty-three people at that moment and could accommodate the

Picards with ease. But the crew of the yawl refused to do even this small service for the most helpless and vulnerable group of all those stranded in the *Medusa*.

Public notary or not, so savage was the father's anger that he snatched up a musket which had been dropped on deck by one of the soldiers embarking in the raft, leveled the barrel at the crew of the yawl and swore to kill every one of them. Even then, his legal background did not desert him entirely, for he was at pains to point out that the yawl was the property of the king and that he was as much entitled to have the use of it as they were. Muttering among themselves, but convinced by one or the other of these two arguments, the sailors reluctantly sheered in under the side of the frigate.

The sullen, revengeful men threw overboard the few personal possessions the Picards tried to bring with them, including a small box of vital documents and two bottles of wine. Everything the family really needed would be found already in the pinnace, they snarled.

Ready excuses met them when the yawl ran alongside the boat to which the Picards had been assigned. They did not believe a word of it, for it seemed to the Picards that the arrival of such a large and ill-assorted family as they were had proved as unwelcome to the occupants of the pinnace as they had to the crew of the yawl. Exposure in an open and ill-provided boat to the burning sun and blazing heat of the tropics with such helpless creatures to protect and care for should have seemed a terrifying prospect. On the contrary, at that moment the Picard family were very happy. Clearly, the father's initiative on their behalf had been well timed. Had he not commandeered the yawl, they were certain that the gallant Sub-Lieutenant Lapeyrère would have sailed away without them.

M. Picard was jovial, too. He called out to the crew of the yawl, saying that he would be eternally grateful to them. Perhaps taking this for irony, the sailors replied with indistinct muttering and some open abuse. Raising his voice a little, as if in court, the notary turned to his family and explained gently: "You can hardly blame these sailors for being without shame, when their officers blush at being forced to do a good deed."

The sub-lieutenant affected not to hear and busied himself with being charming to the ladies.

Meanwhile a theatrical comedy, which at any time might have become a sordid tragedy, had been enacted on the deck of the frigate. Lieutenant d'Anglas, lately of the *gardes du corps*, and even more lately of the raft, was the center of it. He cared nothing for the unfortunate soldiers of his unit who were on the raft, because he thought them so stupid as to be unable to appreciate the dangers of their position; but he had been bitterly hurt by being refused a privileged position in the center. Now on board the *Medusa* once more, he picked up a carbine and leveled it at the governor's barge as soon as that craft had begun to move from the ship's side to take up the tow of the raft. To those who did not know of the wound to his pride, this officer's actions seemed to be those of a madman and may have precipitated the captain's flight. Under cover of this uproar, de Chaumareys embarked in his own barge which was lying ahead under the bowsprit concealed from most of those standing on deck.

With the departure of the captain in a well-found boat not overfull, following that of the governor in as sound a craft similarly half empty and towing the raft slowly and awkwardly away from the *Medusa*, the last of the boats had gone. But the deck of the frigate was crammed with people, no fewer than sixty-three, some of whom were women and children.

Lieutenant d'Anglas gave way to a furious despair. To him, the prospect of having his life snuffed out by the suffocating sea, instead of a noble death on the battlefield under the admiring gaze of the army, seemed unbearable. He now tried to kill himself, rather than the governor, and on being forcibly restrained began to cry out for death. His hysterical reaction was in marked contrast to that of M. Bredif, the young mining engineer, who had from the first deplored the disorder of the embarkation. As he told his sister wryly, "I gave the example, and was near being the victim of it."

With more deliberation than Lieutenant d'Anglas had shown, some of the soldiers who had been abandoned began to load their muskets to fire a volley into the departing boats, particularly the captain's, which was nearest and the last to leave. M. Bredif, and their own ingrained submission to authority, prevented it. But the engineer had to use more than forceful argument; he had to seize the firearms from their owners and throw them overboard. He never doubted that it was the right thing to do, but long afterwards some of the survivors from the raft were still of the opinion that it had been wrong of him to prevent the execution of de Chaumareys.

A significant thing, however, is that in all this brandishing of firearms, starting with father Picard and ending with the threat of a volley from trained soldiers, no weapon actually went off, not even accidentally. These incidents show that there was no widespread panic; they were demonstrations of anger, not uncontrolled riots.

Apart from the temporarily deranged lieutenant of the Guard, those still on board the *Medusa* quickly and quietly accepted that they had been abandoned and would have to rely on themselves alone. Although water was washing about inside the hull, it was below the level of the upper deck and superstructure. The hollow noises made by the sea flowing through the hold under their feet, as floating objects below bumped against obstructions on the submerged platforms, gave some kind of comfort to the marooned men and women. Clearly, the frigate must be hard aground and could sink no farther. A full gale might sweep it from end to end and perhaps break up the structure completely, but for the moment they were secure. There was time to plan, to do things as they should be done.

Their initial move was to gather to make a solemn pact. "We all joined together, officers, sailors and soldiers," wrote Bredif. "We appointed a master-pilot to be our leader, we pledged our honor, either to save ourselves, or to perish all together; an officer and myself promised to remain to the last." They talked about making another raft and prepared to cut away one of the masts which was now threatening to topple and was straining an already weakened hull. They methodically lit the galley fire and put a caldron of food on to boil.

But de Chaumareys had not in fact abandoned them, although he had no intention of rescuing any of them in person with his own boat. He came up to the longboat commanded by Lieutenant Jean Espiaux, informed him that there were no more than some twenty people left on board the *Medusa* and that he was to sail back and take them off.

The weakness of this plan was that, of all the boats, it was Espiaux's longboat alone which lacked oars and was at the mercy of the current and the wind, which were driving all the boats away from the wreck. Its strong point, although perhaps the captain did not realize this, was that Jean Espiaux was one of the bravest and most capable officers of the *Medusa*. Aged thirty-three, he was the second lieutenant (or third-in-command) of the frigate. He had fought at Trafalgar, in the *Algeciras,* been wounded twice and promoted for bravery. The following year, 1806, he had been captured in the Bay of Cádiz by the British. In 1810, while being transferred with five hundred other officers from Spain to England, he had escaped while still at Gibraltar by diving into the sea and then made his way through Spain (terribly dangerous territory then for a French officer) until he encountered a French army outpost. In 1811, he was promoted to lieutenant for distinguished services at Guadalquivir. With the first lieutenant, Joseph Reynaud, he had opposed the plans of de Chaumareys but in the catastrophe which had now occurred as a result, the actions of these two officers were to be interestingly different.

There was now an exasperating delay because, although there was nothing wrong with what de Chaumareys was trying to do, as usual he bungled the execution by bad judgment. As the wreck was upwind of the boats, the oarless longboat could not go in that direction by herself. So one of the other boats was ordered to tow the longboat and, when that proved impossible also, what might have been done first was attempted last. The powerful fourteen-oared pinnace of Ensign Lapeyrère was sent at length to the wreck; she secured a line to the frigate, which she then paid out as wind and tide drifted her back to the longboat. Finally, by dint of much heavy hauling in on this line, the weak and unwieldy longboat was eventually dragged through the water to the side of the *Medusa*.

Climbing up her side, Jean Espiaux found himself faced not by a mere twenty men, but by a crowd of more than sixty passengers, of all ages and both sexes, many of them with tears running down their faces at the prospect of deliverance. Some of them threw their arms around his neck in gratitude.

Espiaux said promptly that he would take all of them and this embarkation alone, by far the most desperate, was carried out in the accepted way, known as "reverse order": women and children first, then junior ranks, officers last. Two women and a child were the first to be lowered down to safety. When they were seated in the longboat, the most fearful of the soldiers and seamen followed quickly. As the crowd filled up the longboat, the true nature of the situation became apparent. There was not room for all.

With nearly twenty men still aboard the *Medusa* the longboat was precariously as well as heavily loaded. It seemed incapable of reaching land, giving the impression that it would swamp or upset in the first heavy sea it encountered. Indeed, so terrifying a prospect did it present that some men in it began to get up and start to clamber back on board the wreck. Once on deck, three of these men slipped away and found hiding places down below. They were afraid that some interfering officer would order them back into the longboat and, having experienced its leaky condition for themselves, saw no salvation in it. Other men were already below, dead drunk and unable to make a decision either way. In all, seventeen men either refused to seek the refuge of the longboat, preferring to stay with the wreck, or were too intoxicated to move.

True to his word, the last man of the last *Medusa* party to leave the frigate was Bredif the engineer, followed by Lieutenant Espiaux. Their final action was to hoist the French flag above the wreck. The young engineer paused a moment before getting down the side, then threw his small parcel of personal possessions into the sea. Everyone else before him had done the same. It was tacit acceptance of the state of the longboat. Crowded with what he estimated to be ninety persons, she was riding sluggishly and low, water from her leaks washing about inside her. It seemed as if even the weight of a few small bundles might be too much for the craft.

The state of the longboat and the enormous mass of humanity she was carrying were not known to the occupants of the other boats, which had in the meantime moved away. The young explorer Mollien, who was in one of them, described the scene: the *Medusa* heeled over forlornly on her larboard side, the densely packed unfortunates standing to their waists in water on the raft under the white flag of the Bourbons, which someone had hastily set up. He found it all very moving and regretted later that they had not realized just how near the African coast was, for then the boats could have saved them all, by ferrying in relays.

The boats were now strung out in a line and going southeast before the wind, about a league and a half away. They were not heading directly for the shore but at an angle to it. All of them, with the exception of the yawl, were connected to each other by ropes, the captain's barge being at the head of the line while the governor's barge was at the rear, next to the raft. The approach of the longboat threw them all into some confusion.

Grossly overladen, there was no room for the

crew to trim the sails smartly. Its maneuvers were erratic, as Espiaux was trying to drive in close enough to shout out to the captains of the better-found boats to take off some of his passengers. He needed to get rid of about twenty, a total which could easily have been shared. Reynaud and Lapeyrère each refused to take a single person, although the governor's barge was carrying three heavy trunks (the luggage of the commander-in-chief) and the pinnace ahead of it could have managed a few. The next in line was the eight-oared Senegal port boat captained by Ensign Maudet, too light, too laden and in too bad a state of repair to take any more; but immediately in front, at the head of the line, was the captain's fourteen-oared barge.

Unfortunately, at this moment the longboat sheered in sharply toward the line, and for a moment it looked as if it would blunder across the towrope or drive violently into Maudet's frail craft. The ensign was forced to loose his towrope which connected to the pinnace or risk an accident. Once it had dropped free into the water, the two leading boats—his own and the captain's—drew swiftly ahead. The two boats behind, left to tow the raft on their own, wallowed almost to a standstill and began to drift.

It was a minor mishap, easily repaired, and Maudet prepared to do so. As soon as the erratic longboat was safely clear of them he brought the Senegal boat about in order to reform the line and resume towing. The captain's barge was similarly wheeling around. Maudet called out to de Chaumareys, "Captain, take your towrope again." The reply was shouted back: "Yes, my friend."

Meanwhile the unwieldy raft was acting like a giant sea anchor on the pinnace and the governor's barge. They seemed to be tugging at it in vain, veering around it at the extremities of their ropes without apparently moving it at all. The impression of sheer futility, of a task far too great, was heightened by the swift mobility of the boats of Maudet and de Chaumareys as they maneuvered in the distance and began to return. Lieutenant Reynaud, seated in the stern of the governor's barge, directly in front of the raft, called out, "Shall I let go?"

M. Clanet, paymaster of the frigate, gave a defiant "No, no!" and was supported by several others.

Then the towrope connecting the bow of this barge with the stern of Lapeyrère's pinnace was slipped off unobtrusively. Reynaud was to say that this was cast off by the crew of the pinnace and Lapeyrère was to deny it. But cast loose it was, leaving only the governor's barge to tow the raft alone for a moment or two.

Now Reynaud was in a difficult position, convinced that the whole idea of the boats towing the raft any distance in the open sea was a practical impossibility and under pressure from Governor Schmaltz and his entourage to let the raft go. Schmaltz had always been impatient of slowness and inefficiency, and the deadly drag of the raft must have been a torment to him. Although reminded of the oath he took while still aboard the *Medusa* not to desert anyone, he insisted that the rope be cast off and was seconded by many.

Obediently, Reynaud began to loosen the towrope at the stern. Then he flung it into the water. He had to do this in clear view of many men standing to their waists in the waves, staggering for a foothold on the raft, which was now left to wallow on its own, two leagues from the *Medusa* but twelve leagues or more from shore. The governor was afterwards to tell a cunningly articulated story of how the men at the front of the raft had pulled on the towrope to draw his barge nearer to them and how a wave had made them let go, and so the boats had too rapidly taken up the slack and stretched the rope so much that it broke. As Savigny was to remark: "This manner of explaining this last desertion is very adroit, and might easily deceive those who were not on the spot, but it is not possible for us to accede to it, since we could even name the person who loosened it." That person was of course Reynaud, who subsequently admitted the fact that it was done, and done at the orders of Governor Schmaltz.

The captain's barge and the Senegal boat were now approaching in order to resume towing. Seeing Reynaud's boat drawing ahead of the raft they passed close and de Chaumareys hailed the governor's barge.

"What are you doing?"

Reynaud shouted back, too ashamed to admit the truth, "The rope has just broken."

"What do you intend now?"

Many persons heard Reynaud's shouted reply.

"We abandon them!"

Midshipman Charles Rang, who was in the captain's barge and was one of the few officers who had supported de Chaumareys, testified to this dialogue. At that moment, he added, "We could not see the least movement on board the raft, not even a cry was uttered. They seemed reduced to nothing. . . .

"There is no doubt that the handling of the pinnace caused the boats to scatter and to abandon the raft. But they alone cannot be blamed for this. The separation was taken as the signal for common escape. Everyone sailed ahead and took care of himself first. In a short while we were out of sight of the raft.

"When we left them, we all thought they were bound to be lost. We knew that they had not enough food and we could only hope that they might possibly meet a ship. It was the most fragile of hopes," Rang added, deadpan, "for it was most unlikely that a ship would sail in the area where we were then."

The sodden, weary men on the raft were unable to believe that they really had been left to die. Any excuse for hope was at once seized upon. The first evidence they thought they saw was in the movement of Espiaux's longboat, which had remained in the vicinity. They watched intently as her foresail was lowered to the halfway position. Then it came down completely, as if to slow her speed for the task of taking up the towrope.

This was in fact Espiaux's intention, a resolution only made possible by the cries of anger from his passengers as it became clear to them that all the other boats were leaving the raft and were not just reforming. But their resolution did not match his, for a closer approach to the raft revealed the dangers. To pick up the tow they might have to come so near that any desperate man could leap on board their boat. Certainly, a shoal of swimmers could strike out from the raft and grasp the gunwales to haul themselves up out of the water. That would mean the swamping of the longboat and the deaths of them all. There were muttered objections.

"I know, I know," pleaded Espiaux. "I haven't the least intention of coming in dangerously close, my friends. And I know we can't tow them on our own. But once *we* take up the tow, the other boats may follow our example." He paused, then added: "I promise you this, if the other boats don't come back and join us, I'll not risk your lives to save the people on the raft. I know I can't perform miracles."

But too many of his passengers were unwilling to face the risk. The spectacle of the other boats, all five of them in better condition than they were, fleeing for the horizon, decided the matter. There went the commander-in-chief of the whole expedition, the captain of the *Medusa* and the first lieutenant. Obviously there was no hope.

"Very well," said Espiaux. "We are probably doomed, too, like those on the raft, but let's face it to the last. At least we'll try. *Vive le roi!*"

The men began to cheer. Although some thought it madness, others found it sublime, a gesture of defiance and hope. The cry was heard far off by the men in all the other boats and they took up the shouting also. The calls echoed a long way over the sounding board of the sea.

The staccato chanting convinced many of the men massed on the submerged raft that rescue was only just out of sight, only just over the horizon, that the men in the leading boats had sighted a passing ship and were speeding away to attract her attention.

They rationalized their hopes. They thought they saw the explanation. For had the boats continued to tow their raft, progress would have been so slow that the distant ship might have passed before they had come close enough to be sighted. The actions of Espiaux's longboat provided a convincingly final touch, for had she not appeared to be about to take up the tow? Then she had hoisted her sails again and made off in the wake of the other boats toward the coast.

The men on the raft were patient because they knew that the onshore wind, which so rapidly carried the boats away from them, would be unfavorable for the rescue ship, which would have to beat laboriously out to sea against it in order to locate them.

They gazed intently at the horizon for the first sight of her topsails, but none appeared. Steadily, the sails of the boats grew smaller as they drew away until they could be seen only now and then as a boat here or there reared to the crest of a distant wave.

Finally there was no sign of any sail at all.

And then they knew.

# 5

# "Land, Land!"
## (*Morning, July 5,*
## *to evening, July 6*)

Abandoned, buried to their waists in the sea, many of the shipwrecked men cried out in terror and despair. Endlessly, in every direction, the waves heaved and sparkled to the horizon. There was no glimpse of a sail, no sign anywhere of land. Above was the blazing sun of the Sahara, the oppressive, suffocating heat of the tropics. In the chaotic rages and emotions of the morning everyone had forgotten food, but it was becoming all too plain to each man that he had not eaten since the previous day. Curiously, it was hunger they felt now, not thirst, and it was hunger which terrified them all, for its insistence emphasized their utter helplessness.

Everyone experienced this first wave of despair which had succeeded the initial stupefaction at their desertion by the hierarchy of the ship. It was as though the world had crumbled. The officers abandoned on the raft felt this also but concealed their emotions. They pretended to be unafraid and to see some hope still in the desperate situation. By degrees they produced a veneer of decent calm, although inwardly everyone trembled.

Alexander Corréard was gnawed by self-doubt and useless anxiety, for he had no one but himself to blame. Twelve out of his twenty civilian engineers had been set down to go on the raft, while he and the remainder had been listed for places in the boats. He had argued with M. Schmaltz that all his men ought to be with him, that they had promised to follow him wherever the service might require and that he, in his turn, could not desert the majority of them. Failing to persuade the governor, Corréard had taken his place with the dozen engineering workmen condemned to the raft, without realizing how fatal that course might prove. With only two exceptions, one of them the excitable Lieutenant d'Anglas, all the army officers had made the same decision as Corréard. If the men under them were listed to go in a boat, they would go in that boat and command them; if the men were ordered onto the raft, then their place also was on the raft.

The officers strove to calm the men and at the same time control their own fears and regrets. Gradually they all realized that with the favorable wind, and the tide due to become favorable also within a few hours, the ungainly raft could have been dragged appreciably nearer to shore had the boats continued to tow it. They might not have been in sight of the coast that night, but the following day they surely would. At least they would have been moving; there would have been hope. Instead, they had been sacrificed deliberately; they were sure of it. As the thought sank in, there was now an outburst of hatred. They swore vengeance, if ever they should get out of this alive. Everyone felt the emotion, even the officers. And the officers encouraged it, fanning the men's feelings with their own genuine rage, thankful that the channeling outward of their tension could swamp their fear and bind them together in a union of the deserted.

Stupefaction—despair—revenge—that was the sequence of the first morning. And it was followed by a measure of acceptance, disturbed by outbursts of fury, as the more thoughtful among them began to think of what to do and then discovered that the raft was bare of necessities. There was no compass, no chart, no anchor. The lack of a compass, the least necessary item had there been a competent navigator or seaman on board, was what disturbed and enraged them most. There were renewed shouts for revenge against the men who had abandoned them without a thought. Then Corréard remembered that he had seen a pocket compass in the possession of his foreman Touche Lavillette, and he asked him if he still had it.

"Yes, yes! I've got it with me," the man called back.

A tremor of hope and joy ran through the drenched, packed mass of humanity standing uncertainly on the submerged timbers of the raft. The ridiculous little instrument, about the size of a large coin, seemed a talisman promising safety. It was passed from hand to hand toward the nominal commander of the raft, Midshipman Coudein, who was in great pain from the wound on his leg, now raw from the salt water in which he had to stand. A few hours later, the compass fell from his grasp into the water and disappeared forever between the openwork timbering of the raft.

The lack of a chart as well as a compass brought a sense of loss, of being utterly without bearings, of being unable to make the simplest calculations of distance and direction, except at dawn and sunset. How far away was the land and what sort of coast was it. Wasn't there an island of Arguin, much nearer to them than the coast, where they might take refuge? How many leagues were they from it and which way did it lie?

In truth, given the clumsy, careless design of the raft with its rows of projecting spars—each one a drag in the water—compasses and charts were pretty much academic. More important was the lack of an anchor, for the raft did drift with the winds and tides, and sometimes it drifted in the right direction. A good anchor, to hold the position gained when wind or current became adverse, would have been invaluable. Bit by bit, moving only when the natural drift was landward, the cumbersome construction would have come eventually to shore. Such a steady shoreward movement, although it might have taken some time, would have kept hopes alive.

But there was no anchor. There was not even a commander of the raft, for the unfortunate Coudein was in agony, unable to move, unable to supervise. His place was taken by two men, Corréard, the engineer, and Savigny, the ship's doctor. The former attended to the rations. He made out a nominal roll, with everyone allotted a number (so far as was possible, the crowded conditions on the raft making a head count difficult). Then, because everyone felt hungry rather than thirsty, he distributed the contents of the flour container which had fallen into the water, together with a three-quarter measure of wine, which was to be the daily ration. The full measure was probably a pint. He does not specify, but remarks only that this was "the best meal we had the whole time we were on the raft."

Probably because of his experience at sea, Savigny undertook to organize the setting up of a mast to take a sail. For a pole he used one of the *Medusa*'s masts which had been incorporated in the raft; he had it cut in two pieces to serve as their mast and yard. It was impossible to step it properly in a recess, but they managed to erect it more or less upright by using a lot of rope to make stays and shrouds. No rope had been included in the stores loaded onto the raft, but a length of rope was washing around the raft—the towrope to the boat which had freed itself from them. They used that.

When the sail billowed out triumphantly, many thought they would soon be able to confront the men who had left them to die. In case they saw a ship sooner than they sighted land, pistols and gunpowder had been hung at the top of the mast as a signaling device. All that could be done had been done, and the very act of working to save themselves had produced a new attitude of determination and hope. But it soon became apparent that however well they trimmed the canvas, the raft would move only crabwise and then only when the wind was directly behind the sail.

The two spars interlocked in a V-shape at one end of the raft only gave the impression of being a bow because they were on top; there was no bow. Indeed, there was no hull. There were no lines at all to the contraption, for the spars and beams projecting far out from the sides made the width nearly equal the length, apart from causing turbulence and drag in the water.

Although the hulk of the *Medusa* was still in sight, it was only a low-lying dark object at least five leagues away. And those leagues were in the right direction. One way or another, partly by towing, partly by the drift of the current, partly by pressure of the wind, the raft was that much nearer the shore in the evening than it had been in the morning. Savigny and Corréard believed that the *Medusa* had struck some twelve or fifteen leagues from the coast, so that if the boats should return for them once they had lightened themselves by landing the passengers, the ordeal of the shipwrecked might not be unbearably long. It might even be ended that night, if the boats had gone to unload at the island of Arguin instead of carrying on for Africa.

Before the coming of the night they prayed, alone on the sea. They prayed with fervor and with hope, gaining comfort from the belief that there was a protecting spirit, that God would not abandon them. This was the fragile unity which the more dominant characters among the officers had created out of nothing in the first day of their strange new command. The castaways were divided by nationality, by color, by caste, by age, by occupation, by experience and, most dangerously of all, by the marks of the branding iron which indicated whence many of the soldiers had been recruited—the jails of France. They were divided also into the strong and the weak, but as events were to show it was not physical strength or weakness which would determine who would live and who would die.

With darkness came a rising wind and wild seas driving out of the night. Because only the upper parts of their bodies were above water, the castaways were battered and buffeted, hurled this way and that by the foaming waves. And as the raft swayed and tilted unsteadily beneath them, the soldiers particularly tended to lose their footing. This struggling, helpless mass of humanity might have disintegrated completely and been washed away in the darkness had Savigny not found men still cool and determined enough to help him search for short lengths of rope and to tie these to the timbers of the raft. Now, with some of the castaways holding on to ropes, the formless mass of people struggling individually to keep their footing and to stay above water was given cohesion and anchorage.

Some time after midnight the wind blew with even

greater strength, the waves were higher. The castaways became like would-be swimmers struggling out to sea through surf—very tired swimmers, however, for they had had little to eat and no rest at all for nearly a day. Some were swept away over deep water but managed to struggle back; others simply disappeared into the night, helpless in the waves. Weary men fell among their struggling fellows and at last were too weak to claw themselves upright again. There were those whose feet became trapped in the openings between the timbers of the ill-constructed raft and in their exhausted state could neither free themselves nor stand upright. The night was very dark and no one could make out what was happening more than a yard or so away. The only relief was the glinting foam of the breaking wave tops all around them in the blackness.

Someone cried out in the night that he saw fires. Then others, staring at the horizon, thought they saw them also. A long way away, something seemed to be flickering repeatedly in the gloom. At once they thought of the gunpowder and pistols hung for safety well above water at the top of the improvised mast. One after the other they lit gunpowder charges, which burned and sparked slowly. As one died out, they feverishly lit another. But there was no answering signal. If it was a ship out there, or one of the boats returning for them, they were not keeping a very good watch. Perhaps a noise and a bright flash might attract their attention. Several of the pistols were loaded and fired into the sky. The flame momentarily lit with an orange glow the exhausted, stubbly faces of the suffering men. The sound of the reports rang in their ears. Slowly, at deliberate intervals, the firing continued.

\*       \*       \*

The longboat was in desperate straits, lying so low that the gunwales amidships were only a few inches above the sea. Every wave of any size came over and water washed about the floorboards. Bailing had to be continuous but few of the soldiers or sailors were prepared to do it. After abandoning the raft, they had struggled all day toward the coast of Africa, lagging behind the other boats. Indeed, none of the commanders of the other boats wished to have Espiaux's longboat anywhere near them. They were fearful on two counts: that Espiaux would try to unload some of his mass of passengers into them and that this might be done by force. When the five serviceable boats had left the castaways to their fate on the raft that morning, they had heard several young army officers in the longboat shout out, "Let us fire on those who fly!" At least, that was the polite translation of their words given by one witness. "Shoot the cowardly bastards!" might have been a more strictly literal version. At any rate, this story had been passed rapidly along the line of boats. It was especially worrying for their commanders because a number of their own people took the same basic view and if given armed encouragement might have seized control from them and tried to aid the castaways on the raft.

Just such an incipient revolt occurred on the first evening, as soon as the leading boats sighted the coast of Africa. They had cast off from the hulk of the *Medusa* at about seven in the morning of July 5. The towrope to the raft had been loosed about two hours later. At about ten o'clock there was a distribution of provisions in the fourteen-oared pinnace commanded by Sub-Lieutenant Lapeyrère. A small glass of water and a quarter of a biscuit already soaked by the sea were handed out to each person. The water went down at a gulp but few could touch the biscuit yet. The heat was suffocating and the sun blazed down without mercy. The tender skins of the very young children began to redden.

This day the strong northwest onshore wind, which had come up each day after sunset, began to steepen the waves much earlier, howling at gale force. The sea became covered with the curious jellyfish known as the Portuguese man-of-war, which is really a colony of animals attached to a gas-filled float, pale blue and shot with pink, which serves as a sail. The boats were being driven toward the land, but the jellyfish were trying to avoid it. For them it meant death, not life. They could be seen with their sails to the wind at an angle, apparently in an attempt to escape, and seemed to be in a regular formation. The young midshipman, Charles Léonard Rang, who was in the captain's barge, was curious enough to lean over the side and scoop one of them out of the sea in order to examine it. Soon he felt a tingling sensation in his hand which grew to a burning heat. Some of the creature's tentacles reach a length of several feet and contain stinging cells which are very powerful, although not fatal to a human being.

The water was whitened also with the floating shells of dead cuttlefish. Almost every one of these was covered with flying insects which, unable to combat the gale, had taken temporary refuge on these drifting islands of dead bone.

The crisis came in the evening when from the gale-tossed boats the land was sighted, a thin line of white and burning sand beyond the breakers. All the boats except Espiaux's longboat, still laboring seaward and nearly swamped, gathered together. Safety of a sort lay just on the horizon and several officers proposed that the more overloaded and less well-provisioned boats should run for the shore and allow some of their passengers to disembark and then form a march party for a long walk toward Saint-Louis.

Other thinkers were more radical. They demanded that the bulk of the passengers from all the boats should disembark at the coast immediately ahead and that while these people set up a temporary base camp, all six boats should be formed into a rescue force. Three should go back to the *Medusa*, take off the men left on board the hulk and as many provisions as possible and then return to the base with the rescued men and these supplies. The other three boats should meanwhile go in search of the raft and rescue the castaways, bringing them back to the base as well. Only then should a boat be dispatched to Saint-Louis to bring a ship to their aid.

This was near enough what the governor and the captain had agreed to do, had solemnly sworn on the French flag to do, before ever they left the *Medusa*. It was, however, more practical because it dispensed with the raft as a means of transport. But now, Colonel Schmaltz and Captain de Chaumareys had second thoughts. Their barges were well-found, well-provisioned and far from overloaded. Their chances of making a direct run for Saint-Louis by sea were good. So they forbade anyone to land and ordered all the boats to go south in convoy with them to the mouth of the Senegal River. Some officers protested that the town of Saint-Louis, which is on an island near the river mouth, must be a hundred leagues away, a desperately dangerous distance for some of the boats to sail along this open coast.*

*The distances and times given are those estimated by the witnesses. As their charts were poor and they did not in any case know where they really were, the figures must not be taken literally. This being the evidence, they cannot now be corrected, but the distance to go was probably 250 miles. The *Medusa* may have stranded as far as 40 miles offshore. Only a modern discovery of the wreck could give an accurate position.

There were some voices to declare that this final abandonment of the raft was a shame and a dishonor to France. There was no shaking the determination of their seniors. Both the commander-in-chief and the captain, who was very much under the influence of the governor's dominating personality, insisted that all the boats should anchor for the night where they were and sail for the Senegal River in the morning.

Night fell and as the boats plunged at their anchors there was little sleep, people dozing fitfully in cramped and uncomfortable positions. One man in the pinnace cried out suddenly that he saw ghosts and witches out over the water and uncanny, wavering lights. No one else could see them, although he pointed desperately. They assumed it was some phosphorescence in the water that he had seen, if in fact he had seen anything at all. Even a distant wave might cause that. They were now beyond scientific explanations, so M. Picard and one or two others also pretended to see the lights and pleasantly suggested that Arabic sorcerers must have set fire to the sea to prevent the infidel from approaching their coasts. Very likely it was just phosphorescence, although some doubt must linger, for at about this time the castaways on the raft were burning gunpowder flares and firing pistols to attract attention.

Meanwhile, the ninety or so persons packed into Espiaux's longboat were in trouble many miles away from the five boats which had kept together in front. Later than the other boats, they too had glimpsed that shimmering line on the horizon which was Africa and the cry of "Land, Land!" went up from them all. With the wind blowing strongly and the longboat moving rapidly toward the shore, their spirits rose. Then there was an ominous thumping, more a sensation than a sound, a slight shudder of the timbers below them. They were bumping on a sandbank covered by only three feet of water in the trough of the waves. Lieutenant Espiaux got the heavily laden craft off into deeper water and by constantly sounding the depths worked his way farther out to sea for the night.

M. Bredif at least was relieved, for he was more afraid of Africa than the sea. The water could only drown him whereas the Arabs, he thought, would march him off over the desert to Morocco or Algiers as a slave.

The sea did its best that night, the waves running very high. With so little freeboard, the longboat was vulnerable to a single mistake, however slight. Unless the boat took each wave at exactly the right angle she would be swamped. As wave after wave came roaring down on them, the helmsman skillfully headed into it, so that the crests parted broken around the bows. Even so, several times an unpleasantly large amount of water came smashing aboard, and the men bailed frantically for their lives. Any other boat enduring those circumstances would have been lost, thought Bredif. It was a superlative performance to maintain the same unvarying skill hour after dark hour, within seconds of disaster.

As even the longboat, lagging well behind the others, had sighted land before sunset, it is probable that had all the boats towed the raft toward the coast then the northwesterly gale, blowing obliquely toward Africa, would have proved a blessing. The raft would certainly have been moved many miles nearer the shore. Whether that would have made much difference we cannot know.

\*      \*      \*

The gale which battered the group of anchored boats that night, which made the hours of darkness perilous for Espiaux and his men, which swept the raft from end to end so that the castaways seemed engulfed in the waves, also sent its spume soaring high over the black, shuddering bulk of the *Medusa* lying stranded far to seaward. There were seventeen men still alive inside her broken hull. Some were there by choice because they thought she was a better refuge than the raft or Espiaux's longboat. Others had been too drunk to make any rational decision. But by nightfall they had scoured the hull thoroughly, climbing down into the darkness to where the waves washed about underfoot to search for provisions. They came upon prize after prize: biscuit, bacon, wine, brandy. Enough to last seventeen men for a long time. Then they had sought out living quarters for themselves, each man finding his own "den" in the creaking structure of the ship.

Although her keel was fractured, her holds flooded and her stern gallery smashed in, the *Medusa*'s hull was far from falling to pieces. The frames, beams and planking were solidly bolted and pegged together, with lavish use of great timber brackets called "knees" to support them at the angles. The ship's bottom was bedded down into a hollow in the soft sand and mud, so that it could not move, and the seaward slope of the Arguin Bank served to break the force of the waves and weaken them by degrees before they struck the wreck. The best refuge of all that night was the ship, better even than the best boats, immeasurably better than the doleful raft. This night proved that there had been no valid reason for the precipitate mass abandonment of the wreck of the frigate. When dawn came on the second day of the mass flight, July 6,

1816, her foam-streaked sides still crested the waters like a cliff.

* * *

By daybreak the sea gale had died to a whisper and the waves were flattening, although a swell still rolled over the banks from the open Atlantic. From Lieutenant Espiaux's longboat, barely afloat, the land was distinctly visible. Soon the hot wind would begin to blow out from the Sahara, carrying seaward with it tiny particles of sand which would fall like rain upon the boats. But the sight of that arid, burning waste sparked hope in the sodden, despondent men. They demanded to be set ashore at once, although virtually without provisions. They were given most of what biscuit remained and firearms as a protection from the Arabs. Espiaux took the longboat in as close as he dared and then anchored in the shallows. A mass of men and some women scrambled over the gunwales and splashed into the water. They began to wade ashore to whatever fate awaited them in the Sahara. There were sixty-three of them in all.

Lightened of two-thirds of its heavy burden, the longboat now rode higher and more easily in the water. Bredif, who preferred the terrors of the tumultuous sea which had driven the majority ashore, estimated that the number of people left in the boat besides himself was twenty-six: If the identification of this place was correctly near the Mottes d'Angel, he calculated that those sixty-three unfortunates had some eighty or ninety leagues of desert shore to traverse before they could get to Saint-Louis. He was glad when Espiaux again headed for open sea.

An hour later they sighted four of the five other boats—the governor's barge, the captain's barge, Lapeyrère's pinnace and the yawl. Espiaux had the sails lowered and lay to in order to wait for them. When he said that he intended to take in a few people from the more overloaded of these boats, there were shouts of protest. But the lieutenant was adamant. "They have refused to take any people from us. Let us do better, now we are lightened. Let's offer to take some from them."

He hailed Sub-Lieutenant Lapeyrère in the pinnace, calling out that he now had room in the longboat for more people. Did the Picard family want to come aboard? Did anyone want to be ferried ashore? Lapeyrère shouted back that his pinnace was all right, although it was obviously far more crowded than the two barges. Then the amazed men in the longboat saw the pinnace abruptly turn away from them, using her oars to get clear of the stationary longboat more quickly. The other boats also hauled off in concert, as though they too dreaded to come near the longboat, which indeed they did. Espiaux could see that there was some sort of conference going on, for the little yawl was going from one boat to another, as if carrying messages or instructions.

What the passengers in the longboat did not know was that morale had broken down in the other boats. The men had been betrayed from the top so many times that everybody now suspected everybody else of the worst motives for anything proposed. And there had been an incipient mutiny in the pinnace that morning. Less than an hour before, a group of sailors, some of them armed, had demanded to be set on shore. When Lapeyrère refused they threatened to commandeer the boat, using their firearms. The officer had leaped at one man who was menacing him with a musket, and in the struggle they both nearly went overboard. M. Picard, hanging on to

Lapeyrère's clothes in order to save him, lost his hat. In the blazing sun that could have been fatal and he immediately let go of Lapeyrère in order to pick the hat out of the water.

It was in these rather ruffled circumstances that the encounter with the longboat had taken place. Also, all the boat commanders had tender memories of how yesterday the army officers with Espiaux had threatened to fire on them for cowardice when they had abandoned the raft and how a quartermaster had actually leveled a musket at de Chaumareys. They did not know that it was Espiaux who had prevented the man from firing and looked upon the lieutenant as an enemy of the worst sort. Some also suspected that the longboat's unruly crew had mutinied and were out to save themselves at the expense of the luckier people in the better boats. All were convinced that the offer to take passengers from them was nothing but a trick. Even the Picards were brought to believe this. They were sure that the longboat was only apparently two-thirds empty, sure that she was still packed with men, sure that they were crouching low behind the gunwales ready to leap into the other boats as soon as they came near enough.

One keen look at the way the longboat, lightened that morning of the weight of sixty-three people, was riding much higher in the water should have dispersed their suspicions. But it took more than that; it took near-disaster to do it. An hour after the boats had shunned Espiaux's craft the wind rose and soon the frail yawl was in difficulties. It was the smallest by far of all the boats, yet it carried fifteen men. From the governor, from the captain, from Sub-Lieutenant Lapeyrère there was no assistance to be had. At last, in despair, the crew took the sinking yawl down to Espiaux's longboat, lagging far behind them.

As it came alongside, Bredif gave a shout of joy. He recognized in the yawl his friend de Chasteluz, safe and sound. He called out to him and, the two boats pitching and tossing wildly alongside each other, de Chasteluz made a leap for the longboat, tottered uncertainly for a moment on its side, was grabbed by Bredif and dragged down to safety. One by one the other fourteen men chose their moment and jumped the gap between the two hulls. One of them was M. Richefort, part author of their misfortunes.

It really was a fortunate sequence of unplanned events, thought Bredif. If the sixty-three men and women from the longboat had not absolutely insisted on going ashore, against Espiaux's advice, then the overloaded craft could not possibly have saved anyone. They would have had to watch the yawl and its crew go down in front of their eyes, for the better-found boats had abandoned it as they had abandoned the raft. Virtue had brought a reward, too, he realized. Only minutes before, soaked through from bailing out the leaking longboat, he had taken off his clothes to dry them in the hot sun and, in so doing, had lost the purse containing 400 francs in gold, which represented half his wealth. The other 400 francs he had given previously to de Chasteluz for safekeeping, and only moments after the loss, by the wildest of coincidences, he had helped to pluck de Chasteluz from the sea.

It was now about nine o'clock in the morning. By noon the heat was intolerable. Some were almost unconscious and Charlotte Picard felt that death was near. The sky was covered with a hot mist which was really sand from the desert; it collected on the boats and was sucked into their lungs as they tried to breathe. Through the mist the sun glowed like an ominous red disk and the surface of the sea shimmered and danced around them. There was no horizon. Although the boats lapped slowly through the water, they seemed becalmed in some limbo where the only relief from torment was to chew on something, a lead musket ball or a fragment of leather, to get at least the illusion of moisture in their mouths.

*       *       *

The same sun glowered redly down on the idly rolling raft; the same fine rain of dust fell upon the sea-drenched castaways around noon. But it had been a very different dawn, as the fury of the nightly gale spent itself and a thin bar of light streaked the horizon. As the shadows dissolved and men could look into each other's faces again, they saw that during the night the raft had become an abode of death. About a dozen corpses lolled grotesquely in the water, their legs caught in the gaps between the timbers of the raft under their feet. Hopelessly trapped amid the swaying, shoving crowd of men buffeted by the seas which had swept over them, they had become too weak to struggle free and had choked and gasped their lives away in the darkness.

There was a sudden cry of distress and a swirl of movement as two young men recognized a motionless body as that of their father. They began to weep with pity until a more objective onlooker noticed that this "corpse" was still breathing, although faintly. Savigny, the doctor, applied first aid at once and by degrees the unconscious man was made to breathe more deeply. When he finally opened his eyes, his sons helped him up and held on to him desperately so that he would not fall again.

The number of men dead or lost during the night was conjectural. At ration time, fresh serial numbers were given out to all the survivors, but Corréard and Savigny were sure that some of the soldiers had cheated by calling out more than once in order to obtain an extra ration or two. The survivors were still so crammed together that it was hard to prevent this abuse. Further, the number of people actually on the raft to begin with was known only in round figures, roughly 150. The number of rations claimed on this morning was about 130, and if this figure had been correct it would have meant that 20 men had gone. But the raft had been lightened of more than 20 men. The sea must have taken most of them, the fury of the gale sweeping them bodily off the raft and out into the black wilderness of tossing water.

There was no general loss of morale; hope was still high. The hulk of the *Medusa* was no longer in view and there was no sign of land, but among the packed, suffering mass of people there was the certainty that the boats could not really have abandoned them and that, as the officers said, as soon as they had landed their passengers on the shore opposite the *Medusa*, they would come back again in search of the raft. The oppressive, suffocating heat which was tormenting the people in the boats had the opposite effect on men standing to their belts in the waves. The calm, almost dreamy isolation of their existence as they drifted in the mist was soothing after the black fury of the gale. If only this would continue, they could endure.

The weak, however, were already giving up. Not the physically weak, but the immature or emotionally unstable. The previous day, a gentleman called Griffon du Bellay (the governor's secretary) had tried to drown himself in despair. Savigny had brought him back to the raft, where his talk was vague and disconnected. Shortly afterwards, he again threw himself into the sea but then caught one of the far-projecting crosspieces of the raft and clung to it. And so he was saved again. Perhaps these were gestures.

On this, the second day, however, there were no gestures. Three men gave up. Two were youngsters, the third a baker. They said good-bye to their friends and companions, then there was a splash and they were gone. In others, the breakdown on this day was less dramatic but was increasingly to affect everyone on the raft (and some people in the boats as well). Here and there a happy cry would break out as some castaway sighted land. But only he could see it. A little later a man would point wildly to the boats approaching them, or to a ship. But there were no boats, there was no ship. These men, having lost hope of external aid, had withdrawn to a dreamworld of their own, rejecting the unspoken horror which inwardly must have lurked in all—that they would drift and drift under the scorching sun until long torment at last brought them peace.

*　　　*　　　*

At four in the afternoon, the terrible and extraordinary heat of that molten day was lightened by the freshening onshore breeze from the northwest. In the pinnace, going south for Senegal in company with the other boats, Charlotte Picard noted how the fresh sea air revived them all. The dust-laden mist from the land vanished and the sky became wonderfully calm and clear, an indication of a good night, she hoped. For the second time that day, rations were issued by Sub-Lieutenant Lapeyrère: a small glass of water and one-eighth of a biscuit. Everyone, she thought, appeared reasonably content now. Conditions were more bearable, all the boats were speeding through the water purposefully and some time the next day, after a good night's sailing, they should be in sight of the mouth of the Senegal River, a short distance from the town. They would have a tale of adventure to tell, but nothing really unbearable would have happened.

At half past seven the sky clouded over with ominous swiftness. A strange gloom came over the sea and the waves began to rise. Over the coast of Africa the clouds were visibly boiling as the cool winds from the sea were sucked in toward the superheated air of the desert. These clouds looked like a hideous chain of fire and smoke. Bluish clouds, streaked with dark copper tints, detached themselves from the billowing activity above the land and were sucked individually out to sea, where they merged with the overcast.

Miles away on the raft, the effect was shocking. The demonstration of their helplessness, of their idle, uncontrolled drift to nowhere, was plain. The horror of the oncoming night seized them. They shouted that they had been deceived. There were no boats, the boats would never come for them. There was no hope. The efforts of some twenty determined men, mostly officers, who had managed to instill a measure of calm and purpose evaporated in an instant. There were shrill cries of terror, hoarse shouts of fury. And then the gale broke on them with sudden and appalling violence, sweeping across the sea. The waves rose mountainously around them, half blotting out the sky.

The raft, drifting far from land, became an oasis of white and broken water in the darkness. The boats, fleeing to the south, half swamped by the seas, were caught dangerously inshore and tried to claw their way seaward, the thunder of breakers bursting in the coastal shallows sounding continually like a distant, growling bombardment. Somewhere in the howling sandstorms ashore, the sixty-three men and women who had landed from the longboat were hiding in the dunes; the first night of their long desert march was spent cowering before the fury which raged on sea and land alike.

Far out in the Atlantic, somewhere on the driven wastes of the Arguin Bank, the storm pounded at the stranded *Medusa*, spray hailing as high as her strangely lopped masts. The whole hollow structure shuddered and groaned; loose timbers banged and thundered incessantly; water rolled, surged, sucked and cascaded noisily through her submerged hold and lower deck. The very plank seams began to work and open under the crouching bodies of the seventeen men left marooned inside her, each one huddled into an individual refuge of his own choosing.

# 6

## Terrible Darkness

## *(Night of July 6 to 7)*

Something very strange had begun to happen to the castaways even before the gale overwhelmed them. Savigny, the doctor, felt lethargic; he knew he should keep awake, but his eyes closed and he could do nothing about it. He drifted away into dreams and visions. He was wandering through a splendid countryside where everything was a delight to the senses. A small spark of reason still remained and told him that it was a trance, that he must stay awake. He started nervously, was able to ask for some wine and gradually recovered a little.

In some men the symptoms were furious and impatient shouting. In others they were the reverse. One man turned to his comrades and in a calm and matter-of-fact manner said, "Don't worry, I'm off to fetch help. See you soon." Then he walked off the raft into the sea and disappeared.

Another man was calling, "I want my hammock, I want my hammock! I'm going for a sleep down below. Only for a minute, mates, but I must get a bit of shut-eye."

The gale swept upon them. The seas rose mountainously and as the submerged timbers of the raft tripped the waves, they broke in foam over the heads of the castaways. More than half floating, lacking the full force of gravity to pin them down, the mass of men (among whom was one woman) were driven irresistibly from the back of the raft to the front. Flexing and trembling in the surge, the projecting timbers and spars at the sides gave but slight footing now. Only around the mast in the center was there a semblance of solidity. Those men who were on the outside struggled briefly for a footing or a hold of some sort or floundered desperately toward the mast. But in a moment scores of them were swept away, their heads bobbing in the waves, arms flailing. The crush in the center, where the officers stood around the base of the mast, was terrible. Men slipped and disappeared under the water, other men lurched and fell on them. The waves stifled them or plucked them away.

The fury of the seas would inevitably have destroyed them all but for the direction of the wind, which was behind the sail they had rigged to the mast. The advance of the mountains of water appeared to be slowing down. Really, the raft was beginning to give way before the wind, moving obliquely shoreward. And it was lighter now, much lighter. Much of its original load of humanity had been shed.

The rolling combers pursued the raft, slowly heaving it up on their bulging crests. One moment, one side of the raft was tilted up to the sky, then a few moments later it was the other. The officers, trying to keep a footing in the center round the mast, began to call out for the men around them to rush first this way, then that, in order to balance the structure. But this attempt to control their destiny did not last.

Sure that they would all be drowned long before daybreak, many of the soldiers and sailors felt like having a last fling. They knocked a hole in a wine cask which was in the center of the raft and as each man still had the tin drinking cup he had been issued, all made merry. Seawater soon spoiled the wine through the hole they had made, and curses of disgust rent the air. They drank on empty stomachs. But worse, most were suffering from the tropic heat to which they were not accustomed, from the dehydration and lack of salt which accompanies exposure in such conditions, from almost total exhaustion after two days without sleep or rest of any kind, and from the hysterical excitement which danger and the prospect of imminent death can create.

Nothing the officers could say or do could stop this last desperate orgy. All their efforts achieved was to spark resistance, an uncoordinated revolt of individuals. Among the soldiers recruited from the jails of Toulon, Brest and Rochefort were Spaniards, Italians, Portuguese and Negroes, as well as Frenchmen. But it was a giant Asiatic, a soldier from a colonial regiment, who made the move which turned drunken grumbling into an insane action. When shouts of "Get rid of the officers!" were bellowed, he strode into the middle of the raft waving a boarding ax above his head. Towering over every other man there, he gave an impression of hideous power and determination. His curly hair was short-cropped, his sallow-skinned face dominated by an enormous gash of a mouth and a large nose. His physical strength was enormous. With a single blow of his fist he felled man after man who stood in his way. He waved high the ax at an officer who tried to stop him. For long minutes he dominated the raft, while behind him lesser individuals cried out to him to cut the rope bindings and let the raft go to pieces.

No real blood had been shed yet. The critical change came when the colossal and crazed Asiatic leaped from the middle of the raft to the edge and, with crashing blows of the boarding ax, began to sever the cords which held the timbers of the raft together. Restraint vanished in an instant. The curved blade of a saber rose and fell and the demented giant sank to his knees and collapsed, the first victim.

Shouts of fury from his friends and cries of alarm from those still in part possession of their senses formed the castaways into two opposing factions in an instant. Soldiers, but not all the soldiers, formed the largest part of the suicidal faction. The officers, passengers and engineering workmen, but not all the workmen, formed the basis of the survival faction. The soldiers among the mutineers drew sabers or bayonets; other men flashed out their knives. Like a moving hedge edged with sharp steel points, they advanced on the officers grouped at the foot of the mast. The points were presented, not raised to strike. But as the crowd closed on the officers one frantic mutineer lifted his saber for a deadly stroke—and was at once cut down, pierced by many wounds. The crowd stopped unbelievingly, shocked by the swiftness of the retribution, and retreated, still screaming with rage.

Now they used cunning. While the mass confronted the officers' party with the bristling steel blade points, blocking their view of the back of the raft, some of the mutineers started to slash unseen at the ropes. One man pretended to slump against the low railing at the side, as if exhausted, while stealthily he began to cut the cords with a knife. A servant who saw this told the officers what he was doing and a concerted rush was made at the man. The first officer to reach him was at once attacked from behind by a soldier, but the wild stab of the knifeblade only pierced the officer's coat. Swinging around, he threw the soldier into the sea and, a moment later, his saboteur comrade after him! Instead of further cowing the mutineers, it had the opposite effect.

What up to now had been a wary confrontation of the respective masses encouraging individual champions at once became a general combat. "Lower the sail!" yelled someone, and a tide of raging humanity surged forward and swarmed around the mast, slashing at the yard and shrouds, cutting the stays. The mast fell, pinning a captain of infantry, knocking him unconscious and nearly breaking his thigh. He was plucked up and thrown into the sea. His friends saved him and placed him on a barrel so that his head would be above water. The mutineers swarmed upon him and were going to cut out his eyes with a penknife. The officers' party lost all restraint. Their heavy sabers flashing, they cut and slashed their way through the ragged lines into which the mutineers had drawn themselves. Men screamed in agony, clasping sudden gaping wounds gushing blood, and collapsed into the water. Some of the civilian passengers joined the officers in the merciless struggle. All had momentarily forgotten how completely outnumbered they were.

\*     \*     \*

Alexander Corréard thought he was in Italy, a tourist with all the time in the world. That seemed a fine thing, he was so tired. Somewhere far off he could hear shouting, screams, curses. That was strange, but he was too weary to bother. Then, near at hand, there was a shout like a trumpet blast. "To arms! To arms!" He stirred and shook at the remembered command. "To arms! Or we're finished! Help us, comrades!"

Shakily, he staggered to his feet. The trance was leaving him, but only because he willed it to go, and that was a hard fight. Armed with his saber, which was but poor defense against the dreadful lethargy which only slowly drained away from him, Corréard got his engineering workmen together in a group at the front of the raft. Many were ex-soldiers and one was a former sergeant of the Old Guard. But this was not war; these were deluded fellow countrymen who had lost their internal struggle against whatever malaise it was that plagued the wretched castaways. Corréard told his men not to hurt anyone if they could help it. That was easier said than done, for the mutineers who were pushed overboard from the struggle at the back of the raft were carried by the waves to the other end, where they climbed aboard again.

Mutineers came at them from the back and from the front. The sharp steel of knives, sabers and bayonets threatened them from two sides, as did also a new weapon, for many of the rioters had picked up empty muskets to use as clubs. The workmen stood stolidly in line, presenting the points of their sabers calmly, as a withheld menace. Reluctant though they were to fight their fellow countrymen in earnest, they soon had no choice. Groups of demented but armed mutineers rushed on them. The hoarse, sharp breathing of men in combat with cutting and clubbing weapons requiring great physical energy to use showed how deadly the fight was. Man after man was slashed and torn, many repeatedly. Corréard had his flesh opened by a blade several times, but he hardly felt it at first.

He heard a voice crying out from the sea for help, was told that it was one of his own men by the name of Dominique, who had fought on the side of the mutineers, and immediately Corréard jumped in after him. Seizing him by the hair, he dragged Dominique back to the raft. It was still fairly dark, but they were able to find the wound and, judging it extensive, his comrades bound it up for him with a handkerchief, for he was losing a great deal of blood.

While Dominique still appeared half drowned and half dead, another tumult arose and there were more cries out of the heart of the dark sea. Some of the madmen had thrown the canteen "girl" and her husband overboard. She was actually a middle-aged woman, having served the Napoleonic armies in many campaigns. The despairing calls of the drowning woman aroused Corréard again, in spite of loss of blood from his wounds. Sensing his growing weakness, this time he tied a rope around his waist before jumping into the gale-lashed sea. Then the pair were hauled back to the raft, the woman invoking the aid of her favorite saint. Meanwhile the head foreman of engineers, the ex-sergeant of the Guard, Lavillette, rescued the woman's husband. To keep them from collapsing into the water which swept over the raft, the man and his wife were placed in a seated position upon some dead bodies, with their back supported by a barrel. Neither was fully conscious yet.

*　　*　　*

Almost as suddenly as it had begun, the fighting died. The mutineers, although they utterly outnumbered the officers' party, retreated to the back of the raft and were quiet. Some fell at the feet of the officers and begged pardon, which was instantly granted for all were aware of the mysterious malaise. Those who still had some control over themselves achieved this only by immense internal effort. Now the moon came out and lightened the narrow space which had been a battlefield and which was still strewn with dead and wounded, while the storm still howled and raged around them.

The canteen manageress and her husband recovered very quickly. Finding themselves in each other's arms, instead of in the raging surf where they had been driven by swords and bayonets, they cried with happiness. The woman's first rational thought was to find out who had saved her, and then to pour thanks upon Corréard. Finding that insufficient to express her feelings, she searched her pockets for the only possession she still had left—a little box of snuff—and gave it to him. Seated on a corpse, she handed him the magnificent present which Corréard, who did not use snuff, had to accept.

Feeling at a loss for conversation, but immensely moved by the gesture, Corréard ventured to observe, "Didn't I hear you mention our good Lady of Laux just now? There's a department of that name in the Upper Alps. Do you come from there?"

"Indeed, yes, sir. But I left there twenty-four years ago and ever since I've run a canteen. I was in the campaign in Italy, and many others. You see, it's a useful woman whose life you've saved!

"Often, I've risked death on the battlefield to help those brave men. I always let them have my goods, too, whether they had money or not. Sometimes, my debtors never came back, poor fellows. But after a victory, why, then others would pay me more than they owed. So you see, I too had a share in the victory!"

She positively glowed at the thought that her life had been saved by a Frenchman. But Corréard was drifting away again. He was in Italy, traveling across a splendid plain. He started drowsily from his trancelike state when an officer nudged him and stated gravely, "I know we've been deserted by the boats, old chap, but don't worry. I've just written to the governor and he'll be here in a few hours."

"That's good," murmured Corréard drowsily. "I suppose you had a pigeon, or the letter wouldn't have got there so quickly."

They were all lost in these private dreams. Some were back in the *Medusa*, in their own quarters. Others called out to passing ships for help. One man saw them approaching a harbor with a splendid city built on the heights above it. Others again dreamed that their dreams were of hand-to-hand combat ringing with cries of despair. When they awoke, they thought it had all been a dream. Illusion changed places with reality. They asked if anyone else had heard those disturbing sounds and other men would reply yes, they had; but it was just a vision, merely the effect of exhaustion.

Savigny recognized a delirium, like a burning fever where a thousand visions pass through the mind but few can be recollected when the patient wakes up. It was a fever of the night, he noted. The night brought a natural terror much enhanced by the brutal situation they were in. With daylight, people became calmer. But dawn was many hours away. It was not yet midnight.

*       *       *

Although they thought the crisis was over, the officers' party—fewer than two dozen of them—grouped themselves in the middle of the raft and kept their weapons close. For an hour they all lay quiet, hopelessly outnumbered. Afterwards, they wondered how they had survived so long against so many. The truth was, the tradition of the Napoleonic armies lay with them, whereas most of the men who wore the uniforms of soldiers were the rejects of society, degraded by the newly reestablished practice of branding. In the mass conscript armies of France which had dominated Europe for twenty years there had been a revulsion against flogging and branding. It was argued that such treatment broke a man's spirit and that he was never any good afterwards. Napoleon's conscripts went to war no more willingly than anyone else; they missed their homes and families; they found military life both harsh and boring. But they did not feel misused or degraded or that they were outcasts rejected by society. The prisoners whom the Royalists had formed into a regiment had had the mark of society's rejection permanently and brutally imprinted on their bodies by the branding iron, like cattle. Small wonder, thought the officers, that in the delirium which affected all on the raft, most of these men lacked the inner strength to retain some spark of sanity. Further, they had mixed wine with their fever.

Just before midnight, the mutineers rose again. They were now without restraint, beyond all reason. Those who had lost their bayonets or knives clawed and bit. They surged at the officers like a wave. The officers' group held together, then drove back the yelling madmen. Wild blows cut cloth and sometimes flesh. With clothes rent to tatters the officers fought on. Savigny's right hand was slashed by a knife, rendering two fingers useless. He was bitten in the leg and in the shoulder. Four mutineers seized one of Corréard's workmen. One held him by the right leg and began biting into the sinew above the heel, while the others belabored the man with the flat of a saber or the butts of their carbines. His screams reached Lavillette, ex-sergeant of the Guard, who led the rush to free him.

No sooner had they saved this man than the mutineers seized another, a junior army officer called
Lozach, shouting that they were going to be revenged
on Lieutenant d'Anglas. In vain, Lozach protested
that he was not d'Anglas. "You bastard, now you'll
pay for what you did to us in garrison! Remember
the Ile de Rhé? We haven't forgotten!" The terrified
Lozach, who had seen as little service as the man they
took him for and who it appears was almost equally
disliked, gave a last shout of despair as the mutineers
were hurling him over the side. That told the hard-
pressed officers that there was still a chance to save
his life, and they rushed to his rescue in small groups,
aided by some of the workmen. Savigny, Corréard,
even the disabled Coudein struggled forward, as well
as Lieutenant L'Heureux and Sub-Lieutenant Clairet
and the indomitable ex-Sergeant Lavillette.

In the struggle the workman Dominique, who had
deserted them earlier for the mutineers, whom they
had saved and helped nevertheless, was seen fighting
again on the side of the madmen; this time he was
killed. Lozach was rescued and dragged back to the
middle of the raft, and this caused them more trouble
than almost anything else. The mutineers bayed
around the group like vicious dogs, demanding that
d'Anglas be given up to them. In vain the officers
shouted back that d'Anglas wasn't on the raft at all.
He had gone back to the frigate before they had been
cast off. They had seen it for themselves. Still they
howled for d'Anglas. Somewhere in their disordered
minds they perhaps remembered that Lozach, an
officer who had seen service only with the Vendean
bands of Saint Pol-de-Léon, and who was not popular
with the officers either, had also imposed harsh pun-
ishments for trifles. Perhaps it was just that they remembered a hated face.

Momentarily cheated of their chance to avenge dim barrack square memories, the mutineers turned on an easier victim. Midshipman Coudein, the nominal commander of the raft, who had been injured aboard the frigate weeks before, had now been wounded in his effort to save Lozach. Exhausted, bleeding and totally incapable of further fighting, he was hunched out of the water on a barrel and was trying to protect Léon, a young sailor boy only twelve years old, from the maddened rushes of the struggling men to and fro across the submerged timbers of the raft. He and the lad were easy prey. Coudein, boy and barrel all together were hurled off the raft into the stormy darkness. Not quite done in, and still holding on to the boy, Coudein flung out his other arm and grasped one of the projecting spars of the raft. Eventually he was able to get the youth back on board.

\*     \*     \*

There was one thing and one thing only which could be said in favor of the raft—that, as a design, it was far betted fitted than any boat to survive a gale. Its openwork construction guaranteed that. The waves rose and fell through the gaps as if through a grid. And it was almost impossible to overturn.

Even in the best-found of the six boats morale reached breaking point that night. They were all running before heavy following seas with deep hollow troughs and immensely high crests. They were being pursued by these waves and could not travel fast enough to outrun them. This is one of the most dangerous situations possible, the rudder having little or no effect. But, nevertheless, if the boat swings slightly so that a following wave strikes at an angle, she is likely to overturn. And even if she can be kept straight at the critical moments, a breaking sea can roar right in over the stern regardless, filling the boat and probably sweeping the helmsman from the tiller. A fair amount of luck and extreme skill are required to survive.

Midshipman Charles Léonard Rang was one of the two men holding the tiller of the captain's barge, the other being the sailing master. Rang was the son of an émigré but had joined the navy in 1809, immediately after a successful incendiary raid by the British on the French fleet at Rochefort. Possibly his motive had been revenge. Apart from a cool, detached intelligence, he had both youth and experience on his side. In a quiet way, he was to describe the silent horror of the pursuit of the boats by the waves.

"That night was terrible and deprived most of the men of the small amount of courage still left in them. It was very dark at first, but when the strength of the wind finally cleared away the thick cloud which was hiding the land, then the moonbeams lit the huge waves which were breaking around us and allowed us to realize fully the horror of the position we were in. The master and I were steering and everyone else was simply staring at the waves running after us, while we were trying to avoid the next one astern."

The situation was the same in all the other boats, but some men were so exhausted with the continuous roaring and pounding, the lack of food and drink, the impossibility of proper rest, that they just dozed off where they were.

\*     \*     \*

M. Bredif was climbing in the Alps. The splendid scenery entranced him. Best of all he enjoyed the shade, as he walked out of the sun under the trees.

How much better things were now than during the war! There was that terrible time, in the forest just like this, when he and his sister had hidden from the Cossacks who were overrunning Kaiserslautern. Surely there must be a waterfall near here? There was the sound of a torrent running through a gorge, and why, he must be hanging over it. His face was wet with spray!

The engineer's body jerked with the mental effort of preventing himself from falling into the swift river, and his eyes opened. He was indeed suspended over water, from the side of Lieutenant Espiaux's longboat, and the roar of the torrent in his dream had been the lashing of the waves against the side.

The awakening was not pleasant. His head was stiff, his neck wracked with pain. He opened his ulcerated lips, but his parched tongue licked only at a bitter crust of salt which had formed in his mouth from the spray. The terrible shock of disillusion made him despair, and for a moment he thought of ending it all with a quick leap over the side. Then the weakness passed and he determined to endure.

At least the longboat was still afloat. The helmsman himself had doubted that she would survive long in the confused and raging seas that had sprung up with the storm. He had thought it impossible to dodge every giant wave and if they shipped only one over the stern, he had said, it would be a quick death. No one had laughed.

The silent horror they all felt was increased by a hollow, booming thunder sounding far off in the night but becoming more audible and menacing as the hours went by. Believing that they had covered a much greater distance than was really the case, they took the sound to be that of the waves breaking on the bar of the Senegal River. The thought that they were nearly opposite Saint-Louis was heartening, and, in order not to overrun their destination during the hours of darkness, they shortened sail and the boat almost hove to.

This was an error which was to have serious consequences, as they later realized. The booming was indeed the sound of breakers but merely of those tremendous rollers typical of West Africa. Lieutenant Espiaux's longboat was still more than sixty leagues north of the Senegal.

*　　*　　*

The fretful crying of the children mingled with the howling of the wind and the hissing roar of the waves which buffeted Sub-Lieutenant Lapeyrère's pinnace. Tears streamed down the young Madame Picard's face at the helpless, shuddering cries of the suffering child in her arms. The little body was aflame with thirst. But she had bared her breast and found she had nothing to give.

The agony of her parents was beyond Charlotte Picard's powers to describe. The young children, too young to understand, were racked by thirst and hunger, and every moment tossed violently this way and that as the brute waves smashed at the timbers of the pinnace in never-ceasing vicious motion. M. Picard and his wife had brought their large family to this and yet were powerless to help, let alone protect them from the dangers of the sea.

The wind howled and screamed over their heads like some live beast, increasing in force and power every minute. The driven waves climbed still higher until one great monster rose up at them like a mountain and swept the boat from end to end. The torrent of water drove the women and the children from their seats in an instant, carried overboard the little luggage they had brought with them, ripped a sail from the mast and plucked it away. Only the father, clinging on with both hands, still kept his place, while his wife and the six children were washed and thrown about the boat, screaming.

Miraculously, the pinnace recovered. But M. Picard was more affected than his family. He was in despair. The financial loss he had suffered from the wreck of the *Medusa* spelled ruin to his family if they should survive at all. And there was nothing he could do to help them survive. Even if there had been only a single person looking to him for help, he was powerless to give it. His family at once flocked around him, but it seemed to make matters worse. He clasped and hugged them all, tears streaming down his face. Inwardly, he was saying good-bye to his loved ones and blaming himself for their fate.

The shock the family had had from the terrible power manifested by that giant wave was shared with every other soul in the boat. But the reactions showed in different ways. Many of the sailors became quiet and still, shaken and bewildered; others cheered and encouraged one another. The children clung tightly to their parents, sobbing without pause; some through their tears, gulped out pleas for a drink, while they vomited up the seawater they had just swallowed. Others asked for nothing, just sobbed their hearts out, wanting only to stay with their parents until the seas closed over them.

Thunder growled and thumped out over the water and the lightning flashes showed an indescribable wilderness of black waves streaked with white foam. Almost everyone in the boat was helping bail out the water which continually burst over the sides, but still the floorboards were covered with it. They soon found the reason—a large hole in the side where a plank had been stove in by the power of the sea. Instantly, they began to stuff it with anything at hand—old clothes, sleeves of shirts, shreds of coats, shawls, useless bonnets —and hoped that the plug would hold.

About the middle of the night the winds died as abruptly as they had risen and the waves began to flatten out and lose their force. When the sky lightened, with the sun still hidden, they did not know which way to go, for the compass had been smashed in the storm and there was no land in sight anywhere.

*　　*　　*

As the same sky lightened over the raft, now driven far, far to the south, the miasma of the night evaporated with the darkness. Weakened, but no longer feverish, the survivors could take in the full horror of the scene. There seemed only about sixty of them left. Their numbers had been more than halved during the wild fury of that night.

Of those who had been lost, Savigny estimated that no more than a quarter had been swept off the timbers by the gale or had simply committed suicide by allowing themselves to be carried away. The majority had died by being cut down or battered to death in the desperate hand-to-hand conflicts which had swept back and forth across the half-submerged structure. He based this guess on the fact that many of their bodies still littered the raft. Only two were from the officers' party and neither of these was an officer. The wounds among the survivors were too many to count or to compare.

On every face was the deepest despondency as they realized what they had done to each other.

When, slowly, they began to take stock of the situation the numbing truth came home. In the madness of the night, the mutineers had thrown into the sea the bulk of their drinking supplies. Both barrels of water and one of the wine barrels were gone. Only a single barrel of wine now remained. That would not last sixty men very long, even on half rations.

# 7

# Intolerable Pressures
## *( July 7 and 8)*

July 7 was the third day adrift for the castaways on the raft. The third day of close confinement. The third day of helplessness. The third day of exposure to extreme heat and burning sun with insufficient drink and food.

The third day was notable for a reduction in the sense of irritation felt by the castaways. With so many gone overboard or sprawled dead on the raft, there was more space; their sense of confinement and restriction was eased. There was also a faint sense of hope once more, of at least going in the right direction, of doing something to aid themselves.

Soon after dawn the sea became calm and this enabled them to set up the mast again. The coast was not in sight but all thought that they could perceive the distant shimmer of heated air from the burning desert. Having seen so many illusions, they were not entirely convinced now; but it seemed logical that land was just over the horizon. All night the gale had been blowing them inshore at an angle to the coast. That much was sure. All the same, they had undoubtedly reached a watershed and half had passed over the other side. Some thirty men were far-gone and, thought Savigny, clearly dying. "The half of our men were very weak, and bore on all their features the stamp of approaching dissolution," he wrote. For them, rescue would have to come this day or it would be too late.

Unless they could find food. They dreamed of food. Men had even fought for food during the night, attacking other men and demanding that they be given a wing of chicken or a loaf of bread. Although the water had gone overboard, there was still a little wine left. But not a man had touched food of any sort for two days. Their last "meal" had been a little sea-soaked biscuit on the day they were abandoned. Proper food had not passed their lips since the evening of July 4, nearly three days before.

They thought of fish and despite their exhaustion set about devising ways and means to catch some of the live meat that was so prolific in the sea around them. They made hooks out of the identity tags carried by the soldiers, but the raft was such a crazy mass of timbers that the lines became entangled and useless. These were meant to catch little fish. But a shark would feed them all. They bent a bayonet into a curve to make a shark-hook and saw one of the streamlined monsters make a dash at it. The shark bit but was not hooked. Instead, the bayonet was straightened out.

They were still standing to their knees in water. For three days no one had been able to lie down. They could rest only by standing together in a mass so tightly packed that when a man dozed off momentarily, he did not fall down. A shark could have swum over the raft to feed on them, but they were beyond fearing the great fish. They thought only of catching a shark in order to eat it, but they were too weak to attempt any form of food gathering which required great mental or physical effort.

There was fresh meat on the raft, a great deal of meat: the bodies of their companions who had been killed during the night. Some of the castaways began to cut the corpses with their knives, stuffing the bits of flesh into their mouths and devouring them with desperate urgency. Many men abstained, including almost all the officers; but it was soon clear that the men who had eaten felt better for it and might live a little longer. Hope of being found by the boats or by a ship from the squadron was still with them. More men decided to try to save themselves in this way but, shuddering at the thought of uncooked human flesh soaked in seawater, tried to dry it before eating.

Many could not overcome their repugnance. The spectacle of other men eating made them desperate, however. They tried to consume bits of leather hacked off their swordbelts or cartridge pouches, washing the morsels down with a little wine. Some men gnawed at pieces of clothing, others chewed at pieces of leather from their hat bands, the grease and dirt giving an impression of food. One sailor tried to eat excrement but could not force himself to swallow.

Midshipman Coudein later reported briefly: "Among the unfortunate people spared by death, the most starved ones rushed onto the remnants of one of their brothers, tore flesh off the corpse and fed themselves with this horrible meal. At that moment, a great number of us did not touch it. Only a short while later, we were forced to do so."

The long day of July 7 was calm and so was the night which succeeded it. For once the onshore gale did not blow, but they were now beyond all attempts to trim the sail to a favorable wind. They were re-signed to letting the raft drift wherever the winds and currents happened to take it. When darkness fell they tried to sleep, swaying together in a dense mass with the waves washing about their knees. From long exposure to the sun their skins were dry and blackened and their legs, from immersion in salt water, were puffy and sore. Added to the torment of hunger and thirst, these agonies caused men to cry out in pain, continually waking those who were asleep on their feet.

When the sun rose on the morning of July 8, the fourth day of their ordeal, they could see that another ten or a dozen men had failed to survive the night. The effect was salutary. Even the fastidious man came to know that he was under sentence of death and that execution could not be delayed for more than a few hours if he did not eat. The bodies were rolled off the raft to lighten it.

All bar one. That single exception was reserved as a meat ration. The previous day the object had been a man, to some of them more than that—a friend. They had even shaken hands with him, hands trembling with fatigue and fever, and vowed to survive together or die together.

This day also was calm and fine and a little flicker of hope returned. At about four o'clock in the afternoon a shoal of flying fish passed under the raft and found the spaces between the projecting side timbers a trap. They were tiny fish, smaller than a small herring, but the castaways flung themselves on the struggling creatures and scooped them up. Nearly two hundred were caught and put in a barrel; eaten raw, this food seemed delicious.

In the morning an ounce of damp gunpowder was found, and by afternoon the organizing group managed to dry it in the hot sun, so that it would burn. In the same parcel there was wrapped a steel, some flints and tinder. A fireplace was constructed by cutting a large hole in a wooden cask and putting damp material underneath. The cask was placed on a barrel to keep it well above the waves which still washed over the raft, and inside the cask a fire was lighted, the principal fuel being dry linen. Some of the fish were cooked in this way and were hungrily devoured. The entire catch would not really have sufficed to satisfy one man, so some human flesh was added as well. The mixture of fresh fish with the meat made it less loathsome to eat. For the first time all the officers ate some human flesh, and from now on they continued to eat it.

However, this was the last hot meal they were to have. The wooden fireplace caught fire and in putting out the flames the essential materials were lost. There was neither powder nor tinder left. But they felt better, definitely better.

*　　　*　　　*

The castaways on the raft suffered predominantly from hunger, and the pressures turned them all by degrees to cannibalism during the two-day period of July 7 to 8. In the three ill-found boats it was otherwise. Thirst was their principal torment and this also grew to be intolerable during the same two-day period. There was a little to eat, mostly biscuit, in these three boats, but whereas there was a tiny water ration in the longboat and the pinnace, the men in the Senegal port boat had nothing at all to drink for two days.

The gale had separated all the boats and on the morning of July 7 each one was alone. The pinnace commanded by Sub-Lieutenant Lapeyrère was out of sight of land when the darkness lightened before dawn. With a broken compass, it was steering erratically until the sun rose. Then it was sailed toward the sun and the sand dunes of the Sahara.

Some of the sailors had been sufficiently desperate to drink seawater, which had increased their thirst. They urged Lapeyrère to land on the coast and look for water, but most of the passengers were too afraid of the Arabs. In any case, they all expected to reach the Senegal River the next day, not knowing how wrong the sub-lieutenant had been in his calculations. Nevertheless, the sailors demanded to be set on shore at once, so Lapeyrère agreed to take them in as close to the breakers as he could and let them swim to the beach from there. Eleven men agreed to risk this, but when the boat was near enough to see the actual height and fury of the surf through which they would have to swim, they changed their minds. They went back quietly to their oars.

The day's ration was distributed shortly after, and when it had been given out, what remained for the future was four pints of water and six biscuits to be shared among more than forty people. As the pinnace coasted southward everyone looked anxiously for some gap in the breakers through which the boat might be safely steered, but all they saw was a party of Arabs. They headed out to sea again, still believing that they would sight the river mouth the next day. One more day of pitiless sun blazing down on their heads from directly above. Almost all of them, including Charlotte Picard, now drank salt water. To her shame, she also observed that some of the sailors drank urine. But it hardly mattered. Laura, her little stepsister, only six years old, lay dying at her mother's feet. Her cries for water were so pitiful that her father conceived the idea of opening one of his own veins, so that she might drink his blood. He was prevented by a man who observed that not all the blood in his body would prolong for one moment the life of his child.

The coming of the onshore wind in the evening

was a blessing. It gave some relief from the heat and the glare, but it was not so strong as to endanger the boat. They were able to anchor fairly near the shore and everyone was able to sleep peacefully.

On the morning of July 8 the sails were hoisted again, but the wind soon fell away to a dead calm. They began to row but the men were too exhausted to make much progress and a halt was called for the distribution among forty-two people of the final ration: six biscuits, four pints of water. When this had been consumed, which did not take long, there were no more supplies of food and drink in the boat.

The very finality of it emphasized that they now had to make a choice between two alternatives: to risk a slow death from the sun by continuing to row toward the Senegal or to risk a rapid death from the sea by attempting to get through the breakers to reach the shore of the Sahara. The majority favored the latter, although death by drowning appeared to be more a certainty than a risk. But then, if the calm continued and they were forced to row, all would be dead long before they could reach the mouth of the Senegal. With her crew slowly and painfully pulling at the oars, the pinnace crept in toward the coast. Dunes of white and burning sand could soon be made out, and then a few small trees. The prospect did not look very promising, even if they survived the passage through the breakers. Only the splashing of the oars broke the mournful silence into which they had sunk. Then a sailor started up and pointed:

"Look, the Moors!"

Petrified with terror, Charlotte Picard saw what he was pointing at: a number of men walking very quickly along the crest of one of the dunes. The pinnace turned out to sea immediately, to get away from the beach. Even in spite of the breakers, they all feared that the Arabs might somehow swim out to the pinnace and capture them. This was the slave coast of Africa and to the Moors human beings were as valuable as animals.

After several hours the pinnace again approached the coast, when several figures were seen standing on top of a very high dune. The Arabs were everywhere! . . . Waiting for the shipwrecked men and women to be cast upon the shore. . . .

*       *       *

Lieutenant Espiaux gave M. Bredif the task of making out a new list of the men in the longboat and of distributing the water ration to them from a central point. The passengers had changed considerably since the previous day, July 6, when sixty-three men and women had insisted on going ashore and soon after fifteen men had been saved from the sinking yawl. There were now only about forty people in the longboat, less than half the number who had embarked directly from the *Medusa*. Even so, they had little water left. As each man came to him for his meager ration, Bredif poured it out from a tin cup while he held the list underneath its lip, so that if any tiny droplet of moisture spilled it would fall on the paper and could still be used for moistening his lips. Only a few men drank seawater and Bredif observed that this seemed to worsen their condition.

The longboat was alone until about midday on July 8, when another boat was sighted, lying still in the water. This proved to be the Senegal port boat commanded by Ensign Maudet, with its crew and passengers in a state of mutiny. The twenty-five men in it had suffered more severely than those in the longboat. All were determined to go ashore and seek water, as they now had had nothing to drink for two days. The angry debate then raging was whether to coast along until a safe approach to the beach could be seen or whether they should turn into the breakers immediately and take their chance of drowning. The sailors demanded to be landed at once, emphasizing their wishes by waving their sabers. The officers who had pistols, opposed the plan. For a moment, it seemed that the kind of butchery which had taken place upon the raft would be enacted also in this boat, but the officers capitulated. The boat's two sails were hoisted and with oars beating the water the Senegal boat gained speed for the attempt to surf through the breakers. For long minutes the passengers in the longboat watched its progress.

When they saw that the boat survived the passage of the breakers, although it filled with water on the far side, and that the men were able to wade through the shallows to safety, the sailors in the longboat were encouraged. They recklessly demanded a chance to do the same. Espiaux said that he would land them if he could but would not risk the longboat itself because he for one thought they had a better chance to make Saint-Louis by sea. Those who agreed with him grouped themselves around the water supplies and drew their swords to defend it. Espiaux put out an anchor so that the longboat could be drifted close to the breakers on a line but could still be hauled off to safety. The sailors, however, cut or untied the line and the longboat was heaved by the swell into the broken water. The first breaker went right over their heads, leaving the boat three-quarters filled with water but still afloat. A sail was hoisted which took the water-logged craft straight in toward the beach.

Bredif was virtually naked as he had been drying out his clothes at the time the decision had been taken; he did not put them on again because they might hamper his swimming. His friend de Chasteluz could not swim, so as the floundering boat was flung shoreward by the breakers, Bredif took the end of a rope which de Chasteluz was fastening around himself. Bredif planned to swim to shore with the rope, then pull in his nonswimming friend like a hooked fish. The last breaker filled the boat entirely and it sank. Bredif threw himself overboard and was surprised, and relieved, when he found that his feet touched the sand. He was standing only chest-deep in the sea.

Relieved of anxiety about his comrade in the water, Bredif got back into the sunken boat and started to look for his clothes and his sword. Some of them had already been stolen by quick-witted sailors and he could find only his coat and a spare pair of pantaloons. He had no shoes, and a Negro at once offered to sell him an old pair for 8 francs.

The sailors had also saved the barrel of water which represented the total of their drinking supplies. Once they had it safely on the beach, they fought among themselves for a drink. This was much too much for the half-naked and infuriated Bredif. He burst into the crowd, hurling them aside, snatched the barrel from the man who was gulping down the liquid and swallowed two good mouthfuls before losing the barrel to some one else. They did him as much good as two bottles, he reckoned; without them he could not have lived more than a few hours longer. As it was, he was wet through, stripped of most of his clothes and all his possessions, with no water to drink and with only a few soaked biscuits for a food ration. And, like all the rest, he was afraid of the Moors, whose ferocity was legendary.

The forty men of the longboat waited until they were joined by the twenty-five men from the Senegal boat which had been wrecked a short distance to the north. Then they set off to march along the beach because the sea breeze made the edge of the sea a little cooler than the interior of the Sahara and the damp sand was easier to walk on than the fine, shifting sand of the dunes inland. They had been tramping southward for only half an hour when they saw another boat, the third to be wrecked that day, coming in toward the beach under full sail. As it drove violently on shore, to be stranded in the shallows, Bredif tore off his clothes again and dashed into the water to help, for he could see that there were women and children aboard.

*     *     *

The pinnace was also driven to shore by the thirst of all the occupants, but by common consent. There was no dispute in their case as the wisest course to take. What had prevented them from landing until now was the belief that the people they had first seen ashore were Moors. After several hours of slow progress they again saw on a dune several people whom they took to be Arabs. But when the distant figures began waving at them, they looked more attentively. As soon as they realized that these men were also castaways from the *Medusa*, they replied to their signals by hoisting a white handkerchief to the mast top and then set about looking for a way through the breakers. The sea itself was calm; it was the Atlantic swell spending itself on the shores of Africa which made the last lap perilous.

The helmsman was directed to the right, where the waves seemed deceptively lower. Almost at once they saw another group of people ashore, a large group this time, and were close enough to recognize individuals. Charlotte Picard was terrified, for they were now into the breakers. Each wave that swept in from seaward, sensing resistance from the shelving beach after its three thousand miles of uninterrupted passage across the Atlantic, swelled up suddenly and monstrously under the boat. The bow of the pinnace rose high in the air and then dropped shudderingly down onto the face of the wave, throwing the occupants alternately backward and forward. The helm was now given to the old seaman whose skill had saved them during the gale, for at all costs the boat must not swing sideways to the rollers.

The pinnace came safely through two lines of breakers, when they saw ahead a third and final range. Beyond it was the beach and the men from the other boats. They were all trying to signal warnings. Then some turned away as if not wanting to witness what was to happen, while others dashed forward into the shallows to be able to help sooner. The water in front of them heaved itself up to a prodigious height, then fell upon the sand with a hollow clap of thunder that seemed to shake the coast.

That third range took the pinnace as though it were a straw, picked it up, slued it sideways and flung the occupants around like peas. The next wave of the series actually broke upon the floundering pinnace in a vast explosion of water, the groaning of strained timbers, the splintering of oars. All the occupants were suddenly engulfed in boiling foam. As the water drew back again, the pinnace reappeared, immovable, actually stranded on the beach. There was no time for more than a few gasping breaths before the next roller was rearing up. It broke just to seaward of them and a hissing torrent of water came rushing up the beach like a striking snake, covered with white foam.

Charlotte Picard was up to her neck in water and she was a full-grown girl. The four young children were all under the age of six years and quite helpless. Confronted with an emergency that they understood and could handle, the sailors who had seemed so mutinous and selfish produced an astounding burst of energy. In a flash, the grapnel was flung out to hold the boat high up the beach and prevent it from being dragged back out to sea, under the bursting rollers. Then they plunged overboard, scooped up the small children in their arms and ran them up the beach to safety. Returning, they picked up the older females, put them on their shoulders and carried them also up the beach. Charlotte found herself sitting on the sand beside her stepmother, her brothers and her sisters, who seemed half dead. Only her father was missing.

M. Bredif plunged into the surf too late to save any of the children, which had been his intention. The sailors had acted instantly. But he was able to help them get M. Picard from the wreck and up the beach to join his family. Then he went to look for his clothes and once again discovered that they had been stolen. This time his rage was violent and his language uncontrolled. He bellowed out what he thought of petty thieving in these circumstances. Possibly the robber may have felt remorse, for shortly afterwards Bredif found his coat and pantaloons lying farther along the beach.

Four out of the six boats had now gone: the yawl, the port boat, the longboat and the pinnnace. The bulk of their occupants, amounting to about 110 men, women and children, were now ashore in one place with little food and no water at all.

The sixty-three men and women who had voluntarily landed from the longboat earlier, somewhere to the north, with some eighty to ninety leagues to march across the desert, had suffered severely until they found a freshwater lake. Several people died during their march, including a gardener and a soldier's wife. They had no reliable chronicler among them, so little is known. On the evening of July 8, more than 170 of the *Medusa*'s people were ashore from the boats and in desperate circumstances.

The two seaworthy and well-provisioned craft, the barges of Captain de Chaumareys and Governor Schmaltz, were still afloat far to the south. By sunset they had sighted Grieuse Wood, a landmark not far from the mouth of the Senegal River, their destination. Since the morning of July 7, they had been keeping company on an otherwise empty sea. Neither of these two men had appeared concerned about the fate of the longboat or the pinnace or any of the other boats; they certainly did not search for them, but rather carried on southward. Their crews also had suffered from the overpowering torment of the days. Men had become so thirsty that some had drunk seawater and others had satisfied themselves by sucking on lead shot from the pistols and muskets.

In the captain's barge there had been a demand from some of the men to be set ashore in order to find water, but it was not strongly pressed until next day, when their total supplies were found to consist of three bottles of Tenerife wine. The gentlemanly and perhaps politic gesture was made of presenting one of the three bottles to Madame Schmaltz, the governor's lady, in the accompanying boat.

The sailors' reaction was marked. They demanded that a vote be democratically taken as to whether or not the captain's barge should run ashore to search for water. When it seemed that the vote would go in favor of a landing, Governor Schmaltz made a graceful reciprocal gesture. He kindly offered a place in his barge to Captain de Chaumareys and his two officers, Sub-Lieutenant Chaudière and Midshipman Rang. However, the men did not go through with their intention when repeatedly assured that the boats would reach the Senegal within a few hours.

At ten o'clock that night, shortly after sighting the approach marks to Saint-Louis, the shapes of two vessels were seen. They proved to be Captain de Vénancourt's corvette *Echo* and Lieutenant de Parnajon's brig *Argus*.

The corvette, as the senior vessel, hailed the approaching craft, asking who they were.

"Two boats from the *Medusa*."

There was a pause. Then the corvette hailed again, "Who are you?"

"Two boats from the *Medusa*."

There was no reply until the barge carrying de Chaumareys had come alongside the corvette. Then a rope was thrown to them and an officer asked them to come on board at once. Leaning over the side, he called down:

"Where is the *Medusa*?"

For long seconds, no one replied. Not a man spoke. De Chaumareys was silent.

Then Rang said, quietly, "Her captain will tell you in a moment."

\*   \*   \*

These two boats and the raft were all that was left. Of the 150 who had embarked on the raft, still drifting somewhere out at sea, the majority were already dead. Another night of butchery was about to begin. By morning only 1 woman and 29 men would be left alive.

# 8

# Time Running Out
## *( July 9 to 13 )*

By nightfall on July 8, fragmentation was complete among the castaways on the raft. Earlier, there had been a tendency for the people to reject their identity as part of a suffering mass, because they rejected the unfair sufferings inflicted on them for no fault of their own. Then they coalesced into subgroups grumbling among themselves and consoling each other and showing hostility to other subgroups. To begin with, the lines were not firmly drawn. Most of the soldiers were on one side, but not all. Some people were on nobody's side; they were neutral.

Now, however, the jumbled mass of humanity shook down to its basic ingredients and coalesced at that level. The Negroes among the soldiers became Negroes first and soldiers a long way second. Their sense of identity was reinforced by the nearness of their own continent. They felt, from signs obvious to them but not to the Europeans, that the raft was close to the coast and that, once ashore, they at least could survive. Their actions were soon to show that they had been much less affected physically by the suffocating heat and burning sun than the Europeans, whose bodies were seriously depleted of both water and salt. Confidence in their own powers of survival in these conditions enabled them to concoct a plan by which they would survive at the expense of the others. Because they needed greater numbers than they at present amounted to the Negroes approached another newly formed subgroup for an alliance.

Led by a Piedmontese sergeant, these men were all Italians or Spaniards and most had been neutral or had actually supported the French officers. The offer of the Negroes to guide them across the desert, once they were ashore, gave them hope of being able to reach ultimate safety. That in turn led their thoughts toward money, without which they might be little better off. The valuables and cash belonging to everyone, amounting to 1,500 francs, had been put in a bag which had been tied to the top of the mast for safety and was temptingly in view all the time. The sergeant had already stolen some of the wine for his people, an easy task because the officers had put him in charge of it, and seems to have conceived the details of the plan to drive the officers off the raft.

An attempt was made to subvert some of the French sailors. This proved to be fatal to the success of the plot because these men had formed a separate subgroup. The seamen had a basic psychological advantage matching that of the Negroes' confidence in their desert-survival capabilities. A factor behind the despair, resentment and irritation which had afflicted so many and had led in part to the suicidal butcheries was the sheer unexpectedness of being one moment safe on board a ship and the next cast away and apparently doomed to die. Many had been maddened with rage at this abrupt and unfair transition. For an experienced seaman, however, the prospect of shipwreck and possible death in the sea was an accepted occupational hazard—not to be welcomed, but part of the world as it was. Their attitude was professional, calmer; and this bound them together. To them, the plot was crazy; it ignored the difficulty of actually getting ashore on a coast that was not even visible on the horizon.

They told the officers what was afoot and pointed out to them those men whom they knew definitely to be in the plot, but they did not know them all. The signal for revolt was given by a Spaniard moving toward the mast. Once there, he drew a knife and with his other hand made the sign of the cross. The sailors overpowered the man and threw him into the sea. An Italian soldier did not wait to be disposed of in the same fashion. Still holding the ax with which he had armed himself, he jumped overboard. The plot had gone wrong from the outset, the advantage of a surprise rush lost.

Nevertheless, the Negroes and the remaining Italians and Spaniards launched their attack. They were gibbering with rage and crying for Lieutenant d'Anglas to be handed over to them. This had become a kind of rallying cry and it was impossible to reason with them. In the vicious fighting which raged in the darkness, the canteen manageress was again thrown into the sea; she was rescued by the injured Coudein and some of the engineering workmen who remained an organized body led by their foreman, the redoubtable ex-Sergeant Lavillette. Savigny and Corréard cited his courage and effectiveness in close-quarter fighting as a main factor, once again, in the survival of their party. The brief burst of energy which had fueled both the revolt and its repulse was succeeded by exhaustion, nervous as well as physical. The survivors were drained of all feeling and emotion and lay supine until the sun rose.

They could now count the living and see that some twenty men had died during the night, including four or five loyal sailors. Of the thirty people left, many were seriously injured. The canteen manageress had suffered a broken thigh from being thrown between the timbers of the raft, while her husband's skull had been cut open by a slash from a saber. Only about twenty men were still capable of standing upright. And they, like the badly injured, were in agony from long immersion in seawater. The skin had almost been completely stripped off their legs and their bruises and cuts burned with the saltwater irritant. They could not keep silent but cried out with pain continually.

An additional torment was the derangement of the young sailor lad, Léon, who ran about the raft as if demented, calling out for his mother, for water and for food. When he stumbled over the feet and legs of the men, their agony was terrible. They screamed at him not to do it, but without real reproach. They pardoned him everything, for it was hard to see a child dying before he had had a chance to live. Besides, the boy had been very brave and was half a veteran, for he had been on campaign in the East Indies the previous year. He was given more than his share of the little wine they had left, but clearly his life was flickering out like the flame of a lamp when the fuel runs low.

July 9 was the fifth day afloat for the castaways. The only food they had left was a dozen small fish. The wine might last the thirty of them four days more. After that, death would come swiftly for all. They calculated over and over again the simple arithmetic of rescue, and always the answer came out the same. The boats had not come back for them. Therefore, they had either been wrecked in the surf in trying to land on the coast, or they had gone on to Saint-Louis to get help. If—if—they had gone on to Saint-

Louis, they could not reach there in fewer than three or four days. They might have arrived at the Senegal yesterday, perhaps. But then a search and rescue operation would have to be organized, ships would have to be prepared and stored and then they would have to find the raft, which, as far as they knew, might have drifted anywhere. Working out how long that search might take was an unrewarding exercise, for they themselves did not know where they were. But all could see that they had not enough time. They began to think of ways to prolong their existence just a day or two more beyond the four days which was still their final horizon.

\*     \*     \*

The feverishly impatient hopes of the castaways, that with luck the boats might already have arrived at Saint-Louis, were not far off the mark. But they were not the whole truth. One boat had been sunk, three driven ashore and wrecked because the occupants were dying of thirst. All these people were themselves now in need of rescue. Although the captain and governor had sailed into the roads off Saint-Louis late on July 8, the situation was so chaotic that they felt they could not cope with it until the next day. Therefore, although Lieutenant de Parnajon was ready and eager to sail at once in the *Argus*, a full council had to be held before he could be given his orders.

These were from Governor Schmaltz, dated July 9: "You will proceed along the coast of the desert and search for the shipwrecked persons in the most likely places, excluding St. John's Creek, where they could not penetrate, and you will supply them with such provisions and ammunition as they may want. After having assured yourself of the fate of these unfortunate persons, you will sail along the coast up to the point where the frigate lies, because there is a possibility that the men on the raft may have sheltered there, if helped by favorable tides. You will then continue your course toward the *Medusa* and you will do everything in your power to find the three barrels containing 90,000 francs in gold belonging to the king. These three barrels will be found in the storeroom, as they could not be taken away when we left the ship. . . ."

Of course, it was proper for the governor to think of the money belonging to his treasury; but it might have been better if he had ordered a search to seaward for the raft. In effect, instead of the boats bringing a ship to aid the people on the raft, only a single vessel was to be sent out to the aid of the people from the boats—and to save the treasure of the *Medusa*.

The truth which the thirty tormented survivors on the raft could not guess was that they had already been given up for dead. When the news of the shipwreck was discussed in Saint-Louis, it brought the stoic comment: "It's a pity the raft was abandoned, for there were many brave fellows on board. But their sufferings are over now. They may be happier than we are, for who knows how all this will end?"

The arrival of the French Royal squadron in such disarray, with its flagship and many of its passengers lost in circumstances of obvious incompetence made the English governor, Lieutenant Colonel Brereton, unwilling to hand over the colony of Senegal to the new French governor, Colonel Schmaltz. It was this serious situation which was now the prime concern of the senior French officials.

\*       \*       \*

Lieutenant Espiaux had taken command of the combined crews of the three boats which had been stranded at intervals, more or less in the same area, during the morning and afternoon of July 8. Charlotte Picard recalled that he had reproached them for their suspicions and explained how he had earlier landed sixty-three people and so had room for the Picard family. That party was now somewhere to the north, too far away to make contact but sufficiently numerous to hold off small bands of Moors. Espiaux led his group of more than one hundred people southward, sometimes along the beach, sometimes moving inland in hope of finding water. Very often they marched during the night or through a part of the night. Although the sequence of events they record is the same, the actual days blurred in the memories of both Mlle. Picard and M. Bredif.

The first event was a decision to march inland in search of water which they found by digging holes in the sand. The water under the dunes contained more salt than did the sea itself, so they trudged on to an inland plain where Bredif noticed little clumps of tall, hard grass growing. When they had dug here to a depth of three or four feet, they uncovered water which was white in appearance and smelled of sulfur. Bredif risked taking a mouthful, found it delicious and cried out, "We're saved!"

They drank their fill, rested, tried to eat a little of the soaked biscuit they had with them and then trudged back to the firmer sand of the beach to continue their march southward. This event took place on the evening of July 8, according to Bredif, on the morning of July 9, according to Charlotte Picard. The evenings and early mornings, were the most favorable for walking, for in the full heat of the days it was so suffocatingly hot that they could do little more than lie down and try to rest. Both accounts make clear how the presence of the young children of the Picard family were a constant hindrance to the progress of the march party, and it was the underlying fear of everyone that even a small delay during a trek across the Sahara might lead to the deaths of all.

The Picard family's clothes were in tatters and they had lost their shoes in the wreck of the pinnace. It was painful for them to walk on hot sand, let alone over areas strewn with sharp-edged seashells. Madame Picard and two of the older girls gratefully accepted items of men's clothing from the officers, who also took turns carrying the children. The sailors followed their example. The Picards were set at the head of the party so that they would not be left behind if they straggled. Even so, the women and children had a hard time and Bredif recalled a moment when M. Picard could stand no more and for the sake of his family demanded that everyone halt. His position was peculiarly unfortunate, as the head of a group which was keeping everyone back and risking the lives of all; and yet there was little he himself could do. The poor man could hardly carry four children and help his wife and grown-up daughters at the same time.

On July 9, according to Charlotte, the conflict came to a head. Two naval officers complained of the inability even of the adult females in the family to keep up. There was a proposal to abandon them. M. Picard replied bitterly with accusations of selfishness and brutality. These officers and their few supporters put their hands on their swords. M. Picard seized the hilt of the poniard with which he had armed himself aboard the frigate. The females flung themselves in front of M. Picard and loudly implored him to stay in the desert with them, rather than ask for help from Frenchmen who were clearly worse than Moors. This touched an infantry officer, Captain Bégnère, who persuaded his soldiers to stay with the family; and their decision shamed the others into acceptance. Soon afterwards, however, two members of the party left it individually and strode off inland on their own. They were the naturalist M. Kummer and M. Rogéry, a member of the Philanthropic Society of Cape Verde. They thought, doubtless, that their specialized knowledge and experience would give them a higher survival value alone than when tied to a party marching at the pace of the slowest female.

To Charlotte, Africa was a terrible place. That night, she was wakened by the roaring of leopards and the camp was alarmed by the sight of a lion, which proved to be a bush moving with the night breeze. Marching on at sunrise, their scouts sighted two Moorish tents just inland, the homes of shepherds. They were occupied only by Moorish women and children, virtually naked, who struck Bredif as being as "ugly and frightful" as the desert they inhabited. However, they were able to buy or barter food from them, including two goats. They rested here during the worst heat of the day until startled by a cry of "To arms, to arms!"

The alarm was caused by the approach of a small party of Moors and Negroes armed with lances. The French armed themselves against attack and nearly came to blows with the intruders, whom they greatly outnumbered, until by means of sign language the Moors seemed to indicate that they came as guides. Bredif thought them fine-looking men and their well-dressed Negro slave a proud and handsome man. This Negro could not contain his mirth at the evident fear of some of the Negro soldiers with the French party, who still had their swords drawn in alarm. He stepped into the middle of them, placed the points of their sabers to his chest and threw his arms wide in a gesture to show that he was not afraid of them and they ought not to fear him.

Their guides led them to a large Moorish camp some distance away. By the time they reached there Charlotte's dress was further torn and her legs streaming with blood from walking through the prickly shrubs which grew in abundance. The women, children and dogs of the tribe thought the tattered French party as outlandish as the Mooresses had appeared to Bredif. They swarmed around to examine the strangers, pinched them, snatched at their hair, threw sand at them. The dogs bit at their legs, while the old crones, delighted, cut the buttons off the officers' coats or snatched away pieces of lace. At length, the guides drove this crowd away and they were taken to the chiefs, who had a good supper prepared for them, gave them water without limit and charged either nothing or only a low price. Suddenly a Moor approached Charlotte's father with a shout of recognition: "Tiens toi, Picard! ni a pas connaître moi Amet?"

Astounded at finding himself addressed in French by a Moor, M. Picard realized that the man was Amet, a young goldsmith whom he had employed long before during his previous time in Senegal. To him at least he could tell the full story of the shipwreck and its aftermath, which reduced Amet to tears. The Mussulman instantly distributed free a large amount of milk and water to the Christians and had a tent raised just for the Picards. His religion would not allow him to sleep under the same roof with them. They got only a little sleep, however, for the cries of the night watchmen guarding the cattle alarmed some in the French party who had always thought they had been led to the camp merely to be plundered, and they urged everyone else to be well away before daylight. One man, an old naval officer who had been appointed captain of the Port of Senegal, had somehow managed to retain 3,000 francs, but most of the French party possessed little worth plundering.

Seeing that their guests were determined to leave, the Moors appointed guides and offered to hire asses to carry those who were too weak to walk. M. Bredif noted that the men most often overcome with fatigue were those who looked the strongest. He concluded, complacently, that it was mental strength that counted in a crisis. He was happily astonished at his own capacity to endure privations at least as well as the next man. His normally weak stomach had not troubled him at all. He congratulated himself too soon. After only a few hours of walking he fell asleep literally on his feet and would have been left behind had not a straggler found him. At each resting point, the inevitable cry of "On your feet! March!" was the sound he dreaded most.

M. Picard had managed to hire two asses which carried the young children, while he and the rest of his family walked, trying to keep up with the soldiers. When Captain Bégnère saw this, he lent the ass which he had hired for himself to the grown-up girls. He also was no longer a young man, so it was no mere gallant gesture.

Very early on the morning of July 11 the march party again reached the beach to continue their trudge along the shoreline. For those riding the asses, it was a momentous event. The poor beasts, weary of the weights they had been carrying for five hours, broke into a run and lay down amid the breakers, revelling in the cool water. Some of the riders fell off. Charlotte was pinned underneath her animal for a moment and took an involuntary bath. One of her young stepbrothers was nearly swept out to sea, but she managed to grab him. Then they all burst into laughter and continued the march, all happy except for the asses which had been pressed into use again.

At about ten o'clock a sail was sighted. Shortly after, the well-remembered silhouette of the brig *Argus* came into sight. A handkerchief was tied to the barrel of a musket and waved in the air. Keeping out beyond the area of broken water, the *Argus* lowered her sails and hoisted out a boat. It could not get through the breakers, so five of the Moors plunged into the sea and swam out through the rollers toward it. After half an hour they came back, swimming between them three small barrels of provisions. At this demonstration of the Moors' willingness to help, Charlotte felt ashamed of the suspicions they had all had of them.

The provisions consisted of wine, brandy, biscuit and a Dutch cheese. With them was a note from Lieutenant de Parnajon to Lieutenant Espiaux, telling him that convoys of camels loaded with provisions were being sent out by the governor and that the Moors had been asked to give every assistance. The water, wine and brandy mixed with good news, after being so long under the fierce heat of a vertical sun and constant fear, produced an extraordinary joy. Life, which had been a burden to endure, now became precious, noted Charlotte. Lowering and sulky faces split into wide grins. Enemies became friends. The greedy forgot their cupidity for a moment. The children smiled for the first time since the *Medusa* had been wrecked. "Everyone seemed to be born again," she wrote, and added archly, "I even believe the sailors sang the praises of their mistresses." Perhaps she was implying that the suffering men had had until now no thoughts of women, even when they were as naked as the shepherd's wives had been, or clothed in revealing tatters as she and her sisters were.

At about six o'clock that evening it was her father who was physically worn out, for he had thus far walked all the way. He wanted to stop for a moment and sit down. His wife and Charlotte stayed with him. The children and the other older girls jogged on behind the caravan, riding on the asses. The halt was a mistake, for all three instantly fell asleep. When they awoke, it was late, the sun was sinking in the west and there was no sign of the march party. Instead, a small group of bearded Moors was riding toward them on camels. The Picards' instinctive uneasiness returned, but they were in no condition to run away.

The Arab chieftain alighted from his camel and confronted the ladies. For the second time they heard a Moor speak an unexpected language. This time it was English. He introduced himself as Mr. Carnet. He asked them not to mistake him for an Arab, in spite of his headdress and robes. He was, however, friendly with some of the desert chieftains and, hearing that there had been a shipwreck on the coast had hurried forward to help. Their main party was only two leagues away and he could give them a lift there on his camels.

M. Picard accepted the offer with alacrity and was soon perched on a British camel. The two ladies were sure they would fall off the hairy haunches of the animals and preferred to walk. They spent the night at the main camp and the next day Mr. Carnet went off to get provisions. He would bring them to their next halting point, a few hours' walk ahead. By noon, however, the heat had become intolerable—even the Moors had difficulty enduring it—and they searched about for any sort of shade. All they could find were some mimosa and ground plants. But they were better than nothing at all.

Charlotte compared the heat reflected from the sand to the blast from an oven door as it opened. She felt literally suffocated, as though she were about to die. A man called Borner, a smith, saw her plight and offered her a drink of muddy water from his reserve container—an old boot. She seized the boot and drank the awful contents in frantic gulps and with such evident pleasure that others wanted to share. But the remnants were so disgusting that they spat it out.

M. Bredif found the sand so hot to the touch that he could not endure putting his bare hands to the ground. He gathered some stalks and leaves of a creeping plant and made a little shade for his head, which he laid on his coat. But the rest of his body felt as if it were in a furnace, roasting.

Mr. Carnet returned with a small caravan of supplies which included drinking water as well as rice and dried fish. It appears that he was part of a rescue operation set up by the English governor of Senegal, who had not yet handed over to M. Schmaltz and was still in control of the colony. The French governor-designate had contented himself simply with sending out a single ship, the *Argus*.

Charlotte is very coy about the incident which followed the meal. Driven by the heat, the whole party marched for an hour toward the beach in order to plunge into the sea. The Picard girls stayed in the water a long time and then took themselves off to a secluded spot among the dunes, where, she says, they "shaded" themselves with some old clothes they happened to have. Her cousin had an officer's tunic with gold lace and this, she says, attracted the attention of a Moor who, thinking the two girls were asleep, tried to steal the tunic for the sake of the lace. But as soon as he saw they were really awake, he stopped and merely looked at them very "steadfastly." Charlotte was concerned later to deny emphatically a story that she was underneath it and that the Moor had lifted up the covering and had been both astonished and delighted by what he saw, which he had related with gusto to his companions.

At three o'clock next morning, July 13 according to Charlotte, they began their final day's march. Mr. Carnet went on ahead to get an ox. M. Bredif, whose dates do not agree, says that when they rendezvoused with the animal it was "small, but tolerably fat," and a Negro killed it for them by twisting its neck like a chicken. They lit a fire and sat round it, roasting the beef on the point of a bayonet or a saber, or on just a pointed stick. It was many hours to dawn and the darkness accentuated the bearded, sunburned faces of the men, while the constant thunder of the breakers on the coast of Africa and the roaring of wild beasts out in the dark desert made a picture which, thought Charlotte, David or Girodet would have loved to paint. It could be hung in the Louvre and be titled "Cannibals Feasting." And no one in Paris would guess that some of the cannibals had been born beside the Seine or imagine the pleasure to be derived from eating wild plants, drinking muddy water out of a dirty boot or gulping down a delicious roast cooked in smoke. It was a sensation the fashionable, worldly-wise youth of Paris would never know.

Late that morning they were led inland to the top of a dune and saw that the desert had ended. The last part of their march was among green trees haunted with humming birds and parrots. Shortly after, they reached the banks of the Senegal, a freshwater river, and their perils were over. At two o'clock a small boat appeared, being rowed slowly against the current. Two Europeans got out and asked for M. Picard. They said they had been sent by his old friends M. Artigue and M. Lambouré, with a hamper of provisions just for himself and his family. This was a personal gift. Two much larger boats, full of provisions provided by the English governor of Senegal for all the castaways, were on their way from Saint-Louis and would arrive within an hour or so.

In the evening the boats took them all downriver to Saint-Louis, where a great crowd was assembled to greet them. As Charlotte tartly remarked, everyone in the town seemed to be there with the exception of their late commanders, Captain de Chaumareys and Governor Schmaltz. The English governor rode up with his staff, which included Mr. Carnet, to make them welcome. He seemed to be distressed particularly by the plight of the children and the young women.

The most sickly members of the march party were taken to a hospital, and the rest were distributed among private households, for Saint-Louis was only a small trading post. But everyone was glad to help, the English officers appearing particularly eager to have the pleasure, as they put it, of caring for some of the castaways. M. Artigue had no room to put up the entire Picard family, so Charlotte and her grown-up sister Caroline gratefully accepted the offer of an English couple, Mr. and Mrs. Kingsley, to stay with them.

After they had been combed, cleansed and dressed by the domestic Negresses, the two girls were given white dresses which contrasted strangely with their sunburned, almost blackened faces. Charlotte felt faint at the change in her fortunes, which seemed unbelievable, and she was shy when invited downstairs to join their hosts and some English officers at a meal. She could eat little and understood nothing of the language.

A young Frenchman who knew some English was able to ask questions and translate her brief replies. Everyone seemed astonished at the way in which children and young girls had endured such misfortunes. To Charlotte it was all quite unreal, the pleasant room, the kindly, interested people. The miles of burning sand were still underfoot and the walls of the house heaved with the motions of the waves. She asked to be excused, and once in bed, fell into a restoring sleep of total exhaustion.

The young engineer Bredif and some of his companions were taken into the house of two merchants of Bordeaux, Potin and Durecur, who were lavish with their resources. The castaways were completely outfitted and given feather beds or good mattresses to sleep on. But M. Bredif slept badly. The bed seemed to rise and fall underneath him as if on a stormy sea, or else he was trudging from nowhere to nowhere across burning sands.

*     *     *

There was still no news in Saint-Louis of the two men, Rogéry and Kummer, who had struck off on their own from the main party which had escaped the shipwrecked boats and who had gone inland some days before. Nor was there any sign of the party of sixty-three who had landed earlier from the overloaded longboat at a point still farther north, believed to be near the Mottes d'Angel.

But the British were not too worried. They had a standing agreement with the local Moors that any lost or shipwrecked Europeans would be cared for and a reward paid to those who brought them to Saint-Louis. This was why most of the Moors had been helpful rather than hostile to the passengers from the stranded boats.

The raft was a different matter. The search for survivors still at sea was not a British concern, but a concern of the French officials who possessed ships but who did not believe that anyone could still be alive either on the raft or in the wreck of the *Medusa*.

# 9

## "The Eyes of Argus"
### *(The castaways, July 9 to 19)*

The same high sun which burned and suffocated the marchers ashore blazed down on the raft as it drifted idly with the current, out of sight of land. For the castaways there were no waterholes to dig, no Moorish goats to be milked. They could only wait for rescue or for death, whichever came sooner. On July 9, they had worked out that the remaining wine might last them for four days more, until the 13th. They had calculated that although rescue was possible by that date, it might be delayed by many days, in which case the rescue vessel would discover only a raft covered with blackened, sun-dried corpses.

They watched the wine barrel most carefully and on the 11th detected two soldiers secretly drinking from it. They were lying down, apparently innocent, but they were in fact sipping by putting a reed through a hole which they had bored in the wood. The men had already determined what the punishment for this should be, and it was carried out. The two soldiers were thrown overboard.

The boy sailor, Leon, died shortly afterwards. There were now twenty-six men and one woman remaining, a dozen of them badly wounded, delirious and unlikely to last more than a day or two. This judgment was certainly that of Savigny, the surgeon, who gave the best of them not more than forty-eight hours. The logical course which followed from it was debated by the fifteen men who were still fully conscious. The rations of the twelve if given to the fifteen might keep the fifteen alive for six more days. A moderate course of merely reducing the rations of the sick would be cowardice; the sick would die by inches, the fifteen would not last so long. The debate was carried on with a note of despair, because although death had been with them every day for a week, it had been inflicted upon others of their number as if by fate. Both the canteen woman and her injured husband would have to die. What a way to repay her for twenty years of service to the French armies— slaughtered by Frenchmen while she lay unconscious with a broken thigh. Could any of them actually do such a thing?

Eventually self-preservation prevailed, the decision was made, and four volunteers said they were ready to take on the task of execution. Three were sailors; one was a soldier. The remainder turned away while the things were done. Some wept.

The instruments of execution were thrown overboard in an outburst of horror; but one saber was kept in case it might be needed to cut rope or wood. A sour mood set in and during sleep the images of their dead companions returned.

On July 13, an unimaginable event occurred. A white butterfly fluttered over the raft and after darting about, at length it settled down on the sail and folded its wings. It appeared as a visitor from another world, for the universe of the castaways was restricted to a few meters of wave-washed timbers floating over unknown depths and drifting at random with winds and tides. All took the appearance to be quite literally a message that land was near. Some men were so desperate that they thought of munching the creature, but others swore the butterfly was a sign from heaven for them and banded together to protect it.

On succeeding days more butterflies came and fluttered above the heads of the castaways and occasionally a large seabird came near. The butterflies had given them hope and they found an energy they had not thought they possessed. They again tried to catch fish but without success. They then tried to lure one of the birds to settle on the raft, which it seemed almost about to do. This attempt failed also.

The waves which in all but the calmest weather rolled across the raft stung the sores with which their bodies were covered, so that they could not sleep. A low moaning and crying usually marked the position of the raft in the darkness. Several times schools of stinging jellyfish were carried against them by the waves, intensifying their agony.

They found the strength to dismantle some of the timbers at the ends of the raft and from them they constructed in the center a raised platform. It did not keep the sea off them entirely, but it was better. There were holes between the planks of the platform, through which the waves slopped upward and wet them. So they covered it with what old clothing and other personal possessions they could find, which also made it softer. This resulted in a few chance finds among the effects: a lemon, which the finder was forced to share, thirty cloves of garlic and two little bottles of a liquid designed for cleaning the teeth. The latter proved delightful. A tiny drop held on the tongue removed for a few moments the terrible thirst which racked them all.

Each of these discoveries immediately produced

rage and a demand for a share, which was agreed to; very nearly, there was on each occasion a return to the violence which had swept the raft of all but 15 of the 150 people who had embarked on it. But in every case the emotion died without result. It seems that they now had what they needed above all else, even water-space.

They lay all together on the raised platform and took turns telling stories of personal experience, the more sharp-witted egging on the others. The twenty-eight-year-old Clairet had served in Spain and fought at Waterloo. Ex-Sergeant Lavillette, in particular, had many good stories of his campaigns, both by land and by sea. He was fond of recalling Lützen, Bautzen, Dresden, Leipzig, Hanau, Montmirail, Champaubert, Montereau and other scenes of battles, forced marches and privations of all kinds. "And none of them," he would declare, "were anything at all in comparison to what I have to endure on this frightful machine. To start with, I had to be afraid only during the battle, but here I am in danger all the time and, most dreadful, I have to fight Frenchmen, my own comrades. Then I have other enemies—hunger, thirst, the stormy sea and its monsters, the terrible sun. And on this battlefield, although I have fresh wounds among the old scars, they are not tended; I have no means of dressing them. I can do nothing whatever to save myself and, unassisted, I would put my survival at no more than a day or two longer."

Then the conversation would turn to the plight of France, and anger would keep them alive. Military occupation by the armies of Russia, Prussia, Austria, England—armies they had often defeated in the field—was hard to bear. Their resentment could momentarily make their own fates seem of little importance when measured against the national disaster.

In the suffocating, searing heat of midday nothing could banish the torment of their thirst, not even the routine of moistening their parched lips with urine. They kept this in small tin cups which they placed in little pools of seawater to cool. One man never could bring himself to swallow it. Savigny, who kept himself sane and his mind active by continual observation and thought, observed that some men's urine was more agreeable than that of others. Really, it did not taste too disgusting, but in some men, it was true, the liquid had become thick and very acrid. In all men, the drinking of it made them want to urinate again almost instantly. They also drank seawater, but not very much. Although their thirst was quenched for a delicious instant, a moment later it had returned and was even more severe. M. Griffon du Bellay, the governor's secretary, was the exception; he would drink ten or twelve cups of seawater in succession.

They devised a series of tricks to relieve their thirst or to give themselves the impression that they had relieved it, and perhaps also to break the monotony or manufacture a luxury. Some found that pieces of pewter held in the mouth produced a kind of coolness. Washing their faces in seawater could produce relief; so could soaking their hair, or holding their hands in the sea. The most prized sensation was that produced by a single empty perfume bottle. When it was sniffed, the perfume of roses could still be sensed and inhaled and proved extremely soothing. The tiny bottle was passed from hand to hand like a pipe of peace. There were some who did not drink their ration of wine straight off but put it in a tin cup and using a quill sucked at the liquid gradually. They found this very beneficial.

Although the wine ration was minute, Savigny

observed that it could now produce a state verging on intoxication which resulted in discord. The worst occurrence was on July 14, when three normally rational and responsible men suddenly agreed between themselves first, to drink all the wine remaining in the barrel, and second, to commit suicide. They were Jean Coudein, the naval officer and nominal commander of the raft, Sub-Lieutenant Clairet and Sergeant-Major Charlot. No combat had actually ensued, and the other men were still arguing with them, when everyone's attention was diverted by the appearance of a crowd of sharks around the raft. These were no ordinary sharks but monsters nearly thirty feet long, cruising on the surface with their backs high out of the water. They swam within inches of the raft, so near that ex-Sergeant Lavillette was able to strike several of them with a saber. When struck by the steel blade, the monsters would submerge but then reappear only seconds later, quite unperturbed. Probably they were harmless basking sharks which feed on plankton.

The sight of ordinary sharks was commonplace, for they often surrounded the raft. No one cared about them any more. Some of the castaways would immerse themselves completely in the water which continually submerged the front part of the raft; they found this relieved their burning thirst a little. Others jumped over the side for a swim, which had the same cooling, soothing effect. Nothing counted now except relief from heat and thirst.

The sharks did not attack. Almost certainly, the raft had begun to collect marine organisms and probably small and not so small fish in some numbers, as it offered food, protection from predators and shade. The sharks may have been attracted by the fish but were discouraged by the difficulty of getting in among the crevices between the timbers in which their prey could hide. The body of a fish contains a great deal of water—fresh water—and much of the nourishment which the castaways required lay all around and even underneath their feet. But all their attempts at fishing had failed for want of the proper equipment.

Some could still joke. One wag said, "If they send the brig out looking for us, pray God she'll have the eyes of Argus." This was thought very witty and became a catchphrase in the final days.

On July 16, they thought the land must be very near and eight men were still strong enough and sufficiently determined to make an attempt to sail and row there. They made a primitive canoe of solid wood from a single timber some twelve meters long with crossboards fixed and a little mast. The sail was a hammock and for oars they were going to use barrel staves. Fortunately a sailor who was walking on it had to put his weight a little off-center in order to get around the mast, and that was sufficient to capsize the "canoe" and throw the sailor into the water. They decided to give up the attempt and to let death come to them where they were.

Their thoughts that night were very gloomy. It was hard to tell exactly how much wine was left in the barrel, but certainly they were coming to the end of their meager rations. The human flesh which they kept with them for their meals was beginning to stink, and the fact that it was human reminded them of their own mortality. They could not look at it now without feeling oppressed by terror. Daybreak on July 17 brought a cloudless sky, without any shield against the coming blaze of the sun. As the heat began to be felt, they said prayers and the wine ration was given out. They began to savor the momentary delight of drops of liquid in their mouths before submitting to the thirteenth day of torment.

*     *     *

The castaways had assumed the *Argus* would be chosen to undertake any search because of her small size and shallow draft. They had also assumed that everyone would be thinking of them. Their plight had been so much more desperate than that of those in the boats, and their ability to survive for any length of time was clearly more limited. It seemed obvious that to find them would be the main object of any search.

The captain of the *Argus* had received other orders, however. His main task was to cruise along the beaches north of the Senegal River as far as the Arguin Bank in order to look for survivors from the boats who had been cast ashore and to get supplies to them from seaward. This order, while it showed that the French authorities had an accurate idea of how small a chance most of the boats had of making the Senegal on their own, was also unnecessary. The English had an established rescue system based on contact with the local tribes and it was this system which brought most of the boats' survivors without further loss to Saint-Louis. The *Argus*, kept offshore by the breakers, was through no fault of her captain able to contribute little—three small barrels of supplies, to be precise. She should have been directed primarily toward an estimated track of the drift of the raft from the *Medusa*. Her involvement in shore operations may have been mainly a "prestige" operation to show the English that the new French administration was not without resources, initial impressions to the contrary.

Obeying his instructions, Lieutenant de Parnajon, captain of the *Argus*, had cruised northward along the coast, inshore of where the raft actually was, and although his lookouts also searched to seaward they saw no sign of the castaways. On the morning of July 17, he had given up the search and was returning to Saint-Louis with a favorable wind which had brought him within forty leagues of his destination, with failure to report.

Then the wind veered around from northwest to southwest, which was foul for the Senegal, but ideal for making an attempt to locate the wreck of the *Medusa* somewhere on the Arguin Bank, a task which was also included in his orders. On an impulse, de Parnajon ordered the ship put about and the *Argus* began to move northward and out to sea. After two hours on the northwest tack, the lookout at the masthead reported another vessel in sight. It was still too distant to make out what kind of craft it was.

*       *       *

The *Argus* was sighted by the castaways many hours before her lookout saw the raft, because the brig's tall masts were visible for a great distance. A captain of infantry was the first to look up from sipping his wine, which had just been issued, and catch sight of topmasts above the horizon. He gave a shout of joy and everyone was infected with his delight for a moment, feeling that deliverance was certain. Then fear came, a frantic fear of not being seen. The metal hoops were torn off casks and made into a tall flagstaff, colored handkerchiefs were tied to the end, and a man was pushed up the mast by their united efforts, so that he could cling to the top and wave his bundle of flags.

For half an hour hope alternated with fear. There were those who saw the topmasts grow larger, others who thought they were disappearing. Both were correct, for the brig was steering a southerly course parallel to the raft, on her way back to Saint-Louis. When first seen, she would have been coming slightly nearer, but after half an hour she would have been moving away. They could not be sure even that it was the *Argus*, for they never saw her hull.

When the unknown brig had disappeared, they shut themselves in and gave up. They made a tent out of a spare sail and all crowded inside to escape the burning sun; they closed all entrances and tried to console themselves with sleep. But sleep was not what they wanted. Their minds were alight with irritation and despair; they wanted to hit out. A proposition was made that they write on a board a brief account of what had happened to them, which all would sign, and then as a final gesture they would fasten that message to the top of the mast. It would tell the government and their families how and why they had died and by whose hand.

For two hours they lay in the semidarkness, wracked by a torment worse than the violence of the noon sun. At length M. Courtade, who had been master-gunner of the *Medusa*, had to leave the tent to relieve himself. He was only halfway out into the sunshine when they saw his face take on a look of awesome joy, both hands stretched out toward the sea, his breathing so shallow that he could only whisper, "Saved! The brig—it's close, close!"

There was a convulsive scramble to get out of the

tent. Even those whose feet and legs were in such a state that they had been unable to move for the last two days somehow crawled on their bellies out to where they could lie down and see deliverance approaching. Tears ran down their faces; those who could embraced each other, or waved handkerchiefs at the brig which, half a league distant, was bearing down on them under all press of sail.

As it came closer they could make out a large white flag at the head of the foremast, which showed she was a ship of the Royal Navy of France. And shortly after, they could see that this was indeed the *Argus*, and their joy redoubled. When she came closer they saw her sails lowered, and the brig coasted slowly past the raft, her bulwarks and shrouds crowded with men waving hats or handkerchiefs. A boat was hoisted out and lowered to the water, then began to pull across the waves toward them.

The boat was commanded by an officer, M. Lemaigre, and what he saw as he ran alongside the raft must have astounded him: fifteen men, almost naked, faces and bodies blotched and disfigured by the scorching sun, the skin almost stripped from their legs and feet, covered with sores and wounds; fifteen hollow faces with staring eyes from which tears ran down and long unkempt beards to make their appearance more wild and frightful. Only about five could even attempt to stagger across the raft to the boat. The others crawled or simply lay helpless. One of the latter was Alexander Corréard. He had not expected to last out this last day, yet had a presentiment that rescue would come. Dimly, he had felt that a series of events so extraordinary could not be destined for oblivion. Some of them at least would survive to tell the story.

Lemaigre boarded the raft and helped or carried the more helpless castaways to the boat. As, man by man, the wasted figures were brought on board the *Argus*, the crew was silent, but pity and compassion could be read in every face. They were given light food, a broth, with some wine, and their wounds were dressed. The little ship was turned into a hospital. But the fever lingered. Some became delirious once more. An army officer got up and tried to throw himself into the sea to search for his pocketbook and had to be forcibly prevented. Others showed equally strange signs of continuing derangement.

The winds being unfavorable much of the time, the final stage of their journey to Senegal took two more days. The position at which they had been found was many miles from the coast; their belief that land was near had been an illusion, perhaps a fortunate one. The only time they could have been really close to land was soon after their towrope to the boats had been loosed, for just south of this position the coast of Africa juts out seaward for some distance. Lieutenant de Parnajon did not know this, for the wreck of the *Medusa* had not been located and the original position of the raft could not yet be calculated. All he knew was that his discovery of the raft was luck, a fortunate chance inspired by a feeling, as the wind changed, that somehow he ought to search again for the *Medusa*. Now, as he told one of the castaways, "If they made me captain of a frigate, I couldn't feel any more pleasure than I did when I sighted your raft."

On July 19, the *Argus* anchored in the roads off Saint-Louis and the 15 survivors of the original 150 were transferred to a small, decked vessel for the passage over the river bar and up to the town itself, where Governor Schmaltz and a crowd of brilliantly dressed officers, French and British, were waiting to greet them. The moment of confrontation was near.

The men they were expecting to greet consisted of four army officers—Captain Dupont, Lieutenant L'Heureux and Sub-Lieutenants Clairet and Lozach—plus Sergeant-Major Charlot and Jean Charles, a Negro soldier. The navy was represented by a single officer, Midshipman Coudein, Savigny, the ship's surgeon, Courtade, the master-gunner, a sailor called Coste and a pilot named Thomas. The geographical engineering party were represented by their leader, Corréard, and the foreman, ex-Sergeant Lavillette. The list was completed by Griffon du Bellay, the governor's secretary, and a hospital administrator named François. These were the men who were expected to step ashore at the official, multinational reception arranged on the quayside.

What the brilliant crowd actually saw were fifteen shrunken scarecrows, a little more presentable than they had been forty-eight hours before, but a still-living accusation. Five were so far-gone that they would never recover and were to die at Saint-Louis within the next weeks. They included the two army officers, Clairet and Lozach, the master-gunner and the black soldier. Some of the others were to be hospital cases for months.

The castaways saw horror and compassion mingled on every side, a genuine surge of feeling which also contained admiration, for these men had, as it were, come back from the dead. It should have been a heartening welcome, overflowing with joy; but it was not. For among those who had come to greet them were people who should have been ashamed and were not; and one of the hands extended to them in welcome was that which, two weeks before, had cast off the towrope linking them to the boats and had loosed the raft upon its fatal journey.

Fig. 1 Despair and cannibalism on the raft. Another preliminary idea by Géricault. *Gobin Collection, Paris*

Fig. 2 Théodore Géricault. A self-portrait about 1818. *F. S. Jowell Collection, Toronto*

Fig. 3 The abandonment of the *Medusa* as depicted in an anonymous lithograph about 1818. The frigate is correctly shown heeled to larboard with her topmasts down. Of the raft nothing can be seen, only a mass of men standing on it up to their belts in water. *Bibliothèque Nationale, Paris*

Fig. 4 A survivor of the desert trek at the court of the Moorish King Zaide. One of his ministers is drawing a map of Europe in the sand to show the Arabs' familiarity with current events. From a lost watercolor drawing by Géricault.

Fig. 5 The mutiny on the raft. A preliminary study by Géricault employing the device of a "cascade" of bodies. *Stedelijk Museum, Amsterdam*

Fig. 6 The desolate and abandoned *Medusa* at the mercy of the waves, with some of the seventeen men left behind huddled by the stern. From a lost watercolor drawing by Géricault.

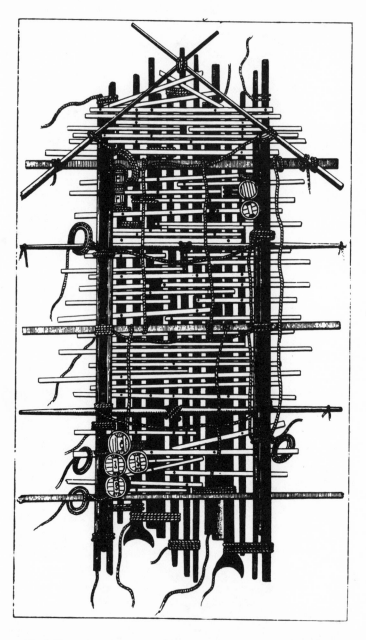

Fig. 7 Plan of the raft (as published in Savigny & Correard's book).

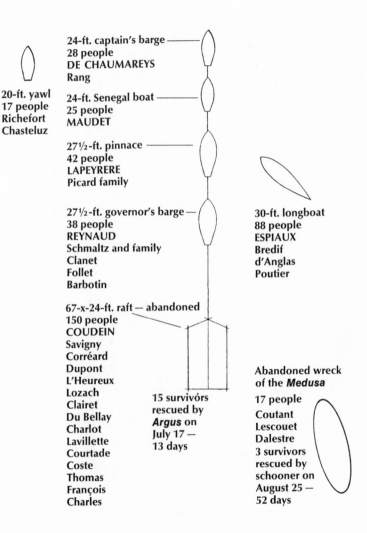

20-ft. yawl
17 people
Richefort
Chasteluz

24-ft. captain's barge ———
28 people
DE CHAUMAREYS
Rang

24-ft. Senegal boat ———
25 people
MAUDET

27½-ft. pinnace ———
42 people
LAPEYRERE
Picard family

27½-ft. governor's barge —
38 people
REYNAUD
Schmaltz and family
Clanet
Follet
Barbotin

30-ft. longboat
88 people
ESPIAUX
Bredif
d'Anglas
Poutier

67-x-24-ft. raft — abandoned
150 people
COUDEIN
Savigny
Corréard
Dupont
L'Heureux
Lozach
Clairet
Du Bellay
Charlot
Lavillette
Courtade
Coste
Thomas
François
Charles

15 survivors
rescued by
*Argus* on
July 17 —
13 days

Abandoned wreck
of the *Medusa*

17 people

Coutant
Lescouet
Dalestre
3 survivors
rescued by
schooner on
August 25 —
52 days

Fig. 8 Raft and boats at the moment the tow was loosed.

Fig. 9 The seventy-four-gun *Duguay Trouin*, built at Rochefort in 1800 and one of the leading battleships in the French line at Trafalgar, 1805, afloat in Portsmouth Harbor in the 1930s. This is the actual ship in which Jean Reynaud, first lieutenant of the Rochefort frigate *Medusa*, served during 1801–2. On right is the forty-six-gun frigate *Trincomalee*, a British copy of a French design, laid down in 1816 a few months before the forty-four-gun *Medusa* was wrecked, and almost identical to her. Some of the essential differences between a ship-of-the-line and a frigate are shown—the hull lengths are almost the same but the battleship is high-built and heavy with guns and men. *Photo: Wright & Logan*

Fig. 10 The frigate *Trincomalee*, now renamed *Foudroyant* and used as a training ship for boys. She has been afloat for nearly 160 years. *Photo: Alexander McKee*

Fig. 11 The stern of the *Foudroyant*, showing the captain's cabin and the rudder. This part of the *Medusa* was beaten in during the gale when the rudder became unshipped. *Photo: Alexander McKee*

# 10

## The Specter at the Window
## (*In Senegal, July*
## *and August 1816*)

Saint-Louis was built on a sandbank about two leagues up the Senegal River. The island was four thousand yards long by six hundred yards wide. Originally, the site had been chosen for nothing more grand than a trading post, with an eye to defense. But it was now the center of government administration and had a population of ten thousand. Only five hundred were Europeans, two thousand were Negroes or free mulattos, seventy-five hundred were slaves. The wide streets, unpaved and covered with banked Sahara sand, were flanked by 150 European houses. The rest of the dwellings consisted of straw huts. It was the poor capital of a poor colony.

Although founded by the French in 1621, Saint-Louis tended to change hands when there was a war. It had now been French twice and British twice and was about to become French for the third time. Some of the settlements on the coast had been founded by the Dutch even earlier than Saint-Louis but had fallen to the French later on. These also tended to become British during a war. Consequently the European hold on the area was fragmented and tenuous, confined virtually to a few places on the coast. The interior was largely unknown and generally hostile, both in its population and because of its diseases.

On July 22, Kummer and Rogéry, the two men who had gone off on their own into the interior sixteen days before, were brought in to Saint-Louis by a Moorish chieftain, Prince Muhammed, who claimed the reward. They had news of the party of sixty-three who had lightened Espiaux's longboat on July 6 at what was thought to be the Mottes d'Angel but may have been Cape Mirik (modern Cape Timiris) still farther north. If so, they had marched four hundred kilometers through the desert in seventeen days, for by the afternoon of the 22nd they had reached the banks of the Senegal. They staggered into Saint-Louis the following day, minus five of their number—four soldiers and a soldier's wife. Among the survivors was the army officer Lieutenant d'Anglas.

Most of the men who had preferred the land to the sea two and a half weeks before had been soldiers. D'Anglas recalled distinctly that the first two days in the desert had been harsh but bearable. On the third day hunger and thirst began to torture them. "Our skin is dried up, our lips are cracked, our tongues are black and have retreated into our mouths. . . . The wife of a corporal, Elisabeth Delus, collapses onto the sand, dead. The sight of this corpse troubles our imagination; it predicts our own fate. But we have neither the courage nor the strength of will to dig a grave for her."

The story which was now beginning to go around in Saint-Louis was that the corporal had buried his wife's body by the seashore, after first cutting off her head, that he then put the head in a beggar's sack and would not be parted from it until he was taken to the hospital at Saint-Louis, where he died of his privations a few days later.

The sequence of the long trek blurred in d'Anglas's

recollections after the first few days, as indeed did the memories of everyone else, whether in the desert, with the boats or on the raft. This was inevitable. But particular incidents remained vivid. D'Anglas recalled the first meeting with the Moors, perhaps on July 11, at which they exchanged firearms and gunpowder for foul-tasting food. Then they were seized by another tribe and made to work for them, unloading camels and digging up roots for a fire. "We change masters without changing our bad luck" was the way he put it, adding that the Arab women were particularly cruel. They threw sand into his still festering wounds.

One day they saw the brig *Argus* out to sea, but they were not seen by de Parnajon. This event, which may have happened on July 13, depressed them greatly. Two days later, perhaps, they met the English (or Irish) political officer, Carnet, wearing his usual Moorish robes and turban which the French assumed was a disguise. More probably it was comfortable, convenient and a subtle compliment to the Arab chiefs who really ruled most of the colony. (Much later, another British intelligence officer, T. E. Lawrence—of Arabia—was to dress exactly in the same way for much the same reasons.) Carnet had brought a supply of rice and beef for them, but so hungry were some of the marchers that they ate the rice uncooked and devoured vast portions of the beef. One soldier, an Italian, gorged himself so much that the next day he lay on the ground with a distended stomach and could not get up. Ignoring his cries and contortions, his comrades pulled him to his feet and helped him forward.

On July 18, the *Argus* was seen again, coasting along the shore, and this time the brig's lookouts sighted them. But de Parnajon could do little more than send encouragment. They were still some twenty leagues from Saint-Louis. Arriving at the banks of the Senegal on July 22, some distance north of the town, they met Kummer, the naturalist, and Rogéry, the explorer, being taken in by another party of Arabs for ransom. These gentlemen's local expertise had not done them much good, but they were able to direct the marchers to the best route.

The march of the sixty-three had been an epic, although only fifty-eight lived to tell of it. All the desert groups had been peculiarly ill-dressed for such a trek, particularly the soldiers in shako-topped uniforms and the scientists in their formal clothes. Rang described meeting the naturalist Leschenaux immediately after he had come in. "He had just covered a hundred leagues in the desert, clad as a scientist who is going to the Academy. The black silk stockings had been so ill-treated that they only covered the upper part of his leg. He showed his usual good humor in all the tales he told us."

All those who had abandoned the frigate on July 5 were accounted for—alive, half-dead, dying, drowned, butchered or lying dehydrated in the desert. So far there were about 140 known to be dead out of some 380. This left only the 17 men left aboard the *Medusa* unaccounted for. They were presumed to be dead, although the wreck had not been found by the *Argus*. Lieutenant Reynaud was preparing a salvage vessel to go out to search for the frigate and recover the 90,000 francs in gold. There was no thought of saving life and no urgency in these preparations.

\*　　　\*　　　\*

The story told by Kummer and Rogéry illustrated the real situation of the colony and the actual role of Saint-Louis. The desert to the north was controlled by the Moors under King Zaide, whom they had met. He also had been interested in salvage, but only of the wrecks of the boats on the shore, and the two Frenchmen had been used as his guides to the wreck sites. The Moors were basically of two races, the most numerous impressing the French with the austere nobility of their features. A minority were ugly and savage-looking. The Moors were quite well informed concerning European events, including the French Revolution and the almost continual wars which had followed, particularly the campaign in Egypt. Almost their only misconception was their impression that Napoleon and Bonaparte were the names of two different French generals. The Moorish king and his aristocratic princes were astonished that, in Europe, it was possible for a mere general to become an emperor; they found this faintly shocking. Their principal wealth consisted of cattle and slaves, but they did have some commerce and manufacture. Rogéry could not have been very comfortable in their encampments, being an early zealot for the abolition of slavery.

The slaves were Negroes basically friendly to the French and more open and amiable than the Moors, whom the Europeans always mistrusted to some degree. Apart from the frequently poor soil, it was the well-organized slave trade which prevented Senegal from being fully cultivated, for the Moors often raided the Negro plantations and villages and life was insecure. Some of the victims were shipped to America from Saint-Louis, where the slave market was. The basic clash of interests between Europeans who wanted to cultivate or mine the land and Arabs who wished to raid the villages for the pick of the black population had not been resolved when Europe was convulsed by war. M. Picard had been one of the earlier colonists and owned the nearby island of Safal where, in 1807, he put down about one hundred thousand cotton plants. When the English finally captured Senegal, in 1809, he had had to abandon the project and return to France.

The English had expected a full French convoy to arrive in 1816, bringing a French governor, a garrison of soldiers and a host of specialists and administrators as well as supplies of all kinds. What happened was the arrival of three French ships not as a fleet but at varying intervals and without their flagship. Then the new governor turned up as a fugitive from the wreck of the most important ship, lost in ridiculous circumstances which soon appeared as something worse when, between July 13 and 23, other survivors straggled in with tales of abandonment and cannibalism. More than a third of the people from the flagship were dead and most of the others were haggard castaways clad in rags and tatters, some needing lengthy hospital treatment.

If the local English had wanted an excuse to delay the handing over of the colony, this was it. The French suspected that they did, for two reasons. First, the year's crop of gum arabic, one of the more profitable exports, was ready to be harvested as a result of the work of the English merchants and planters; naturally, they did not want the benefits of their work to go to the incoming French. Second, part of the English administration and garrison would have to leave Saint-Louis for the nearest English settlements which were in Gambia, then justly known as the "white man's grave"; and the very season of the year which normally proved mortal to two-thirds of any unacclimatized newcomers was just about to begin. Some of the French suspected that the English intended to hang on to the colony forever, but in fact it was to be handed over after a delay of six months, in January 1817.

The day after they had staggered out of the desert into Saint-Louis, the Picards were told that the English governor had instructed the French governor to withdraw the bulk of the French contingent to the Cape Verde peninsula, as he had not received orders from his home government to hand over the colony. The French camp was to be set up opposite the island of Gorée which, because of its favorable climate, was used as a convalescent depot for the sick. Gorée itself was still in English hands but the locality opposite, then called Daccard (now Dakar), was to be French. The French governor, Schmaltz, then gave detailed instructions as to who was to go and who was to stay. The Picards were to go.

The English family, the Kingsleys, with whom the Picards were staying were indignant and went straight to the English governor. He sent back a message by his aide-de-camp that, considering the wretched condition the family were in, they might remain; and all the officers of the *Medusa* likewise. After twenty days with the Kingsleys, the Picards moved out to a hired apartment in Saint-Louis, but they were very poor. As there was no French administration, M. Picard was not receiving his salary as the public notary; most of his money and possessions had been lost in the *Medusa*; and his cotton plantations on the island of Safal had been uprooted and destroyed by wild animals during the years since he had been forced to leave in 1809. He was not even receiving rations from the French stores and they were soon reduced to living on a cheap native diet. They could not afford bread or wine.

In the middle of one such meal an English officer visited them and could not conceal his astonishment, although it shamed the Picards. This officer was Major Peddy, a veteran of the Peninsula War. The very next day the Picards were put on the English ration strength, receiving an officer's allowance of bread, wine, meat, sugar and coffee. This cannot have improved their relations with the French governor, whose meanness toward the family may have been connected with the fact that M. Picard had been a voluble critic of the way in which the *Medusa* had been carelessly stranded and then precipitately abandoned. Underlying the entire chaotic situation, particularly for those in authority, was a time bomb. The knowledge that it was there must have nagged them constantly.

Savigny and Coudein were fortunate, for they were housed and cared for by a French merchant, M. Lasalle. The worst treatment and conditions were reserved for those too ill to be put in private care and instead were taken to the hospital, which was poorly equipped and badly staffed. They were laid on truck beds, without mattresses, and with sheets disgustingly dirty.

The sailors and soldiers were put into one room, closely packed. Corréard was put into another, together with the four surviving army officers from the raft: Dupont, L'Heureux, Lozach and Clairet. The food consisted of ordinary rations, unsuited to the recovery of men brought nearly to death by their ordeals on the raft or in the desert. On the evening of their arrival, Colonel Schmaltz and Captain de Chaumareys, accompanied by a numerous suite, visited them with a grave air of compassion; they were promised money, new clothes and wine to restore their strength. The governor-designate said that he was about to go to the camp at Daccard, but that he had given orders that they should want for nothing in his absence. His wife and daughter were not among their compassionate visitors that day or any other day. The point of this—even the fact that it had a meaning—was not grasped by Corréard or his comrades.

The sick men asked the English doctor of the hospital for more suitable food. He replied that he had no authority to change the ration scale. They passed their complaints to the English governor, Lieutenant Colonel Brereton, without result. Eventually the same Major Peddy who had helped the Picards arrived at the hospital to offer assistance. Apparently he came on behalf of the British garrison officers rather than the British administration, which was bound most probably by inflexible rules. Major Peddy begged the French to accept this aid because of the generous treatment which he and his comrades had received from the French army during the war. The major's intervention came too late to save some of the men. On August 24, Sub-Lieutenant Clairet died in the bed next to Corréard's.

A few days later Corréard was awakened by bugles and drums. Covering himself in a sheet, for he had no clothing, he struggled to a hospital window. They were burying Clairet. Two French officers and two British officers carried the coffin, draped inappropriately with the old lily flag of France. British soldiers and French soldiers and sailors formed the procession, Major Peddy being the senior British officer. This at least was fitting for he also had fought in the Peninsula, although against the army in which Clairet had served. The procession marched out through the gates of the hospital and then Clairet, at twenty-eight a veteran of Talavera de la Reina, Sierra Morena, Saragossa, Montmirail, Champaubert, Montereau, Waterloo and the raft of the *Medusa*, was gone.

Corréard, unutterably depressed, felt sure that he himself would follow soon to the same graveyard, but without such ceremony. Haggard, clad in a white sheet, he must have seemed to those who saw him at the window a specter welcoming a companion.

It was just as well that he could not know then the contents of a letter which Mademoiselle Schmaltz, daughter of the governor-designate, had written to friends in Paris and which was being circulated in the capital. She had avoided visiting the hospital, she said, out of horror at what the men on the raft had done. She could not have endured seeing them without showing some of the indignation she felt at their conduct.

On August 25, the day after Clairet died, the wreck of the *Medusa* was at last found by the salvage vessel, the third attempt. The little schooner, commanded by Lieutenant Reynaud, had first sailed on July 26 with insufficient provisions; contrary winds had forced him to return. The second time the ship was driven back because a gale tore her poor-quality sails to shreds. Some other ship could easily have been sent, but this was not done. The schooner left the port of Saint-Louis for the third time late in August, reaching the wreck fifty-two days after the frigate had been abandoned by her captain and the commander-in-chief. Reynaud's principal task was to recover the three barrels containing the 90,000 francs in gold.

Reynaud reported the *Medusa* as now lying entirely on her larboard side, with only the starboard side showing and even this swept almost completely by high waves. She was therefore a difficult structure to enter, even for his native divers, which he gave as the reason why he was unable to find the gold. However, by cutting a large hole through the planks and framing of her starboard side, his men were able to recover forty barrels of supplies, several sails, some tools, furniture and personal luggage.

The most shocking discovery, however, was of the bodies of three men: gunner Coutant and two seamen, Dalestre and Lescouet. It was not that they were dead, but that they were still alive, although barely. They were the sole survivors of the seventeen men who either had been left behind or had preferred the wreck to the raft as a means of survival. In fact, only one of the fourteen missing men had actually died of privation. The other thirteen had perished in attempts to escape when, after forty-two days on board the wreck, provisions began to run out. In despair, a dozen of the most determined had constructed a raft of their own on which they hoped to drift ashore. This raft did eventually reach the coast, where it was found by Moors owing allegiance to King Zaide, who reported the matter. There was no trace of the men and no one knows their fate. A few days later, another man had attempted to drift to shore, this time by launching himself on a chicken coop. He drowned after covering only a few hundred yards.

By now, the four men left on board were very weak and half crazed. Each had his separate den, which he never left except in search of something to eat, and then only with knife in hand. As long as the wine had lasted, all had been tolerably well, but during the last few days there was only brandy to drink. For food, there was only tallow and salt pork. One man died only hours before Reynaud's schooner arrived at the wreck. The *Medusa* had not broken up, but rather had bedded down in the sand, and although the salvors failed to find the gold they returned highly pleased with their booty. Coutant, Dalestre and Lescouet were weak and incoherent, but they all recovered in due course to testify to the fact of abandonment. The number of known dead now totaled approximately 155, without counting those who were not to recover from their privations.

The day after Reynaud's schooner returned to Saint-Louis the area of the town became a public fair for the sale of the salvaged goods. These included the personal possessions of both the dead and the living. The national flag worn by the *Medusa*, hoisted at last by Lieutenant Espiaux, was also auctioned and cut up to make tablecloths and napkins. The affair was so successful and the frigate so far from being gutted that the merchants of Saint-Louis were permitted to send out a salvage fleet of four vessels on the understanding that the proceeds should be evenly divided between the French authorities (owners of the frigate) and the salvors (who would do the work and take the risks).

The arrangement and the terms were not unusual under British precedent at the time, were indeed fair as regards government property. Modern salvage laws operate on the same principles. What irritated, even infuriated, the wretched survivors was the refusal of Reynaud's party to return their own personal property, particularly clothing, of which they were destitute. They were laughingly brushed off with a remark that these were now a "good prize." Strictly speaking, this may have been correct, except that the proceeds from their sale should have been equally divided between the salvors and the owners, in this case the survivors. But Reynaud, the government salvor, returned nothing and paid nothing. An amusing sidelight was that Governor-designate Schmaltz received as a present from Reynaud some vases he had recovered from the wreck which were shortly afterwards recognized by Captain de Chaumareys as belonging to himself.

There was no compulsion upon the commercial salvors to restore personal property, if found, but a few books and other items were in fact returned to the original owners, without any payment being demanded. This second salvage operation lasted nearly three weeks. Corréard strongly suspected, from the strange fact that the salvaged goods were disposed of through a commercial firm and not a government agent, that Schmaltz had benefited—not directly, not in a way which could be shown to be illegal, because that was not his method, but linked to it by a business friend who was deeply involved in the commercial salvage operation.

It is interesting that at this time Reynaud, who it was felt should have kept very quiet because it was his hand that had loosed the raft, was in fact in the best of spirits and intimate with the governor-designate's daughter. "Well, would you believe it!" wrote a survivor. "This officer would play the fashionable around Mademoiselle Schmaltz, affecting airs of carelessness and coquetry."

Indeed, considering the salvage fleet which worked for weeks on the wreck, one begins to wonder about those 90,000 francs in gold. The type of container was known exactly, the location of these containers was known exactly and the layout of the ship was known exactly. Theoretically, their recovery should not have presented undue difficulties to the native divers, although Reynaud mentions that the interior of the hull was cluttered with displaced wreckage and rubbish. Had they been recovered, they would simply have been barrels as far as the divers were concerned; just three more barrels among many brought up. Disposing of them ashore would present few problems, provided that the salvaged goods were not inspected by a government agent. Those goods recovered by the commercial salvors were not so inspected but were delivered instead to M. Potin, a director of the firm with which Schmaltz had close connections. Nor does this exhaust the possibilities of illegal disposal. It may be that the *Medusa* did not remain a "treasure ship" for very long after her stranding.

These are only speculations. But what was fact, and a fact obvious to all at the time, was that three men had survived for fifty-two days aboard the *Medusa* after she had been abandoned as being in danger of breaking up. Great prizes in the way of stores and supplies were being taken from her intact hull two months afterwards. Without a doubt, there had been time enough for Schmaltz and de Chaumareys to have everyone aboard ferried ashore in relays by the boats. An able and resolute commander would have never abandoned the ship but would have instead dispatched the two best boats to Saint-Louis for help. The raft need never have been used, let alone filled up with men and then cast adrift. There was not the shadow of an excuse for the loss of a single life.

Less than a week after the rescue of the last three survivors of the unnecessary tragedy, the time bomb reached France. Not the feeble, spluttering squib to be ignited by Mademoiselle Schmaltz's letter to her Parisian friends but earthshaking firsthand material. The means of transport had been provided by her father.

On July 29, the corvette *Echo* had sailed for France. She was taking home fifty-five survivors of the shipwreck, many of them invalids, but this was not her main task. The loss of the frigate and so many men, together with the large amount of supplies she had aboard which were destined for the colony, required replacing. The difficulties being made by the British governor also necessitated new orders for

Colonel Schmaltz. The fact was, the whole expedition had been wrecked, not just the *Medusa*. The dispatches the *Echo* carried were therefore vital and would be closely studied. They included two reports, both dated July 29, written by de Chaumareys to glo s over or obscure the size of the disaster and his own responsibility for it.

"My Lord, it is with the saddest spirit that I have the unfortunate honor of informing you about the wreck of the *Medusa* on the sandbank of Arguin.

"Every possible means was undersaken to save His Majesty's frigate. I would have had the satisfaction of doing so, if a strong northwest wind had not been blowing, which destroyed in a short while the efforts that the zeal and enthusiasm of the crew and officers had happily produced.

"The Arguin Bank is much more to the west than the navigational information suggested and it covers a greater distance to the southwest. The sands are continually on the move according to the strength of the current. Therefore the depths vary very much.

In his second report, de Chaumareys described the Excellency know that, out of the 380 men who were on board the *Medusa,* including the 63 men landed at Portendick, the number present now totals 220."

In his second report, de Chaumareys, described the finding of the raft by the *Argus* but failed to mention that only 15 out of some 150 men put on it were still alive.

The figure of 380 appears to omit the 17 men abandoned on the *Medusa* by de Chaumareys, a deadly fact which he would not be anxious to publicize because it would make him guilty of a capital offense. Putting together the various estimates of those carried by the boats and raft, not altogether accurate and sometimes conflicting slightly, the total number of persons aboard the *Medusa* appears to have been approximately 405. When finally corrected to include the deaths of those left aboard the stranded hulk of the frigate (not known until a month later) the number of immediately fatal casualties rose to a total of 155. There were therefore to be some 250 survivors in all.

Fifty-five of them were now homeward-bound with de Vénancourt in the *Echo*. Three were boat commanders: Lieutenant Espiaux of the longboat, Ensign Maudet of the Senegal port boat, Ensign Lapeyrère of the pinnace. Others had been executive officers in the boats: Midshipman Poutier of the longboat, Midshipman Barbotin of the governor's barge. Paymaster Clanet had been an active passenger in the governor's barge and had opposed the casting loose of the raft. There was also the senior surgeon, Follet, a rather old-fashioned and unimaginative medical man.

In the minority, naturally, were the survivors from the raft. There were only two officers: Midshipman Coudein, the raft commander, and Junior Surgeon Savigny, who had led the organizing group.

When assembled together, these witnesses could testify to almost everything that had happened. All were in fact required to submit reports, with the single exception of Surgeon Savigny. This did not stop Savigny. He spent the month-long voyage writing his own narrative of the extraordinary events on the raft. Undoubtedly, he felt that these were so incredible that they ought to be fully detailed, and that, as a doctor, he was peculiarly fitted to deal properly with the psychological and physical phenomena which he had not merely witnessed but experienced as a participant.

On the second day of September 1816, the corvette

arrived at Brest, and Savigny took ashore the explosive pages which were shortly to rend France and echo around the world.

# 11

## "There's One Who'll Never Get to France"

### *(In Paris and Saint-Louis, September to December 1816)*

When Surgeon Savigny reported to the naval authorities at Brest, he was advised to go to Paris and present his report in person. He was told that his misfortunes should procure a sympathetic hearing at the Ministry of Marine, headed by Vicomte Du Bouchage. Not all his wounds had healed and he still wore one arm in a sling. Merely by surviving in such circumstances he had done something extraordinary.

The report he carried, which concerned the raft only, was clear, frank and surprisingly objective in the circumstances. Of course, no mere words could actually describe the experience, but the means by which he and his fourteen companions had lasted long enough to be rescued were detailed without evasion. He did not omit that they survived by consuming the bodies of the slain and by a series of "mercy killings" of those too weak to last much longer.

When Savigny reached Paris on September 11, the news of the loss of the *Medusa* had been public property for less than twenty-four hours. The official *Moniteur Universel* of September 10 had carried one small paragraph placed in an inconspicuous position which read:

> On July 2, at three o'clock in the afternoon, the frigate *Medusa* was lost, in good weather, on the shoals of Arguin twenty leagues distant from Cape Blanc (in Africa, between the Canaries and Cape Verde). The *Medusa*'s six launches and lifeboats were able to save a large part of the crew and passengers, but of 150 men who attempted to save themselves on a raft, 135 have perished.

Savigny's reception at the Ministry on September 12 was noncommittal. Although his report was accepted for the files, the events recounted in it could be damaging, if widely circulated. Savigny was therefore not only astounded but alarmed to read the next day in the pages of the popular opposition newspaper, *Journal des Débats*, extensive quotations from his own report, beginning with the hasty and chaotic abandonment of the *Medusa* and detailing the sufferings of the 150 people on the raft. Although soberly and tightly written, the facts of cannibalism and butchery were in themselves sensational. Nor had he concealed the fact that the towrope of the raft had been deliberately cast off by the first lieutenant of the *Medusa*, amid cries of "Let's abandon them!" No feelings of delicacy had restrained him from making clear that the tragedy was not the result of some natural, inescapable force. It had been man-made.

Nor was the strange story given as from an anonymous source, which might have weakened its authority, for the newspaper stated that the material had been written and signed by Savigny "on board the corvette Echo" on August 22, 1816. The editor had blandly pressed on an exposed nerve by inserting a note to his introductory paragraph which read: "The writer, we suppose, leaves it to the captain and other marine officers, if alive, to explain how the shipwreck took place." The two deadly words "if alive" suggests that the editor may have known very well that the senior officers of the frigate had reversed the established traditions of the sea.

On the day this article was published, the Ministry of Marine sent for Savigny and there was an ugly scene in the office. He was accused of leaking confidential information to the press and when he denied it, was not believed. How had a complete copy of his report reached the offices of an opposition newspaper? Savigny did not know. He recalled letting only one copy go out of his hands. He had given that one to Frigate-Captain de Vénancourt at Brest, partly as a matter of interest, partly because de Vénancourt had promised to have it sent on to an official of the Ministry of Marine in Paris. This had suited Savigny at the time, as he had intended originally to go directly home without visiting the capital. As it turned out, de Vénancourt had indeed sent the report to a senior official in Du Bouchage's Ministry.

The surgeon was now told that it was up to him to prove his innocence of all complicity in the affair. At the same time he was berated, not merely for publishing what he had written but for actually writing it. The astonished Savigny found that the world was upside down. Now he was being forced to defend himself for his sufferings on the raft. That he had been put there by the actions of others was a forbidden thought. He was so enraged that he threatened to resign his commission as a naval surgeon but was persuaded not to by some people in the office who suspected the real meaning of the affair.

Apparently unaware of the tangled web of politics into which he had blundered and believing that truth would be a complete defense, the surgeon rushed to the offices of the newspaper which had printed his report. The editor of the *Journal des Débats* was perfectly willing to give him proof of innocence and with this document in his pocket Savigny returned to the Ministry. Triumphantly, he produced the note, which read: "I certify that it is not from M. Savigny that I have the details of the shipwreck of the *Medusa* inserted in the *Journal* of September 13, 1816."

While Savigny waited, the note was taken away and shown to Minister Du Bouchage. It came back with the reply that His Excellency was not satisfied. While the document appeared to establish the innocence of Savigny, it was not conclusive because it failed to reveal who had passed the doctor's manuscript to the editor of the newspaper.

In an effort to clear himself with authority, Savigny sat down that same day to write an open letter to the official newspaper, *Le Moniteur Universel*. In this he denied having given a copy of his confidential report on the shipwreck, intended only for the Ministry, to any journalist. Further, he denied having any knowledge at all of how the "leak" had occurred. Explaining that the affair had put him in a dangerously embarrassing position, Savigny implored the editor, in the name of justice, to publish his denial officially as soon as possible.

The editor did so two days later, on September 15. But this was too late, for already, on September 14, the *Moniteur* had printed a letter from the minister himself, bitterly and brutally attacking Savigny.

"When the first news of the wreck of the *Medusa* was received, many newspapers attempted with sound and fury to exploit this cruel event for their own purposes," His Excellency had declared. "The very diversity of these reports, which departed from the truth to an extent varying with the veracity or otherwise of their sources, together with the manifold contradictions which they exhibited, caused great confusion in the minds of the public. But how can one describe the emotions one feels when reading in the *Journal des Débats* of September 13 an article actually signed by one of the doctors of the expedition, in which one cannot help but notice a certain note of malignant insinuation and inexactitude regarding the facts in dispute. The author of this article should have remembered above all that he may be held accountable for his opinions to a court-martial which will possess thorough knowledge of the affair. And could the evidence of this witness possibly be accepted, when he has already exposed himself publicly as a biased accuser? That would be stretching the imagination too far."

This letter, with its official reproaches holding a hint of menace, frightened Savigny. It angered him also. The moment he read it, he hurried directly to the offices of the *Journal des Débats* and demanded that the editor supply him with the name of the person who had actually handed over a copy of Savigny's own report. The editor refused. But, under pressure, while still not naming any individual, he consented to identify the organization for which the person worked and wrote out another note, with a sting in the tail: "I certify that it is not from M. Savigny that I have the details inserted in the Issue of September 13, but from the office of the minister of the police."

What on earth did the police have to do with it? When Savigny took this second note to the Ministry of Marine, they understood well enough. It was admitted that he had been the innocent victim of an indiscretion and not a member of a plot. No action would be taken against him.

To find the informant who had passed on the report, they must now look within their own Ministry, that of the navy. He was that senior official, Forestier, to whom Frigate-Captain de Vénancourt had passed a spare copy of the surgeon's unsolicited report regarding the raft. And Forestier was an informant for Élie Decazes, the powerful Prefect of Police, an ambitious politician who was then intriguing against the Minister of Marine, with the approval of the king.

Oddly, but only at first sight, Du Bouchage, opposed by the king, was an ultraroyalist. His strict policy was to give officers' commissions only to members of the nobility and to returned émigrés in particular. His choice of de Chaumareys as captain of the *Medusa* and commander of the Senegal squadron was an example of this policy, and also of its dangers. It was untrue that the Bourbons had learned nothing and forgotten nothing. Louis XVIII could see very clearly the unwisdom of excluding from both the army and the navy the experienced officers who had risen to command under Napoleon, in favor of unskillful and inexperienced aristocrats. In this view he was supported by the Prefect of Police.

The fate of the *Medusa* under an aristocratic émigré appeared an excellent weapon to use against the navy minister and Du Bouchage had rightly scented political machinations behind the printing of Savigny's report. His deadly—and also unscrupulous—denial in the *Moniteur* had been designed primarily to bring about a showdown and to brand the author of the report as a suspect, malignant and mendacious person. For if the report was accepted as true, it could be argued that all the émigrés, such as de Chaumareys, were dangerously incapable. And that made the position of the minister, who had appointed them, untenable.

One aspect of the tragedy, the apparently cowardly abandonment of his men by their aristocratic captain, while possibly not typical, could be made to seem so and therefore tended to undermine not merely Du Bouchage, but the monarchy itself. Political opponents did not lose the chance to draw the obvious parallel —the carelessly shipwrecked *Medusa* and her wretched crew were France and the French under the Bourbons.

The minister's intervention in the *Moniteur* and Savigny's denial published in the same paper the next day increased the controversy and inflamed the scandal still further. In less than a week it had attained international proportions. The *London Times* carried a free translation of Savigny's report lifted from the *Journal des Débats.* The rest of the world's press duly copied and a month or so later the appalled governor, captain and first lieutenant of the *Medusa* were reading in Senegal, in an English newspaper, an English account which was less oblique than the original French.

Captain de Chaumareys, the only one of them who stood to lose his life as a result of the affair, was the least affected. Still complacently cocksure, he was heard loudly declaiming that the loss of the *Medusa* was a mere "bagatelle." Lieutenant Reynaud, playing the gallant to Mademoiselle Schmaltz and babbling away as if he had not a care in the world, while the survivors of the raft glowered silently, was merely disguising his uneasiness. Colonel Schmaltz was fully aware of the dangers looming in Savigny's report. He was also in a position to act, and without scruple. Reynaud was as fully implicated in the abandonment of the raft as he was and therefore had to cooperate.

To start with, it would be their combined testimony matched against Savigny. Two to one. Then his own secretary, Griffon du Bellay, who was dependent upon him, was also a survivor of the raft. There were other survivors still in Senegal, many of them physically weak and mentally exhausted from their ordeal.

With Reynaud, he prepared the draft of a letter to be written by du Bellay and signed by other raft survivors which would satisfactorily explain the casting off of the raft, refute the charge of abandonment and cut down Savigny with the deadly charge of "murder."

The letter, addressed to the Minister of Marine and finally dated November 13, 1816, was a long one. It began by relating how they had read with horror, in the English newspapers, a translation of an article by Savigny in the *Journal des Débats*. They admitted the terrible atrocities which had occurred on the raft but stated that in these excesses Surgeon Savigny himself "had always been the prompter and principal executor." They affirmed that the waves and the currents had combined to cause a break in the tow-rope; they denied that it had been deliberately cast off. They described as a barbarous libel any suggestion that the first lieutenant had ever cried out, "We abandon them!" And finally they accused Savigny of base ingratitude toward the officers of the frigate who had done everything in their power to save him and had in fact succeeded by sending out the brig *Argus*.

If many survivors of the raft could be persuaded to sign this document, then Savigny would be exposed as a lone troublemaker peddling reckless stories to the discredit of others, while he himself was guilty of criminal acts. The campaign was conducted with great care and much trouble was taken. Some of the castaways were ill or dying, racked by fever, troubled by still vivid memories of the heaving sea and the horrors on the raft.

One of these was ex-Sergeant Lavillette, master carpenter and foreman of Corréard's party of engineers. Bredif visited him in the Saint-Louis hospital, on July 23, soon after his rescue. Confidentially, he noted that the sick man was babbling about Doctor Savigny and two or three lieutenants behaving like thugs, committing murder, organizing a horrible system of destruction, so that the unfortunate men on the raft kept on killing one another. He talked about how the number of men decreased every night, how two men came to murder him and how instead he murdered them, one by a cutlass slash to the head, the other by holding his face under water until he drowned. He then revealed how he himself was asked to help slaughter ten or a dozen men the officers had decided must die and that he would not do it, and that because he kept a gun by him, he was respected. In a final moment of lucidity, he added, "After each slaughter, they would kiss, thanking God; after the last one, all the guns were thrown overboard."

In all the feverish babbling there was some truth and in that final sentence set down by Bredif, although it rings oddly, there was absolute truth. But that it was true, why it was true and what it really meant were not to be known for more than one and a half centuries. There were undercurrents in the story of the raft of the *Medusa* which were to be endlessly debated ever after and were not even capable of resolution until recently.

Lavillette signed the document presented to him by du Bellay on behalf of Schmaltz, probably without even knowing what was on it, for he was certifying not only that Savigny had been "the prompter and principal executor" of the killings on the raft, but also that the towrope had broken accidentally and that there had been no deliberate abandonment. This was the important point, for whatever happened on the raft afterwards was the direct result of its abandonment. Whether Savigny was guilty or not guilty, or only part guilty, was of lesser importance because, like all the other castaways, he was merely reacting to the pressures of an intolerable situation created for him by others.

Another easy signature was that of the poor, dying Negro soldier Jean Charles. No one could know then the strange way in which his ordeal on the raft was to become immortal. The signatures of the soldiers Captain Dupont, Lieutenant L'Heureux and Sergeant-Major Charlot were also obtained. Naturally Griffon du Bellay, the governor's secretary, also signed; he had very little option, unless he wanted to wreck his career.

None of the living castaways were at all normal at this time. A distinguished visitor to the hospital, the Prince de Joinville, aptly described it as being like an "antechamber to the morgue." Even those who were not to die soon took many months, and in some cases years, to recover; some never really recovered. One of the latter was Alexander Corréard, the engineer and republican. Even so, his signature to the document was not obtained. It was not for want of effort, and Corréard, because he survived, was able to record the sort of pressures which must have been applied to all the others.

Although still a very sick man, he was slowly getting better, largely as a result of the help given by Major Peddy and Captain Campbell of the British garrison of Saint-Louis. When the governor's version of affairs was brought to him for signature, he noted that it had already been signed as correct by Griffon du Bellay, who owed his life directly to Savigny on at least one occasion. This, he thought, showed ingratitude, because the statement attacked Savigny personally for directing the slaughter from first to last, not just the "mercy killings" during the last days. But what enraged Corréard and decided him to resist were the plain untruths regarding the real authors of what eventually happened on the raft.

He commented bitterly: "One paragraph was employed to prove that the towrope had *broken*. Could I certify to that, when I was myself an eyewitness and had been told by more than twenty persons that it had been *cast loose*? Besides this falsehood, it was stated in one passage that when the raft was left, the words *we abandon them* were not pronounced." Corréard returned the document, unsigned.

Then the pressure came on. "The governor's secretary came several times to the hospital to urge me to give my signature, but I persisted in my refusal. The governor himself pressed me most earnestly one day when I went to him to ask permission to quit Senegal, but I answered that I would never sign a letter quite at variance with the truth and went back to the hospital. The day after my friend, M. Kummer, visited me and pleaded with me to go to the governor and sign this paper because, he had been told, if I continued to refuse, I would not be permitted to leave Senegal. These gentlemen must have indeed been deeply interested in the matter, if they employed such measures toward an unfortunate man, exhausted by a long illness, whose recovery depended on his return to Europe; for this they would not grant him, except on condition of his signing a false narrative contrary to everything he had himself seen."

Of those who did sign, Corréard commented: "They

were suffering from that terrible fever which was then carrying off the French so rapidly, when they were invited by the governor to sign this narrative. Some yielded to the fear of displeasing His Excellency the governor; others conceived hopes of obtaining his protection which, in the colonies, is no trifling advantage; others again were so weak that they were not even able to make themselves acquainted with the paper to which they were asked to put their names."

Corréard persisted in his refusal and Schmaltz had to be content with only six signatures. That of course was in addition to his own testimony and that of Lieutenant Reynaud regarding their own innocence of any desire or intention to cast off or abandon the castaways on the raft. Ideally, that would be sufficient to clear Schmaltz of all blame for the tragedy. The document, which was addressed to Du Bouchage, Minister of Marine, was to be dispatched in the transport *Loire* commanded by Lieutenant Gicquel des Touches, due to sail for Rochefort on the first of December 1816. The reasons for this sailing may not have been known to Corréard, but the governor must have been well aware of them; indeed, they made most urgent the matter of obtaining as many signatures as possible on the document.

A swift passage home in the *Loire* seemed to Corréard his only chance to survive. He sought and found allies among the British. Their doctors wrote out a certificate to the effect that, as his health was not improving, but on the contrary declining, it was imperative that he be repatriated immediately. When Schmaltz received this certificate from what was still the reigning authority in Senegal, with whom he was having most difficult negotiations, he had little option but to allow Corréard to return to France.

In the last days of November, Major Peddy and

Captain Campbell called on the sick man to say good-bye. They were about to leave Saint-Louis with an expedition consisting of 130 soldiers and 400 pack animals which was to explore the interior, for at that time only the coasts of Africa were known to Europeans. The interior was a mystery which might or might not contain minerals of far greater importance to Europe than the Arab-controlled slave trade. From this expedition they did not return because both died of fever. But before he left, Major Peddy had a warning for Corréard: "Since you intend to return to France, I hope you won't mind if I give you some advice. Men are all pretty much the same and though I can't predict exactly how your navy minister will treat you, it's safe to assume that you'll obtain no redress from him. Remember, a politician who has made a mistake doesn't like to be reminded of it. Believe me, my friend, don't take the road to Paris. Go to London. You'll find people ready to help you, when they learn what you have suffered. I have with me 300 francs, which will cover your expenses, either to Paris or to London, whichever you choose. Think about it, and if you decide to go to London, let me know. I'll give you letters of introduction."

Corréard was deeply grateful but also distressed. He found it hard to admit that he would not, sooner or later, receive justice in France. He accepted the money and said that he hoped to be able to repay the debt, with interest, in terms of assistance some time in the future to an Englishman in trouble. They then parted, Major Peddy to his death in the interior of West Africa, Corréard to what he always regarded as a very narrow escape indeed from the same fate.

On November 28, he was put on a small coasting vessel which was to take him and the other passengers out over the bar of the river to where the storeship

*Loire* was lying in the deeper water of the roadstead. Corréard had hardly stepped on board the coaster when he began to shake with a fit of fever. These fits came on him almost every day at about the same time, but on this occasion the direct blaze of the noon sun made his condition even worse than usual. Then the wind fell away to a dead calm so that the vessel was motionless and the sick man, who had been resting against some ropes coiled on deck, began to drift off to sleep. Just before he drowsed off, Corréard heard a voice say, "There's one who'll never get to France."

When he awoke, five hours had passed and he was in a desperate condition, having been left all that time out in the sun. He felt just as he had during the last days on the raft, when he was not far from death. Yet all the other passengers had been taken off nearly five hours before by a boat sent in from the *Loire* to collect them. Only Corréard had been left behind to suffer from the sun on the exposed deck of the coaster; no one had even bothered to wake him. He felt sure that this was no oversight but a final attempt by Schmaltz to silence him forever. Whether or not there was any truth in his suspicions, the *Loire* was still lying out off the bar and as a breeze had now sprung up, the sailors had no excuse not to take him out to her.

The storeship made a good passage home, faster in fact than the *Echo*: twenty-seven days from Saint-Louis to Rochefort, as compared to de Vénancourt's thirty-six days from Gorée roads to Brest. The *Echo* carried home fifty-five *Medusa* survivors, including almost all the junior officers and boat commanders, as well as Coudein and Savigny. The *Loire* rounded off the list of critical witnesses by bringing home among further *Medusa* survivors her captain, de Chaumareys, and his first lieutenant, Reynaud, as well as a sick and vengeful Corréard and the letter originated by Schmaltz. Corréard was determined to warn Savigny of his danger and wrote out an account of the pressures which had been brought to bear on him to sign the Schmaltz document.

The ineffably conceited de Chaumareys, perhaps because he had leaned on Schmaltz as the real leader and decision-maker of the expedition, had no apprehension of danger whatever, although he must have known that a court-martial would inevitably follow the loss of a king's ship.

Lieutenant Gicquel des Touches, the *Loire*'s captain, was to recall that de Chaumareys "was very upset by the loss of his ship but happy to have come out of the affair so well. He spoke in a very free way of this catastrophe. I think I did right in telling him to prepare his defense. I did not hide from him that the impending court-martial would find, without doubt, that there was no excuse for his conduct, and that this was in fact my own opinion. But he did not seem to understand what he had done. When I saw that we were not speaking the same language, I gave up; but for some reason the poor man pursued me for a long time afterwards with his letters, hoping to find in me a very indulgent judge of his conduct. He was without a doubt truly guilty, but shouldn't a large part of the responsibility have been shouldered by the government which had entrusted such men with tasks they were incapable of fulfilling?"

When the *Loire* anchored in the roads off Rochefort from where the *Medusa* had sailed just over six months before, de Chaumareys sat down importantly to write a report for the Minister of Marine regarding the situation in Senegal and, in particular, his own part in organizing the emergency camp at Daccard. At the same time, he demanded leave of absence to visit his estates. Six months before it had been high summer, now it was after Christmas and bitter winter; and the reply he got from the port admiral was just as bitter.

On that admiral's desk there had been lying for more than two months a letter from Du Bouchage, the Minister of Marine. It instructed that officer to report immediately to Paris the arrival of the ex-captain of the *Medusa* and to ensure that "for no reason or pretext whatever" would he be given the home leave which the other officer and under-officer survivors of the frigate might naturally expect. Instead of a leave pass, the port admiral signed an order for the arrest of Frigate-Captain de Chaumareys, Chevalier of the Royal Order of Saint-Louis and Henry IV.

# 12

# Due Process of Law
# (*At Brest and Rochefort, 1816—1817*)

Although the result might be death for an individual, there was nothing dramatic in the way the French legal system went to work. It was entirely cool, objective, thorough and confined at first largely to documentation. There were no theatricals. Nor did anyone concerned with it wear blinders. The warnings went up to the Ministry early that this was no ordinary shipwreck case. On the contrary, it held all the makings of a most dangerous scandal.

Consequently, the public utterances of some individuals were mostly at variance with the facts. It was not that they did not know the truth, but that they did not wish the truth to be known.

The legal proceedings lasted in one form or another for more than six months—from September 1816 to March 1817. The official record of them was to total no fewer than 650 pages, an almost unprecedented length, but was not made public. Its secrecy was enforced by the authority of the state.

Essentially, the proceedings consisted of enquiries into facts, divided into two main phases: that of the *Echo* and that of the *Loire*. The first stage began with the arrival of the *Echo* at Brest on September 2, 1816. She carried fifty-five witnesses from the

*Medusa* as well as the all-important log of the *Echo* herself. By September 18, the minister had decided that Frigate-Captain de Chaumareys must be recalled to explain his conduct before a court-martial. In the meantime the matter was transferred to Rochefort, and a commission of inquiry was held there during most of November.

Then there was a delay, caused by Schmaltz, until the arrival of the *Loire* at Rochefort, on December 27, with the two principal officers of the *Medusa*, de Chaumareys and Reynaud. The transport also brought home a vengeful Corréard and a defensive document from Schmaltz. The court-martial proper was held intermittently on various dates between January 22 and March 3, 1817, and included a thorough and careful examination of de Chaumareys which lasted four days.

The basic documentation provided on September 2, 1816, by de Vénancourt's *Echo* consisted of the official reports of eight officers of the *Medusa* who had traveled in her, plus de Vénancourt's own official report. The captain of the *Echo* could take the story only to the night of July 1/2 when his corvette parted company with the frigate. He stressed that the ships had separated several times before this and that in no case had he received any signal from the *Medusa* as to the course he was to take. However, there was a standing instruction that in case of separation the ships were to sail directly to Saint-Louis. That more or less covered him, being true so far as it went. De Vénancourt was careful to add that Bellin's chart was extremely inaccurate and that the hydrographer of the navy should be informed. This could be read as providing an excuse for de Chaumareys, but it justified first and foremost the action taken by de Vénancourt to steer a night course which would take him well clear of the vaguely defined danger zone.

De Vénancourt's suggestion was acted on and two ships were sent out later that year to resurvey the coast of West Africa, with results that, although they were received too late to influence the court-martial, they did have a distinct bearing on the conduct of de Chaumareys and his advisers.

The critical documents, however, were the official reports of the *Medusa*'s officers. They affirmed that the course of the frigate during daylight on July 2 was south-southeast—directly toward the Arguin Bank; that at 2 P.M. on that day, sixty minutes before stranding, de Chaumareys had refused to take a sounding because it would cause a delay; that a number of men had volunteered to remain on board the frigate and did so; and that the towrope had been cast off because it was found impossible to tow the raft.

Point one meant that de Chaumareys had made a major error in his navigation. Point two meant that he had proceeded with extreme carelessness in waters known to be dangerous. Point three meant that he had not been the last to leave his ship and was therefore technically guilty of a fault punishable by death. Point four, abandoning the raft, might well carry the same penalty. This latter admission by the officers rendered useless at a single stroke all the intricate and industrious work then being undertaken in Senegal by Schmaltz to conceal his vital role in the ghastly tragedy of the raft. However, as Schmaltz had no naval responsibilities, he could not be tried for it; it was de Chaumareys who would have to answer for him.

The report by the raft commander, Midshipman Jean Coudein, was not entirely damning. He stated that although the wind was blowing directly toward the shore and was therefore favorable, the tidal stream proved the stronger force and took the raft to seaward of the *Medusa*. He did not state, because it was a law of nature known to everyone, that the current was bound to reverse its direction and join the wind to take the raft inshore. Nor did he state what seems obvious also, that had the boats anchored during the periods when the tidal stream ran offshore, no ground would have been lost. Coudein neither criticized nor made suggestions but merely stated: "I do not know what were the reasons that caused the boats to cast off the life raft at the time they did. But the fact is that they abandoned us, crowding on all sail, holding the wind as closely as possible until, in the most awful despair, we saw them disappear."

By September 18, all the facts as so far known were on the minister's desk and he had considered them thoroughly. On this day he himself reported to the king. He did not minimize or conceal anything. The affair not only involved the loss of a valuable ship with valuable stores and the death of 132 Frenchmen as so far known, but would also mean the mounting of a new expedition at great expense. There was considerable evidence to show that the ship was lost through faulty calculations, lack of foresight and a lack of elementary precautions. An absolute opinion could not be pronounced, however, until the captain and those of his officers who still remained in Senegal had returned and been heard at a court-martial. This was to be done as soon as possible.

The minister did not consider that the captain alone had been to blame for abandoning the raft; all those in the boats must have been responsible to some degree. Midshipman Coudein had told simply and bluntly what had happened on the raft afterwards, but here the minister did not go into detail. Instead, he wrote: "I spare Your Majesty the narration of the terrible scenes that took place on that raft, resulting from hunger and despair, and of those horrors which were committed during the thirteen days of desolation. I still bemoan the fact that journalists have revealed events that should never have been placed before the eyes of mankind."

The newspaper controversy of the previous week, in which Du Bouchage had thrown official doubt on Savigny's narrative, imputing untruthfulness and malign motives to him, had been no more than a paper battle for the public, after all. The minister had been only too well aware of the truth.

Du Bouchage also wrote to Vice-Admiral Rosily, who had issued the navigational orders to be followed by de Chaumareys, asking him to comment on his own "fragmentary" first impressions. The two reports written by de Chaumareys on July 29 had also arrived with the *Echo*; even to a layman there were great contradictions apparent in them when they were compared to the reports of the officers. De Chaumareys had declared that he had been steering south-southwest away from the bank when the frigate struck, while the officers gave the course at that time at south-southeast, directly into the bank. Du Bouchage asked Rosily for a confidential technical report on the conduct of de Chaumareys, adding that there seemed to him to be imprecisions in the captain's narrative which made it appear that his statements were not firmly based on the log of the frigate.

Rosily reported on September 25, a week later, noting that he had been compelled to use as his primary document the log of the *Echo*, which had been sailing in company with the *Medusa* up to the night of July 1/2. There was no log available for the *Me-*

*dusa,* only the two reports by de Chaumareys in which Cape Blanc, the shoremark for the first "leg" of the dogleg, was stated to have been sighted on the evening of July 1. The log of the *Echo* did not corroborate this. On the contrary, even at midnight de Vénancourt had put the position of his ship, then a little ahead of the *Medusa,* as north of Cape Blanc. It was obvious that neither ship had actually sighted Cape Blanc, so that the start of the seaward turn was from an imperfectly known position. Rosily found it inexplicable that the two vessels had in fact separated during the night when they were both supposedly following the course stated in the reports by de Chaumareys.

But two points were clear. De Chaumareys had not obeyed the Ministry's instruction to head for open sea as soon as the lead showed shallow water and to keep on out to sea until he had passed safely around and was to the south of the Arguin Bank. Nor had he obeyed the Ministry's instruction to take proper soundings at regular intervals in order to stay in safe water and avoid the shallows. These were elementary precautions, given the hazardous "coasting" route laid down by the instructions. Rosily concluded by stressing that if, as the officers said, a course of south-southeast was being followed, the noon sight on July 2 should have made clear that the frigate was heading directly toward the Arguin Bank. "With such conflicting evidence," he wrote, "it is impossible to judge without either having the ship's log in front of one or reassembling all the witnesses."

The ordinary seamen were already being questioned at Brest by Rear-Admiral de Saint-Haouen. The only matter of navigational importance was the testimony of apprentice Bernard Benjamin Chassériau as to a change of course during the early hours of July 2, when the *Medusa* and the *Echo* parted company. The time, he thought, was about 2 A.M., when the soundings began to give depths of only sixteen to eighteen fathoms. Lieutenant Reynaud, who was on watch, hurriedly ordered a change of course westward. The captain, of course, was asleep and did not know what his first lieutenant was doing or what course he had actually steered up to that point.

Seaman Quévélec Mathurin gave confirmatory evidence of the conduct of Lieutenant Espiaux. When all the other boats had abandoned the raft, Espiaux had made a lone attempt to take up the tow, but had been prevented by his men. They had argued that the occupants of the raft, "who had water up to their belts, would rush the longboat and all would perish uselessly." Mathurin also revealed that he had been sleeping in the maintop at the moment the frigate had stranded and had not felt the impact; he had had to be woken up by friends telling him he was shipwrecked.

When the evidence of the seamen had been obtained and added to the written reports of the officers, yet another commission of inquiry was set up. Under Rear-Admiral Maurville, this body was based at Rochefort and worked from November 7 to December 2, 1816. They rationalized the matter by producing a twenty-five-point questionnaire to be answered by the officers, principally regarding the navigation, starting with the hour at which Cape Blanc was seen, followed by an estimate of its distance at the moment of sighting.

The six deck officers (no one asked the surgeon or the paymaster, but they might just as well have) gave six different times for the sighting, varying from as early as 9 P.M. to as late as half an hour before midnight on July 1. Their estimates of distance varied, but not by so much. This was very odd, because the log of the *Echo* made clear that Cape Blanc had not been sighted and never was seen. The deck officers were also at variance in their recollections of the position indicated by the noon sight three hours before stranding. But on one thing they were completely agreed: de Chaumareys had ordered a change of course at 7:30 on the fatal morning of July 2, and that course was south-southeast. This was the really vital point: the time and heading of the second "leg" of the dogleg, the course which would take the *Medusa* back toward the coast of Africa.

The commission noted a curious air of reserve among the officers, which was repeated among the petty officers and other experienced seamen. The missing key to their attitude consisted of one word which was never employed during these proceedings. That word was "Richefort." The captain had rejected his officers and a "vile impostor" of a civilian had in fact been navigating the ship. And the policy decisions, also rightly the captain's, had been usurped by Honorary Colonel Schmaltz. In these circumstances, these officers had ceased to take an interest in anything except the work of their own departments, although they had noted with melancholy resignation the steady march to destruction which began at 7:30 on the morning of July 2. There was little else they could have done, short of mutiny, and that could not succeed because of the number of soldiers on board, all at the orders of Governor Schmaltz.

The commission reported to the minister that there was a clear case against de Chaumareys and that they had formed a poor opinion of the courage and zeal of his officers, with the exception of Lieutenant Espiaux. Now, there was nothing to do but wait for the arrival of the *Loire*, which was, inconveniently, during Christmas.

The next stage of the de Chaumareys case began at Rochefort on January 22, 1817. The president of the court was Rear-Admiral La Tullaye, flanked by the obligatory seven ship-captains. The recording attorney was Ship-Captain Le Carlier d'Herlye and the proceedings consisted of taking more statements. The documents placed before the court included the minutes of the two previous commissions of inquiry, the written reports of the officers and the log of the *Echo* from June 16 to September 2, 1816.

First Lieutenant Reynaud's examination did not produce a favorable impression on the court. Apart from being wordy, he was vague. He thought that Cape Blanc had been sighted at 8 P.M. on July 1 about four or five leagues away, but was not sure. He admitted that he had had the course changed at 2 in the morning of July 2, but he was unable to explain why. He claimed complete ignorance of the change of course ordered by de Chaumareys at 7:30 in the morning of July 2, because, he said, he was too busily engaged with the running of the ship. He could not recall the position of the frigate at noon on July 2, three hours before stranding.

But Reynaud did admit that he had cast off the towrope to the raft at the direct order of Governor Schmaltz. Of the other officers examined, Sub-Lieutenant Lapeyrère was especially firm in his insistence that it was Schmaltz who had been the prime mover in having the raft cast adrift and abandoned. Midshipman Coudein, the raft commander, found the fact of abandonment by men who had been his comrades and were present in court so painful that he begged to be excused from answering questions about this episode and asked the recording attorney to refer to his original report (in which he had written that, for reasons not known to him, the boats had cast off the towrope and fled). It was not Schmaltz who was on trial, however, and indeed the navy had no jurisdiction over His Excellency the governor of Senegal.

Having received little enlightenment from the officers, Le Carlier d'Herlye turned to the petty officers and seamen, of whom he cross-examined thirteen. Again, he met that wall of prudent reserve which masked the real situation in the *Medusa* prior to the disaster. It was only when he questioned three of the petty officers, Granche, Dejoie and Griffon (not to be confused with Griffon du Bellay), that he broke through to the effect which that demoralizing situation had had on the ordinary routine of the frigate.

Both Granche and Dejoie stated that the first sounding they could recall being taken on July 2 was at 2:30 in the afternoon, half an hour before the *Medusa* struck; and that, furthermore, the result was not reliable because the cast had been poorly carried out by the leadsman, and he had had to do it again. This necessarily took some time and the delay was fatal. Griffon, master mariner, testified: "Because of the clumsiness of the leadsman, the sounding was not correct. He cast again and, finding only six fathoms of water, went over to starboard to take a sounding on the other side." Recovering and recoiling a length of wet rope is not done in an instant, but it would be unfair to blame the sailor for his error; the captain has to take entire responsibility for the performance of his officers and crew.

It was clear that the *Medusa* had been a very badly run ship indeed, even if the antagonism between the captain and his officers is disregarded. Although it did not appear in evidence, almost certainly the fact was known to the court. But none of this was evidence of anything other than unfitness for command, which was a reflection on the Ministry as well as on de Chaumareys. The deadly evidence, potentially fatal to de Chaumareys, was contained in the statements of three other members of the crew: gunner Coutant, seaman Lescouet and seaman Dalestre. They were the three men found by Reynaud still alive on board the *Medusa* nearly two months after she had been abandoned. Just by being alive they condemned de Chaumareys to death for not being the last to abandon ship.

Their evidence was disarmingly simple and honest.

Coutant stated: "Believing that there would be more risk by going in the ship's boats or on the life raft than by staying on board, I chose to stay on board."

Lescouet, under cross-examination, admitted to having "taken a little drink," but denied that he had been drunk. He had consciously preferred the wreck to the overfilled longboat or the half-sunken life raft.

Dalestre stated: "I hid so as not to be forced to leave the ship."

Both in the Revolutionary Navy and the Royal Navy of France, the captain, by law, was required to be the last man to leave his ship. It was not just a tradition of the sea, a code of honor, it was a matter of discipline. In no other way could order be preserved in a situation of extreme stress.

The judge-advocate found accordingly, in spite of the conflicting evidence, that five main points could be established without doubt:

(1)  The shoremark of Cape Blanc was not definitely identified, as by instruction it should have been;

(2)  The *Medusa* and the *Echo* parted company, contrary to instruction, without any valid explanation;

(3)  De Chaumareys had altered the course to south-
     southeast without due care and without taking
     any soundings;
(4)  The life raft had been deliberately abandoned,
     but the responsibility here was not that of the
     captain alone;
(5)  In violation of the marine code, the captain had
     not been the last to leave his ship.

Because he was responsible for the loss of the *Medusa*, de Chaumareys had exposed himself to the
punishment of being dismissed from his ship and
suspended from duty; but because he had abandoned
the *Medusa* before seeing that every man got away,
he was liable to the death penalty. La Tullaye, in
forwarding this report to the minister, pointed out
the extreme peril in which de Chaumareys stood
and asked for time in which to question him
thoroughly. He also enclosed a pleading letter from
de Chaumareys.

Instead of considering the matter a mere "bagatelle," the captain was now thoroughly frightened.
He wrote of "a coalition of the *Medusa*'s officers"
against him, of "the fears and passions aroused among
the families of these officers," of the fact that he stood
alone amid a storm of intrigue, stripped even of the
ship's log and his own chart. "I am innocent of
the slanders now assembled against me," he wrote.
"But I am far from seeing myself as being beyond reproach and, attacked by a mass of enemies who have
been preparing their case for five months, I am
frightened of not being able to defend myself from
them all and on all the points." He talked vaguely of
a "route" which he was supposed to have taken and of
how he had a declaration by "four officers" (un-
named) as to another (unstated) "route" he claimed

to have actually followed. And he posed as a victim of the "party spirit" of the Bonapartist officers, who intended to ruin him because of his association with the heroic (Royalist) affair of Quiberon, more than twenty years before.

Both this letter and La Tullaye's plea were unnecessary. Du Bouchage had already written to Louis XVIII asking for a stay of execution so that de Chaumareys could be afforded every opportunity of explaining his conduct. He had concluded: "Although de Chaumareys is guilty of a grave error whose results have been deadly, he has, in other circumstances, given proof of courage and devotion to the Royal cause. He was part of the naval detachment which faced death at Quiberon and was one of the small number of those who escaped the massacre which followed the failure of the enterprise."

# 13

# The de Chaumareys Case
# *(Rochefort, February to*
# *March 1817)*

The *Medusa* was a Rochefort ship, as was the *Loire*. The tragedy was a local story. Many people in the town had relatives or friends who had served under de Chaumareys and there were besides many retired naval people living there. No censorship could hold that story and local interest was intense and well informed. Consequently, de Chaumareys had to be given every chance to explain himself, if he could, and his careful interrogation lasted from February 3 to 6, 1817. After that, judgment would be pronounced.

The captain of the *Medusa* made a poor start. Even during the formal procedure of identification he was caught having lied about his age at the time of reenlistment. Le Carlier d'Herlye, acting as prosecutor, sought to establish what sort of a man de Chaumareys was. In particular, was his seeming vagueness concerning matters of fact a deliberate policy designed to blur the truth or was his mind actually as imprecise as it seemed? It was vitally necessary to do this because the mass of evidence already collected from the officers and men was completely at variance on a number of issues with what de Chaumareys had stated in his written reports of July 29, 1816. It was also at variance with the log of the *Echo* kept by Frigate-

Captain de Vénancourt, while de Chaumareys could not produce either the log of the *Medusa* or even his own charts. It was merely his word against those of the officers and men of the *Medusa*. Early on, Le Carlier sought to establish the lack of documentation.

Asked to explain what had happened to his chart, de Chaumareys replied: "I gave my chart to a midshipman when I got into my boat and by an inconceivable mishap, it was lost. On this chart were marked all the points on the course from our departure until noon on the day the frigate was lost."

The next question and answer established that the chart was Bellin's and that it was part of the Ministry's navigational guide, which included recognition drawings of the various prominent headlands to be taken as shoremarks for position identification.

Le Carlier asked, "At what hour did you identif, Cape Barbas, at what distance was it and what was your position at midday on July 1?"

At this time the *Echo* had been keeping company with the *Medusa*, and Le Carlier had all the answers from de Vénancourt's log. The answer that de Chaumareys gave him revealed that not only had the *Medusa*'s captain identified the wrong headland as Cape Barbas, but even now he did not know that he had done so.

Le Carlier then moved to the next shoremark, the most important. "At what hour did you identify Cape Blanc and at what distance was it?"

De Chaumareys replied without hesitation: "At eight in the evening of July 1, when I expected to. I recognized it perfectly. I estimated we were four leagues west-northwest of it at the time. I estimated the distance we had covered from the average speed of the frigate since leaving Cape Barbas."

As the court had studied the *Echo*'s log, it was

obvious to them that the distance the *Medusa* had covered had been "estimated" from one landmark incorrectly identified to another landmark never seen at all.

The questioning then turned to the course held at night, based on the "sighting" of Cape Blanc. De Chaumareys insisted that his orders for the night had been as laid down in his instructions: that is, a course of west-southwest, sounding every two hours and keeping the *Echo* in sight. He explained: "All I had as a guide for my passage, which neither I nor my officers had navigated before, were nautical instructions issued to me by the Ministry. These instructions advised me to take a southwesterly course for fourteen leagues after sighting Cape Blanc."

In such circumstances, at the most dangerous part of the passage, a captain would normally be on deck. But further questioning revealed that de Chaumareys had been asleep. Indeed, with great indignation, he gave this as his excuse. "To this very day," he declared, "I have been accused of failing to see the corvette *Echo* and to notice that at three in the morning she burned signal flares to draw my attention. I was in my bed. I never had a chance to note the direction of those flares."

By concealing some of the facts, de Chaumareys was making matters worse for himself. The main fact missing from the record was Richefort. The court was not told that precisely because neither de Chaumareys nor his officers had experience of this coast, the navigation had been entrusted to a man who supposedly did have such knowledge. In effect, de Chaumareys had abdicated in favor of someone who was not even in the navy and had such boundless confidence in him that he could sleep the whole night through during the critical time when the hazardous and only partly known sandbank must be close. Even so, the officer of the watch at that time (Reynaud) should have notified the captain that the *Echo* was signaling.

Le Carlier then reached the time of the fatal decision, 7:30 A.M. on July 2. Here, for once, the testimonies of de Chaumareys and his officers showed no disagreement. De Chaumareys agreed that he had come on deck at 6:00 and at 7:30 that morning and repeated that the leadsman had found no bottom at 120 "brasses" (640 feet). "This gave me such confidence that I thought further sounding unnecessary. I then definitely ordered that the course be changed to south-southeast in order to look for the coast."

In his report of July 29, de Chaumareys had stated that he had ordered further soundings to be taken, both at 9 A.M. and at 10 A.M. (as indeed he should have done), but faced by the prosecutor he did not repeat this fable.

Nor did his answer to the next critical question chime with his July 29 report, in which he had stated that the sight taken at noon had shown the *Medusa* at 20° 8′ North and 19° 30′ West, which sounded reasonably professional. Faced by his accusers, de Chaumareys lapsed into imprecision. "At noon the sun was high enough to take an altitude, but I didn't make an observation. In any case, I had little confidence in the latitude taken because the sun was now at the zenith and because the navigational guide told me that one must expect great errors in this area. . . . However, I had every confidence in my reckoning [the distance run from Cape Blanc], although at this moment my memory cannot recall what it was. Indeed, several times during that morning I reflected upon the inconceivable route which the *Echo* was believed to have taken, a route which had taken her away from us to such a great distance that we never saw her at all that day. But with such great confidence in my reckoning, I continued to steer south-southeast."

This does give a clue as to what really happened. If de Chaumareys was relying entirely on an estimate of the distance run since the "sightings" of Cape Barbas and Cape Blanc, and if that estimate had been entirely accurate, it would certainly make him believe that he had completed more of the first "leg" of the dogleg than he had actually done. The *Medusa*'s real starting point was problematical, but if it was perhaps ten or twelve leagues north of where it should have been, then the second turn of the dogleg was bound to be made too early. Even so, even if in fact he had managed to correctly identify Cape Blanc and then made his first turn from the right position, de Chaumareys was still cutting things rather fine, particularly in a largely unknown and imprecisely charted area. To add to this recklessness, a failure to take frequent soundings to give early warning of approaching danger could only be explained by his dependence on Richefort. The court was not told that when the officers protested to de Chaumareys of the extreme danger ahead, the captain had had to turn to Richefort, who at once reassured de Chaumareys that he knew his business and that all was well. But the fact that the real navigator had been Richefort was not admissible in court.

This fact being omitted, the next piece of evidence from de Chaumareys bordered on farce. It must be remembered that a sailing ship can rarely be turned quickly; in unfavorable circumstances, it may take up to six miles.

Three hours after the results of the noon sight had alarmed all the officers, the water had changed color—clearly indicating the imminent approach to a bank—and at last de Chaumareys took action, ineffective as usual. He merely ordered a sounding to be taken. This showed eighteen "brasses" (96 feet). "This caused me extreme surprise," he said. "It made me go over to the starboard side and briefly consult my chart and check my calculations."—this, when a thousand tons of frigate was heading inshore with irresistible momentum.

When the inevitable occurred, de Chaumareys was stricken "as much by astonishment as with grief" to find his command heeled right over, hard aground on the Arguin Bank. He could not understand what had happened, except that the bank was in the wrong position.

Le Carlier d'Herlye produced a copy of Bellin's chart, similar to that used by de Chaumareys, and asked the unfortunate captain to show him, on that chart, three critical positions: where the *Medusa* was at 5 P.M. on July 1, at 6 A.M. on July 2, and at 3 P.M. on July 2, the hour of the stranding. De Chaumareys indicated the three points with great confidence, but not one was correct. The first one, which de Chaumareys showed as near Cape Blanc, could be proved badly wrong by the log of the *Echo*. The last position, that of the wreck itself, he had stated in his report of July 29 to be 19° 55′ North, 19° 24′ West. But he had declared to the court that his own estimate was now 19° 36′ North, 19° 45′ West. (A hydrographic mission sent out a few months later was to establish it as 19° 53′ North, 19° 20′ West.)

Le Carlier asked de Chaumareys to sign the copy of the chart on which he had just marked the three positions, then he himself countersigned it; the clerk of the court, Belanfant, added a final signature.

That ended the navigational questioning. When Le Carlier turned to the abortive attempts to refloat the frigate and then the plans to evacuate her and save the crew and passengers, de Chaumareys again unwittingly revealed his incompetence, although he could confidently state that "these operations were carried out with the greatest order." Incompetence is not a crime. Abandoning men for whom one is responsible most definitely is. The atmosphere of the courtroom changed as the shadow of the death penalty began to loom over de Chaumareys.

The witness stated: "I stayed on board the frigate almost to the last, while I could still see men manifestly engaged in leaving her. They showed a pronounced dread and dissatisfaction with the embarkation."

This presumably referred to the brandishing of a musket by Lieutenant d'Anglas and the threats of the soldiers to fire on the boats which seemed to be leaving half empty—also perhaps to the reluctance of some seamen to leave the *Medusa* for Lieutenant Espiaux's desperately overcrowded longboat.

De Chaumareys went on: "I decided, at the request of several sailors who surrounded me, and to the great satisfaction of all, to get into my barge. I did so and very quickly helped by towing the longboat. I remember that at one moment, when the longboat came alongside the frigate, I positively commanded Lieutenant Espiaux to embark the rest of the men remaining in the ship. He said, 'Don't worry, captain.' On my honor, I assure you I was convinced that the longboat was capable of saving them all. At that moment I was not aware of the danger which threatened the raft, but three attempts to tow it failed and it moved away with the currents. I put before you the despair of the men helplessly adrift on it, the fatal consequences which must ensue. From then on, it was obvious that my command was no longer the frigate, but the raft and the boats which were towing it."

The last sentence was a legal nicety, probably suggested to de Chaumareys by his defending counsel, Frigate-Captain Cuvilier, and M. Mesnard, a Rochefort lawyer, who were to invoke a law of 1765 which gave some latitude to officers faced with circumstances unforeseen in their orders or by any regulation. In effect, de Chaumareys was claiming that in leaving the frigate before the last man had gone, he was not abandoning his command, because the bulk of the men under his command were either on the raft or in the boats and his proper place was with them, where he might still be of some use in controlling rescue operations. The raft, he claimed, had not been abandoned; the towrope linking it to the barge carrying the governor and his spouse and their daughter had broken.

When the interrogation of the accused ended on February 6, La Tullaye, the president of the court, sent his own opinions to the minister in writing. Oddly, he mentioned nothing of the abandonment or even of the abortive attempts to refloat the ship. He gave judgment only on the disputed matter of navigation. He put his finger on the errors made by de Chaumareys: his reliance on an estimate of the distance run along the coast of Africa when his positions were quite erroneous and how a dogleg course begun too far north would bring a ship directly to the Arguin Bank. He regretted that the only documentary evidence he had in front of him was the log of the *Echo*, so that his opinion was only an opinion. But there was one error committed by Captain de Chaumareys which was indisputable. He had not carried out those frequent soundings which would have revealed the navigational mistakes and averted their fatal consequences.

*    *    *

The critical speeches for the prosecution and the defense lasted from February 24 to March 1, 1817, and the vote of the members of the court was taken on Monday, March 3. Tension ebbed and flowed as the prosecutor, Le Carlier d'Herlye, dealt with charge after charge alleged against de Chaumareys and examined the validity of the defense he had made.

The first charge was that de Chaumareys had allowed his squadron to become separated off Cape Finisterre, when the *Loire* and the *Argus* were left behind, contrary to instructions. The prosecutor began severely: "This was an entirely voluntary act on the part of M. de Chaumareys. The fault would be very serious, if the reasons which the accused puts forward are not admitted, for the fact of separation has been proved, and it did not occur because of bad weather. But the accused has claimed that the poor sailing of these two ships considerably slowed the *Medusa*, that the governor of Senegal wished to reach his destination as soon as possible, that it was necessary to prepare in advance for the unloading of the troops and stores from the *Loire* and the *Argus*, and that the instructions given to M. de Chaumareys urged him not to delay because of the approach of the bad weather season."

The court waited to hear on which side Le Carlier would weight the scales. The prosecutor went on: "I think that all these reasons, taken together, justified M. de Chaumareys and I conclude that he should be declared not guilty of dividing his squadron."

That must have given hope to de Chaumareys, but Le Carlier then turned to the navigation of the frigate and, in great detail and with some irony, tore the captain's defense to shreds. Then he turned to his own conclusions and these were remorseless.

"The sinking of His Majesty's frigate *Medusa* was not caused by forced circumstances, because the weather was fine, the sea good, the wind both moderate and favorable. I therefore attribute it to the course taken during the night; to complacency founded on the fact that they could not find bottom at 120 fathoms in the morning; to an overconfidence which led M. de Chaumareys to take the route to the east far too soon and on that course to be taken by the wind farther toward the shore than he had expected; and to a feeling of security which made him neglect the indispensable precautions to be taken in dangerous regions and especially when in close proximity to a bank whose area and position are still not well known to this day."

After that broadside, Le Carlier let de Chaumareys breathe for a moment by mentioning his favorite excuse. "I truly believe," said the prosecutor, "that the edges of the Arguin Bank stretch much farther to the west than is indicated on Bellin's chart, which is the one M. de Chaumareys was using. If his estimated position had been correct, then he would merely have struck the bank after traveling a further fifteen or sixteen leagues, instead of when he did, but if we take the position given in the witnesses' statements, then he would have struck six or seven leagues later than he did."

Le Carlier then stated formally: "I conclude that M. Duroy de Chaumareys should be declared guilty of sinking His Majesty's frigate *Medusa* through complacency and the taking of insufficient precautions; and considering the results of this lack of caution, that he should be condemned to be dismissed from his ship and declared unfit to serve, in accordance with Article 39 of the penal code."

Le Carlier sharply divided the rest of the story into three phases: the unsuccessful attempts to refloat the frigate and then the final abandonment of first the frigate and then of the raft. Regarding the failure to get the stranded *Medusa* off the bank, he pointed to three factors beyond the control of de Chaumareys. They were the lack of a heavily built boat capable of taking out an anchor immediately; the effect of the currents combined with a choppy sea which added to all difficulties and, in particular, to the taking out of anchors in the desired directions; and, finally, the storm which drove the frigate further aground and stove in her hull. Therefore, he concluded, on the charge of causing the total loss of the *Medusa*, de Chaumareys should be found not guilty.

So far, the balance had swung evenly: for de Chaumareys on the first charge, against de Chaumareys on the second charge, for de Chaumareys on the third charge. If the pattern continued with the fourth charge, that of the abandonment, and de Chaumareys was found guilty, he would face death, for this charge alone carried the death penalty. On the face of it, there could be no finding other than that of guilty, for he certainly had not been the last man to leave the *Medusa*. His sole defense had been a rather shaky legal subterfuge.

The prosecutor kept everyone, and not least de Chaumareys, in suspense for a very long time while he meticulously turned over the facts to examine them from all angles, and in the light of various codes and regulations. His opening words must have struck a chill into the heart of the accused.

"The unanimous statements of all the witnesses, and the replies of M. de Chaumareys, leave no doubt that the longboat was no longer alongside the ship when he left her and that there were only a few men still on board after the departure of the longboat." That seemed to mean that de Chaumareys was technically guilty, but Le Carlier went on to consider what did or did not constitute an infringement of Articles 56 of 1763 and 66 of January 1, 1786. "Both of these state that the captain of a sinking ship must not, for any reason whatever, leave the ship until the last moment," he pointed out.

Was he saying that the captain had waited until the last practical moment, until the longboat had taken on its quota of passengers and left only a few men and himself behind? Or did he mean that, with the departure of the longboat, only the captain's barge remained, and if de Chaumareys got into that without embarking every last man and woman left on board (there were some sixty, not "a few"), then he was guilty of abandoning any who remained behind? Or was the fact of the return of Espiaux's longboat, after de Chaumareys had abandoned the *Medusa*, being left out of account? Or was its return the result of an order by the captain? A command which might justify his claim to have left the frigate to control the rescue operation instead?

"I am going to examine with you, gentlemen," continued the prosecutor, "the penalties applicable to that charge which would render the accused liable to capital punishment; that is, if I paid no attention to the circumstances which accompanied the infringement of Articles 55 and 66 previously mentioned, but demanded for him due application of that penalty so liberally stipulated by Article 35 of the penal code for ships of August 22, 1790." Those were the savage regulations of the Revolutionary Navy.

"In my report I have been guided by a just and

severe impartiality regarding the guilt of M. de Chaumareys which, equally, must be the basis of the conclusions which my duty obliges me to take in indicating the penalties which I believe to be applicable to the misconduct alleged by the prosecution.

"You will recall, gentlemen, that in his interrogation and in the debates which followed, M. de Chaumareys alleged, and his defenders have repeated it, that he directed the details of the frigate's evacuation and controlled the disorders that tended to accompany it. M. de Chaumareys and his defenders have invoked in his favor Article 1285 of 1765, by which His Majesty, not being able to foresee all the tasks and orders which may be necessary, orders only that in unforeseen circumstances an officer conduct himself generally for the greatest good of the Service and in accordance with the laws of honor. Now, it is alleged further, that he had to directly supervise the embarkment of a large part of his crew onto the life raft as well as into the boats, and that he saw this as more important than passively remaining on board his frigate in order to try and make the rest of his men leave the ship."

The thinness of that excuse must have seemed even more flimsy when spoken by the prosecutor, in framing a reply to it, than it had when put forward as a legal nicety by the defense. The court waited, and for de Chaumareys this must have been the worst moment of the long ordeal, for Le Carlier to reject the plea out of hand. Indeed, several members of the court expected that the prosecutor would instantly demand the death penalty. For a moment it seemed that he was going to.

"Even if I try to temper the severity of my minister, any indulgence cannot go beyond the bounds of equity," declared Le Carlier. "I cannot admit that these extenuating circumstances are sufficient to clear the accused of all guilt. On the other hand, I cannot entirely refute the validity of the motives he has given to excuse his infringement of Articles 56 and 66. Therefore, although I cannot regard them as extenuating circumstances for his grave misconduct, I can put them in the balance to weigh in favor of the accused when the question of the death penalty is considered."

The shadow lifted from the room, and from de Chaumareys, and there was a certain amount of astonishment at this promise of leniency. It was with lessened tension that the court listened to Le Carlier continuing to prove why he thought de Chaumareys was guilty.

"Unlike M. de Chaumareys, I do not see his command at the last divided between the life raft and the boats which lay alongside the *Medusa*. I always visualize the frigate as sinking and not completely evacuated when he left her. The regulations foresaw the case of a sinking vessel. They are very clear and do not leave the captain the option of making up his own mind where his presence is most necessary. But I am persuaded that it was not through any weakness, which it was the intention of the law to punish severely, that M. de Chaumareys left his ship before the moment laid down by the regulations. I believe it was only an error of judgment which led him to make a false interpretation of the various articles in the regulations."

"Even so, gentlemen, if some doubts do arise concerning the actual intentions which M. de Chaumareys alleges motivated him at this time, can we forget those principles which direct all men called to judge their equals to weigh the doubts in favor of the accused? Can we forget this, above all, when it is a case of capital punishment? Guided by this principle and by my conscience, I would exclude from my conclusions a penalty which the legislative could only have wished to be used for cowardice or for treason."

The prosecutor blandly continued: "But if I do not find in the conduct of M. de Chaumareys any fault specified by the regulations which would warrant capital punishment, I am far from declaring him not guilty. The fact that he infringed the articles and did not remain to the last minute in the frigate renders him liable to punishment. I conclude, gentlemen, that M. de Chaumareys should be declared guilty of not leaving his ship as the last man; and that, in addition to the penalties to which he is already liable for the loss of the frigate, he should be condemned to serve a term of five years in a military prison, if His Majesty so desires."

Le Carlier was compelled to explain why he was asking for a type of punishment which, for this offense, was not laid down in the regulations. He stated that he was aware of various precedents and then took refuge in a variation of de Chaumareys's own plea, that if the 1765 regulations admitted that all offenses could not foreseen, then neither could the penalties.

The final charge concerning the conduct of de Chaumareys after the frigate had run aground was potentially almost as deadly as that from which he had just escaped. It was the accusation that he had abandoned the raft. And here, the captain's ingenious plea that he had left his ship while there were still men aboard her because he had wanted to save the people on the raft and direct the boats could with ease be argued against him.

Le Carlier d'Herlye set out to argue for him, at great length. He said there were two ways of looking at the matter. "First, the *Medusa* being entirely abandoned [sic] by all the men who were now reformed on and around the life raft, should this craft be regarded as forming, with the men, the physical basis of a new command under the direction of M. de Chaumareys? If so, his abandoning of it would imply that he had infringed the articles already mentioned. Or, alternatively, should the life raft and the six boats which accompanied it be regarded as distinctly separate craft, each one under the command of a particular officer and forming part of a division under the orders of M. de Chaumareys? I am utterly of the opinion that the second way of looking at things is that which is usual and just. The boats cannot be regarded as forming part of the life raft which, anyway, could not help or protect them against bad weather as a ship does; on the contrary, it was from the boats that the life raft would receive help."

This was extremely dangerous ground, but Le Carlier pressed on. "I therefore consider the life raft and the boats as a division of seven craft, whatever their size or type, following the commands of a chief common to all. One of these boats being in trouble or sinking, it is certain that the others must give it as much help as possible. But if bad weather or other forced circumstances do not allow the rescue attempt to continue, or even to save the crew of the craft in distress, the commander of the division is not guilty of having abandoned it."

As Le Carlier continued, his meaning began to emerge slowly, underlying what he did not say rather than his spoken words. De Chaumareys had revealed that, on occasion, his orders had not been carried out; but he had never named the officers who he said were to blame and had taken all the responsibility himself; he had never accused anyone. Now, Le Carlier was doing it for him.

"In this case, the boats of M. de Chaumareys and his companions were already crowded. Perhaps they could have taken more men from the raft, but it is evident that the boats would have been rushed and sunk in doing so. This fear, well founded I believe, appears to have been the reason which prevented any of the boats from going near the raft. Even in the letter written by M. Schmaltz to the minister this motive is revealed. I must observe, however, that M. de Chaumareys made both his own boat and the Senegal boat go about and return to take up the towrope again, but by the time they had done so, they found that the other boats were no longer towing the life raft and were making no move to renew the tow. Therefore I conclude that M. Duroy de Chaumareys should be declared not guilty of abandoning the life raft."

That was the nearest that His Excellency the governor of Senegal ever came to being declared guilty of the same offense.

Saturday, March 1, was given over to speeches for the defense. They hardly needed longer, as the prosecutor had done most of their work for them. On March 3, the members of the court voted. Although one was for the death penalty, most votes were cast for three years imprisonment. In addition, the name of de Chaumareys was to be struck from the navy list and he was to forfeit his orders and decorations.

\*       \*       \*

Le Carlier had previously written to the minister in confidence, explaining why he intended to be merciful. "I hesitate to pronounce the death penalty because in my soul and conscience I do not judge that the accused deserves death for having left the frigate before he should have. He did not commit this offense from weakness or to save himself, but to put himself in a place where he would be of use."

No doubt this was a delicate letter to write for, putting politics aside, many believed that the principal fault lay with the government and, in particular, with the Minister of Marine. As the captain of the *Loire* had noted, "Chaumareys was without doubt truly guilty, but shouldn't a great part of the responsibility fall on the government which entrusts such men with employment for which they are not fitted?"

There were some who thought that even the mild sentence passed on de Chaumareys was too harsh. An officer who was serving at Rochefort and had closely studied the trial wrote to the minister. He was concerned first to bring out what the trial had concealed, in case Du Bouchage did not know. "The captain committed major errors from the first. He immediately alienated his second-in-command, who in turn involved the other officers, by taking as his confidant in the navigation of the ship a passenger who was to be the port captain of Saint-Louis."

The writer made the significant point that not a single nautical document, chart or log was produced to show with certainty how the *Medusa* was navigated before the stranding. The implication may be that they were deliberately destroyed or "lost" because they were incriminating.

Impatiently, he short-circuited the endless tale of the errors committed by de Chaumareys and asked: "What do they prove? Failure, unfitness for leadership, inability to cope with difficulties, and a quite unusual lack of safety precautions. But by no means a coward. At present, he is regarded as solely responsible for this disastrous event, because it was he who was in command and also because he had the generosity not to transfer one part of this fatal responsibility to any of his subordinates. But these men, have they all done their duty?"

He examined the separation in the night of the *Medusa* and the *Echo* and concluded that Reynaud, officer of the watch in the frigate, and de Vénancourt, captain of the corvette, were jointly responsible. De Chaumareys had nothing to do with it. Had the two ships not separated, there might have been a stranding but there would have been no disaster.

He condemned Reynaud again for casting off the towrope to the raft without a direct order from his captain and asked pointedly: "Was it M. Schmaltz and his entourage who gave this advice? Further, this boat (holding Reynaud and Schmaltz) saved only forty people from the frigate. I have been told that this boat had on a previous occasion carried no less than seventy soldiers with their arms. If this is true, then it could easily have taken off the seventeen men remaining on board the *Medusa*."

The writer concluded by explaining that this was not merely his opinion but that of a number of other officers who were not directly involved and were therefore unbiased. They all thought the sentence too harsh and that, at the least, de Chaumareys should be returned to the navy list and be given back his rank.

In a sense these three men who sympathized with de Chaumareys were too detached. Neither Le Carlier nor des Touches nor the anonymous naval officer from Rochefort had any real contact with the *Medusa* tragedy.

But to men like Savigny and Corréard, who had by a small margin survived the horrors which had been the direct result of the multiple errors and muddles made by de Chaumareys, the court-martial and its judgments appeared to be mere whitewash—an example of the "old boy net" at work to protect its own. But they were far from blaming de Chaumareys alone. Although the minister was their prime target, they were extremely bitter about the conduct of Schmaltz, Reynaud and several of the other officers. Charlotte Picard also was to give a very poor impression of the behavior of some of the officers on whom de Chaumareys had to rely.

It is all very well to point out, as some French academic historians have done, that the testimony of Savigny and Corréard is "biased and suspect" and to endeavor to discount it because there were political and personal overtones. The affair was indeed political and politics could hardly be avoided, but their original involvement was quite involuntary (except that Corréard chose deliberately to take his chance on the raft with his men). They knew, as few others did, what the results had been.

Above all they knew that the example set by the leader is all-important and that in this critical aspect de Chaumareys had failed lamentably, as had his co-leaders, Schmaltz and Reynaud. They had been tried in the only court that counted—that of a true, character-revealing emergency—and had failed miserably. They would have done better to have died with their men.

By the strangest of coincidences, unknown at that moment either to the French or to the British, as the court-martial trying de Chaumareys for the loss of his frigate was actually sitting and arriving at final judgment, an almost exactly similar series of events was taking place many thousands of miles away, but to a British frigate.

# 14

## A British *Medusa*
## *(The* Alceste *in the*
## *South China Sea,*
## *February to March 1817)*

On January 21, 1817, while Le Carlier d'Herlye was still studying the documents in the de Chaumareys case, the British thirty-eight-gun frigate *Alceste* was leaving Whampoa in China, carrying 257 persons, including a V.I.P. and his entourage. The captain, Murray Maxwell, was a battle-experienced officer. He and his ship had been partly responsible for probably ruining one of Bonaparte's campaigns by capturing his artillery at sea before he could attack. Although that had occurred in 1811, he was to be reminded of it in the strangest way before he saw England again.

The V.I.P. on board was Lord Amherst, then the British ambassador to China and a very much more distinguished official than M. Schmaltz, for he was later to become governor of Canada and later still governor-general of India.

It is probable that, as with the *Medusa,* some of the *Alceste*'s guns had been removed to make room for passengers. A slightly smaller ship, she carried 150 fewer people than the *Medusa* had.

The British frigate was bound for home through the South China Seas. In their danger and mystery these more than matched the coast of West Africa.

While today the Arguin Bank alone stands out as unsurveyed on the charts, the South China Seas contain a space of one hundred thousand square miles similarly unsurveyed and unknown, labeled simply "The Dangerous Area." Furthermore, there was no safe route far out from land over deep water, such as the *Medusa* could have taken. For no fewer than 1,500 miles there was nothing but shallow water, nothing deeper than 40 fathoms (240 feet). In an area where typhoons were frequent, this meant that extraordinarily dangerous seas could develop. The time for the passage had been well chosen, however, and the winds were favorable.

The route recommended then for sailing ships (but not now for steamships) passed through the Bangka Strait, immediately before the Sunda Strait. This is nearer the equator than the Arguin Bank, so that the heat was intense. The route was chosen because it was comparatively well known. Nevertheless, Captain Murray Maxwell of the *Alceste* kept the leadsmen sounding continuously, because there were hundreds of submerged shoals in the area, some of which rise so steeply from deep water that neither a sounding lead nor a modern echo sounder can give much warning.

On February 17, the *Alceste* struck one of these steep-to reefs at speed. Maxwell let go an anchor at once, to hold the frigate on the reef in case she was badly holed. The British ship proved to have struck on rock, not sand, and was so damaged that the pumps could not control the inflow. Maxwell's plight was worse than that of de Chaumareys, for his ship was doomed to start with. If she was moved off the reef, she would only sink. He was, similarly, many hundreds of miles from all help and off an inhospitable coast populated by potentially dangerous natives. The nearest land was much closer, only three miles, but it was merely an island with no obvious landing place.

Significantly, the captain's first thought was for the V.I.P., Lord Amherst, and his entourage. The ambassador and his suite were embarked in a barge and a cutter under the command of the first lieutenant, Hopper, the equivalent of the *Medusa*'s Lieutenant Reynaud. Hopper was ordered to land this party on the island first of all and then return with the boats. Hopper had to travel six miles to and along the shore because the mangroves prevented any landing being made opposite the scene of the wreck.

Meanwhile, Maxwell hoisted out the other four boats and ordered the construction of a large raft to be towed by the boats. On this raft he put no people, only large and heavy stores. The smaller and more important items, such as water, food, arms, ammunition and tools, he had placed in the boats. When the barge and the cutter returned empty from landing the first party, Maxwell embarked the rest of his crew in the boats and they all headed for shore, towing the raft the full six miles. By nightfall, they were all safely ashore and setting up a camp.

The next day, it was discovered that the island was waterless. There was little chance of their being sighted by a passing ship, so a council was held and it was decided that the ambassador and his suite should embark again in the barge and the cutter under First Lieutenant Hopper to try to make Batavia in Java, some two hundred miles farther south. Given good weather, this should take them four days; but it could easily be longer. When they arrived at Batavia, they were to send out a relief ship to pick up the island castaways, who by that time would be very short of water. The men in the boats were given enough water to provide a ration of one pint per man per day for four days only—little enough for Europeans exposed to the sun in a latitude 3° south of the equator, but more than the castaways on the island would have.

The procedure bears strong resemblance to some aspects of the abandonment of the *Medusa*, particularly that of the second-in-command being given charge of the boats designed to take the V.I.P. to safety as rapidly as possible. But there the similarity ends. Captain Maxwell did not accompany them. He remained behind on the island to control the castaways, who numbered two hundred men and one woman. No one was abandoned, not on the wreck, not on the raft, not in the boats, not on the island. The captain was where he should be, with the bulk of his command.

Also, unlike de Chaumareys, Maxwell knew what to do and he saw that it got done. Above all, he was not complacent; he foresaw various hazards and set out to be ready in time. He changed the camp site to the top of a small hill, for better defense; he had the provisions stowed in a cool cave under formal guard by armed marine sentries; he had his crew digging like beavers in the tropical heat to find water, and when they were twenty feet down into the earth, they found a little water seeping into the clay at the bottom; and he sent out a boat party to the wreck to salvage supplies and arms. His seamen were still digging at midnight and shortly afterwards the first bottle of muddy water was filled and pronounced fresh.

Immediately, there was a rush to the well by the thirsty men. Maxwell stopped it and posted an armed guard over the digging party; he also proclaimed that no one—no one—would get any water at all from the well until there was enough to give a ration to every-

body. By noon next day, February 20, a pint of well
well water per man was served.

On the fourth day, February 21, a boat party of
unarmed seamen salvaging the wreck were surrounded
by several local war vessels—proas armed with swivel
guns at the bow and manned by eighty Malays. The
British pulled madly for the shore, pursued by the
Malays. Maxwell counterattacked at once. Armed
seamen jumped into two of the boats by the shore and
rowed out to confront the proas, which gave up the
pursuit of the unarmed party. Then a lookout reported more proas, landing armed men on the island
about two miles away.

Maxwell assumed that attack was imminent and
that it would be ruthless. The sea-Dyaks usually
murdered everyone aboard any ship they captured and
it was rumored that some tribes practiced cannibalism.
He ordered that all effort be concentrated on defense.
A stockade, flimsy but still sufficient to stop a rush,
was rapidly built around the hilltop. The marines
had thirty muskets and bayonets, but only seventy-
five rounds of ball cartridge. The gunner had had the
foresight to save the gunpowder charges from the
carronades on the upper deck, so there was spare
powder, but no shot. He improvised by using broken
glass from the bottles instead of lead for projectiles.
There were a dozen cutlasses, but most of the two
hundred men were still unarmed. Again, the British
improvised. Spearshafts were made from branches
and small trees; knives, chisels and nails were used
to give them unpleasant points. Scouts were sent out
to keep watch on the Malays and they reported that
the Dyaks seemed principally interested in plundering
the wreck.

The next day, Captain Murray Maxwell of the
British Royal Navy decided to talk peace with the

Malays, rather than fight them. He sent an officer down to the landing place to go out in a boat and wave a green bough in token of his pacific intentions. It was a sensible move, for the main interest of the Dyaks lay with the wreck and the metal objects it contained or was built of; to them, this was treasure beyond price, whereas what the British needed was food and water. But the Dyaks were suspicious and ferocious; it was impossible to negotiate. What they wanted they would take.

That was exactly Maxwell's own view. He decided to recapture the wreck from the Dyaks, using his best-armed men embarked in three boats under Second Lieutenant Hay, who was now his second-in-command. As the attack went in, the Dyaks threw their plunder into the proas, set fire to the *Alceste*, and made off. This was helpful, for Maxwell faced the same problem in getting at the stores of the *Alceste* as had Reynaud in his salvage attempt on the *Medusa*. He had decided to burn off the upperworks anyway so that he could get at the decks below. Reynaud did not do this, perhaps because he claimed that the *Medusa*'s hulk was continuously wave swept.

All that night the flames from the burning frigate illuminated the eerie mangrove swamps and the improvised stockade with flickering lights and shadows. In just such a situation in the desert the French castaways had been frightened by a lion which proved in the morning to have been a bush waving with the wind. Showing less imagination a British sentry cried, "Halt! Who goes there?" to a hunched shape prowling out in the darkness and pulled the trigger when he received no reply. At the crash of the shot, every man was armed and at his post. Then it was discovered why the intruder had failed to answer the challenge— it was a Malayan baboon.

The next day was Sunday. While the captain took Divine Service in the camp, two boats went out to the charred and smoking hulk of the frigate and obtained a good haul from the opened decks—barrels of flour, cases of wine and one cask of beer. The latter, for a party of British castaways, was an immense boost to morale.

For several more days, Maxwell was concerned with getting as much arms and ammunition as possible out of the wreck and with improving his fields of fire around the stockade. But he did not neglect his boats; he had sentries watching over them all night and his officers, unlike most of those commanded by de Chaumareys, were efficient and alert. At dawn on February 24, Second Lieutenant Hay sighted two proas with canoes towed astern stealing into the cove where the British boats were kept. He at once manned the boats and went out to attack. The Malays cut loose their canoes to allow the proas to get away faster, and one of the proas brought a swivel gun to bear as the British ran alongside to board. Fired blindly, it hit nothing and then the British seamen were in among the Dyaks with cutlass and bayonet. Within a minute or two, four Dyaks were dead, two were prisoners and five were overboard and vanished.

Later that morning, a second Dyak fleet of fourteen proas was approaching the wreck of the *Alceste*. One vessel was much larger than the others and appeared to be a flagship, carrying perhaps a raja. They took possession of the wreck and the "raja" was seen directing their salvage operations.

On March 1, 1817, Captain Maxwell's castaways saw yet another division of fourteen proas join all the others; and during the night yet more were noticed arriving, but the light was too bad to count their number exactly. The buildup for a major attack seemed to be taking place.

On the morning of March 2, Sunday, twenty of the largest proas approached the shore in line-abreast while the remainder clustered closely around the wreck of the British frigate. Still in line, the twenty approaching vessels anchored as one just offshore and to the beating of gongs and brandishing of spears the Dyaks opened fire with their bow-mounted swivel guns. No landing was attempted.

Maxwell believed it would come that night, under cover of darkness, which would render ineffective the fire of those of his men who were armed with muskets. It may be that the Malays were merely demonstrating —that, in effect, they were simply saying, "Your ship is now ours, keep off." Or they may have been genuinely enraged by the killing of their men in the raiding proa a few days before and were itching to get at the perpetrators. Or, because the islands on which they lived were short of protein food, they relished the thought of meat, and there were two hundred live carcasses on the island.

The British captain was certainly right to prepare for the worst. He gave them a rousing speech which was also coldly informative. "My lads," said Maxwell, "you must all have observed the great increase in the enemy's force, and the threatening posture they have assumed. I have reason to believe they will attack us this night. I do not wish to conceal our real state, because I do not think there is a man here who is afraid to face any sort of danger. We are in a position to defend ourselves against regular troops, far less a set of naked savages, with their spears and krises. It is true they have swivels [swivel guns] in their boats, but they cannot reach here. I have not observed that they have any muskets, but if they have, so have we.

When we were first thrown on shore we could only muster seventy-five ball cartridges—we now have sixteen hundred. They cannot send up, I believe, more than five hundred men; but with two hundred such as now stand around me, I do not fear a thousand— nor fifteen hundred of them. The pikemen standing firm, we shall give them such a volley of musketry as they will be little prepared for; and when they are thrown into confusion, we will sally out, chase them into the water and ten to one but we secure their vessels. Let every man be on his alert, and should these barbarians this night attempt our hill, I trust we shall convince them that they are dealing with Britons." The seamen greeted this harangue with thunderous cheers, which must have carried ominously to the Dyaks and spelled out the message for them.

The speech, obviously a carefully constructed one, nevertheless reads oddly when compared to the only equivalent recorded comment by Frigate-Captain de Chaumareys in his situation, and this comment had to be wrung out of him by an officer calling out from the raft to ask if all was ready? "Yes, yes, I have provided you with everything that can be necessary." And when asked who was to command he replied, "It is I; in a moment I shall be with you," before he disappeared and got into his own barge.

On the morning of March 3, Captain Maxwell reconsidered his position, which appeared increasingly desperate. There had been no attack by the Malays during the night; all had been quiet. But they could now count a further ten proas among the Dyak fleet, which had obviously come in during darkness. The odds against the British were increasing every day, and the relief ship was long overdue. He had estimated four days for the two boats to reach Batavia; if all went well, a relief ship might arrive within a week.

But now seventeen days had passed, seventeen days on reduced rations of food and water. There was a gloomy feeling in the camp that somehow the two boats had met disaster on the way to Java, so that no help would ever come.

Maxwell decided not to wait while his men got physically weaker and the Dyaks became numerically stronger every day; there could be only one end to that. What he needed was to escape and there were not enough boats to take all the men simultaneously without overloading them to the swamping point—exactly the situation which had faced de Chaumareys seven months before, although in detail the problems differed. De Chaumareys had evaded his problem, so that a series of forced and unprepared abandonments took place, for which he was now being tried, luckily by sympathetic judges. Maxwell's judges were going to be the savage and ferocious Dyaks with their spears and long, curved knives.

Maxwell was not going to abandon, however, he was going to attack, and for that he needed boats—boats the encircling Dyaks had. The only thing which he would abandon would be the raft. To tow it would slow the boats too much and any men he had to place on it would be exposed without cover to the fire of the proas' swivel guns. These were the equivalent of huge, heavy shotguns on swivel mountings which could fire destructive blasts of musket balls, glass, shingle, old nails or any other hard object. To tow men on a raft while exposed to a hail of such shot from scores of proas was simply insane. Neither could he leave some of his men behind on the island to be massacred.

He determined on a night attack by part of the force and began to work out an ingenious and risky plan. Maxwell had originally had six boats and a raft, just as had de Chaumareys. He had sent two boats, lightly loaded and therefore seaworthy, two hundred miles to get help. He had four boats left. He would divide these into pairs and each pair would capture a single proa by simultaneous boarding from both sides. While the boarding party manned the captured proas, the four boats would return to shore to pick up more English seamen. The attack would continue until enough proas had been captured to take all his two hundred men comfortably; then they would escape. Without the encumbrance of the raft, they would be as fast as the enemy, and to the Dyaks' swivel guns they could oppose their musketry fire. Some might die, but they would die fighting.

Orders were being issued for this attack when the lookout reported a distant sail in the direction of Java. A squall obscured it and some thought that it was only a chance glint of sunlight on part of the raincloud which had really been seen. But half an hour later, a signalman with a telescope confirmed that it was not merely a sail but a square-rigged vessel, either a ship or a brig. The Malays, having no hill to climb, did not immediately see the approaching European vessel; when they did, they showed confusion and alarm.

Maxwell instantly decided to turn that to his advantage. He ordered the main body of his men to capture some of the nearest proas by moving toward them unseen through the mangrove swamps and then wading out to the Malay craft. But the Dyaks were alert and, in daylight, could see the British as soon as they left the cover of the mangroves and began to push out through the water, holding their muskets at chest level to keep them dry. The swivel gun of the nearest proa swung around and a blast of shot smashed into the mangroves and lashed the surface of the water. The British marines, breast-high in the sea by now, stopped and aimed their muskets while trying to keep steady against the slap of the waves and the surging power of the tidal stream. They claimed no hits. The Dyaks, caught between an aggressively minded force of British on the shore and the British ship approaching from seaward, left the scene entirely, no doubt waiting for a safer time before returning to plunder the wreck.

The rescue vessel, the Honorable East India Company's armed ship *Ternate*, had been sent by Lord Amherst on the same day that he had safely reached Batavia. Captain Ellis, who commanded her, came ashore in the evening and described the scene on the stockaded hill—how wild the castaways seemed, unshaven and in ragged clothes, armed with cutlasses and crude pikes, and how, when the word of command was given, the apparent mob of ruffians fell in smartly under their officers.

On their way home to England in a chartered ship, the party touched at Saint Helena on June 27, 1817. The ex-emperor of France received them and when Lord Amherst presented Captain Murray Maxwell to him, Napoleon bowed and said that he recalled the name from the Adriatic where Maxwell, in 1811, had helped take two frigates carrying two hundred field guns for the French army. "Your government must not blame you for the loss of the *Alceste*, for you have taken one of my frigates," he said.

Like de Chaumareys before him, Maxwell was returning home to stand trial by court-martial for the loss of his ship. However, he was able to show that soundings were being taken continually before the stranding and that the submerged shoal was not marked on any chart. The verdict was not guilty. When it came to considering the actions he had taken after he had abandoned his ship, the court could only express its marked approbation. In a desperate situation, he had not lost a man—not to the sea, not to sickness, not to the Dyaks (although he had inflicted casualties on them). He had brought them all home. Shortly afterwards, he received a knighthood.

This was admittedly an unusual case, of an extremely efficient and determined captain who not merely coped with all problems as soon as or even before they appeared but aggressively kept his enemies on edge. The affair has been largely forgotten, although it provided a striking lesson in leadership. Had Maxwell failed, however, had he been complacent, inefficient, halfhearted and utterly without foresight, then most of his men might have been massacred and possibly eaten by the Dyaks. A terrible scandal would have resulted, there would have been calls for vengeance and a punitive expedition might have been mounted. The affair of the frigate *Alceste* would have become widely known.

\*　　　\*　　　\*

De Chaumareys's court-martial had ended, the sentence had been reviewed and he was safely inside the château-prison of Ham when on April 4, 1817, the hydrographic mission under Ship-Captain Roussin, which had been sent out to resurvey the coast of West Africa and in particular establish both the position of the Arguin Bank and the site of the wreck of the *Medusa*, sighted a remarkable object to the southeast.

In the corvette *Bayadère* with the small dispatch boat *Epervier* in attendance, Roussin was methodically sounding the approaches to the bank and taking bottom samples with the lead at the same time. He was finding a pure sand bottom ten leagues out from the bank giving about fifty fathoms and reducing to forty fathoms as he approached to within five leagues. Closer in still there began to be much broken shell mixed up with the sand and the depths had reduced to twenty-five fathoms. That was quite a considerable slope, leading up to the bank itself. This Roussin reported as "a vast platform of sand, of the same nature as the surrounding coast and consisting of the same alluviums which had helped to shape it. Its mass, as hard as that of the actual coast, is similarly covered with sand and broken shells. It has an abrupt slope on the seaward side. By taking a large number of measurements, the base of this slope was shown to be eight fathoms deep." As the bank was wholly submerged all that could be seen was league after league of tossing wave tops, giving to the inexperienced eye an impression of a vast open ocean. It was anything but that. It was a series of steep terraces, unexpectedly becoming more and more shallow.

Early in the morning of April 4, the little dispatch boat *Epervier,* sounding ahead of the corvette which was her base ship, reported that she was approaching the Arguin Bank. That was at 0330. At 1100, continuing the same course, the color of the water had changed abruptly and the agitation of the sea clearly showed the presence of a large, submerged obstruction which was causing the waves to rise steeply around it. At 1400 hours, or 2 P.M., the *Epervier* signaled, "Something remarkable, southeast."

Lieutenant Legoarrant of the dispatch boat climbed the mizzenmast for a better look. "I saw the wreck of a large vessel on the Arguin Bank and thought it was the frigate *Medusa.* I warned Captain Roussin of the danger. Simultaneously, the bottom over which I was sailing shallowed by three fathoms, which now gave only six fathoms under me, so I turned and came around the corvette's stern." Six French fathoms are thirty-two English feet, but the dark shape of the wrecked vessel was still miles away and inshore of the survey vessels. Roussin was determined not to come too near. From the initial sighting at six miles he closed in only to four miles, from where the carcass of a ship could be seen clearly through a telescope.

He reported formally: "The frigate *Medusa*, wrecked on the Arguin Bank, appeared in front of us. The color of the water indicated a shallow area and also that the bottom was very uneven. I only approached to within four miles, but this was enough to fix the site on our chart of the Arguin Bank. She can be useful for a very long time yet, as the waters do not seem to ruin her. There is every reason to believe that her bulk, by fixing the sand around her, will form a kind of islet of which she will be the lower part. Already the reefs appear only in her vicinity and about half a mile from her bow and stern. In addition, her heel to larboard, which faces west toward open sea, is the most favorable one to withstand the waves without damage. The bulwarks only are ruined. The bowsprit is still in place and the entire wreck is very prominent above the water, so that it can be seen from two leagues away. I do not doubt that much can still be salvaged from her—cables, guns, shot and especially the 90,000 francs in gold. The heel of the ship will make the salvage of her contents easy."

So there it was, the wreck of the *Medusa*, found one month after the court-martial of her captain. He had stranded her on July 2 and abandoned her on July 5, 1816, after about sixty hours. And she had been found on April 4, 1817, nine months after he had abandoned her in haste, without preparation, without thought for the lives of his men because he was convinced she was going to break up at any moment and drown them all. And now, here she was, high enough out of the water to be seen from six miles away, with only her larboard bulwarks broken down. The significant detail was that her bowsprit was still standing. That meant that the internal beams, knees and bracings of her basic structure were still strong.

That the "fix" which Roussin obtained of her position did not agree with either of the two other positions de Chaumareys had given was nearly irrelevant in face of the brute fact that she need never have been abandoned. There had been sufficient time to send the two best boats to Saint-Louis, carrying the governor and his entourage, and for the *Echo* or the *Argus* to sail to the rescue of the remaining men and women left aboard. But that would have meant de Chaumareys's remaining, too.

Not one life need have been lost. There were no seagoing Moorish pirates to attack the wreck and if there had been, there were hundreds of armed soldiers aboard. There were only the waves, the unavailing storms which had proved impotent to crush her hull through nine long months. There had been no need to loose the raft with its crowded cargo of 150 souls to their ghastly and fatal despair under the blazing sun of Africa. No need to put them on the raft. No need for a raft at all.

# 15

# "Shadows of Officers"
## *(France and Senegal, 1817—1821)*

On January 1, 1817, the British handed Senegal over to the French and evacuated their garrison and administration.

This meant a turn of fortune for the Picard family as M. Picard could now take up his official duties as notary public in the new administration and begin to receive pay and allowances. He was still a comparatively poor man, however, because of the large size of his family, the loss of his fortune and possessions in the *Medusa*, for which he had not been compensated, and the war's destruction of the fruits of his work on the plantations at Safal.

Schmaltz was now confirmed in his powers as governor and remained a bitter enemy, determined to crush all criticism of the *Medusa* affair which could hurt him personally. His defense to the charge of abandoning the raft, purporting to be a letter from his secretary, Griffon du Bellay, had reached France in the *Loire*. The denial of the abandonment, of the idea that the towrope had been cast off deliberately, signed by six survivors of the raft, all of them then under his orders, must have made strange reading in Paris. All those who were in France had already testified that the tragedy of the raft had begun with the casting loose of the towrope by Reynaud, and some had added that this was done at the order of Schmaltz himself. When Reynaud also left the governor's sphere of influence and appeared before the Rochefort court in January 1817, his firsthand testimony corroborated the evidence of the other officer witnesses. No doubt Du Bouchage recognized another politician at work behind the letter apparently emanating from Griffon du Bellay.

But the public was not to know that. After all, the minister himself had publicly cast serious doubts on the accuracy of Savigny's narrative. From this flowed a situation which for Savigny and Corréard was to prove awkward, irritating and even dangerous. They were forced to beat vainly at the air against official denial and harassment, in order to prove what they both knew to be true, what the navy knew to be true, what the minister knew to be true. Indeed, in some respects the minister was better informed than they were, for he had at his disposal the machinery of government to carry out the necessary lengthy and extensive inquiries.

As soon as Corréard came ashore from the *Loire* at Rochefort, he was taken to the hospital where he was visited by Savigny. Knowing what was in the governor's letter which had also arrived in the *Loire*, Corréard warned the surgeon. Schmaltz had done more than construct an edifice of defensive lies. He had sought to focus discredit on Savigny and thus destroy the original published narrative. This had admitted both cannibalism and that, in the later slaughters on the raft, the sick had been sacrificed to save the strong—not at all the sort of admission that a politically minded person was likely to make. As the only doctor present, it was likely that Savigny had taken a leading part in the decision and in the selection of the victims. Indeed, whether he had acted rightly or wrongly, Savigny had been the effective leader during those thirteen terribly days. Schmaltz had seized on this fact to accuse Savigny of being the instigator of all the horrors on the raft, instead of a victim fighting back.

It was necessary to counter the Griffon du Bellay letter, with its six signatures, by similar documentation. To start with, Corréard wrote out a personal statement supporting Savigny and, as an eyewitness, giving the lie to Schmaltz. "I certify," he wrote, "that I have refused to sign a memorial drawn up by M. Schmaltz, which was addressed to His Excellency the Minister of Marine and tended to disapprove of the conduct of M. Savigny on board the raft, as well as to refute some parts of the narrative of our shipwreck, inserted in the *Journal des Débats,* September 13, 1816. Further, the events related in this memorial appear to me to be so entirely false, and so contrary to all that we owe to M. Savigny, that it was impossible for me to put my name to it."

Armed with this document, Savigny set out to approach those survivors of the raft who were still alive and had reached France. The first two were quickly found.

From Midshipman Coudein, already at Rochefort for the court-martial, Savigny received the following: "I, the undersigned, appointed to command the raft of the *Medusa* frigate, certify that M. Savigny, the surgeon who embarked in the said raft, has given on all occasions, in the unhappy situation in which we were placed, proofs of the greatest courage and coolness, and that on several occasions his prudence was of the greatest service to us, suggesting to us means to maintain good order and discipline, of which we had so much need, and which it was so difficult for us to obtain."

Nicolas François, the hospital administrator, certified similarly that "M. Savigny, by his courage and coolness, succeeded in maintaining good order upon the raft and that his prudent arrangements saved the lives of the fifteen unfortunate persons who were rescued by the brig *Argus*."

Savigny applied for permission to lay these documents before the minister. After a wait of two months a letter arrived from Paris, dated May 10, 1817, but it did not contain the good news he had expected. On the contrary, permission to state his case to the minister was refused, and, further, as long as the present minister remained in office, Savigny was told that he could expect no promotion. The surgeon was so furious that he resigned.

Corréard, who had lost 10,000 francs in the wreck of the *Medusa* and was now without either means or employment, journeyed painfully to Paris, the marks of suffering still upon him, and sought both compensation and a post from the Ministry of Marine. Compensation was refused and there were only vague offers of possible employment in some distant colony. What hurt as much, as far as Corréard was concerned, was the refusal of a decoration, the cross of the Legion of Honor, for which he had applied. This medal had been granted recently for exceptional conduct in circumstances of peacetime disaster, such as the overwhelming of a frigate by a hurricane and the entombment of a party of miners. What particularly annoyed Corréard was that aristocratic teenage clerks working at the Ministry already wore this ribbon, for meritorious but unknown services.

The unsuccessful application may be an important clue as to how the raft survivors viewed themselves and their disputed conduct. They were of course national celebrities, which was not unpleasant, but one at least felt that the mere fact of survival in those circumstances, let alone a significant contribution to the quelling of disorder, was an achievement in its own right.

Yet one can see how the civilized cynics of Paris could have exercised their wit, had decorations been awarded to men who had survived by eating their comrades. However, even Charlotte Picard, who had come well out of a somewhat lesser ordeal in the desert, felt the same sense of being set apart by what she had endured and lightly mocked her clever Parisian friends. Her faithful description, plus Corréard's action, are a true barometer of the feelings, and therefore the motives, which underlay the coming Savigny-Corréard affair.

They found that their every effort made through official channels to obtain restitution was blocked by inflexible argument. Corréard was told that none of the survivors of the raft had any claim on the Ministry, he least of all. They put their finger on a paragraph of an agreement covering the exploration side of the Senegal expedition, which stipulated that all correspondence with the Minister of Marine should be undertaken through the governor of Senegal, under whose orders they were and without whose approval they could undertake nothing. In short, Corréard was to be ruined and denied even the chance to protest. Attempts to obtain the intercession of the king were easily blocked by the Ministry. Corréard was so enraged by his treatment that he boiled for years even to think of it. The same malignant power reached out for Savigny. The pair were to be harassed, crushed financially, tricked and maneuvered into silence. They were speedily reduced to poverty and despair. The cause of it all was the unauthorized printing by a newspaper of part of Savigny's short and confidential report.

The policy of deliberate and unscrupulous oppression by the Minister of Marine drove them into a corner. They reacted by assuming that the minister was an enemy and treating him as such, striking at him in the way which, he had clearly shown, he liked least. What the minister wanted was less publicity about the *Medusa*. What he would get would be more, much more.

Together, Savigny and Corréard sat down to rewrite and expand Savigny's original brief narrative and to make it a book by adding further material which had come to light, plus a good deal of general information about the situation in Senegal. Their work was published in November 1817, bearing some signs of hasty and scrappy compilation by two authors trying to collaborate and finding it easier said than done. The work was sensational and scandalous. It was delightful to the public to try to work out who the villain mentioned as M. —— might be, and then to deduce toward the end of the book that the authors could mean only M. Schmaltz, or the first lieutenant, or the aristocratic captain. People compared notes, ideas and impressions. The game spread like wildfire across France. And here and there, but especially in the footnotes, were delightfully ironical and only near-libelous denunciations of M. —— (the Minister of Marine) and M. —— (the present governor of Senegal).

But it was not a game. France was full of disgruntled veterans of the Napoleonic wars, retired on half pay or no pay, who hated the aristocratic incompetents who had flooded into the country to take advantage of her final defeat. And recognizing how dangerous it was to antagonize them, the king could take wry satisfaction in the storm that was beginning to blow about the ears of M. Du Bouchage. Let it blow a little longer and that man's dangerous policies could be swept away.

The book sold out within a few months and a second edition was prepared, enlarged with further material, which was published early in 1818 and went into English translation almost instantly. The furor and wave of sympathy created by the book brought in assistance from various quarters. When he heard about it, ex-Sergeant Lavillette, then recuperating in France, contributed a legally phrased certificate in support and withdrew his signature from M. Schmaltz's report which he had signed while in the hospital. This was deadly for Schmaltz.

On November 1, 1817, Lavillette stated that he had been the chief workman under the orders of M. Corréard, engineer and geographer, and one of the members of the commission appointed by the Ministry to survey Cape Verde and its neighborhood. He went on to certify that "in the month of November 1816, a memorial was presented to me to sign, by order of the governor of Senegal. At this time I was in hospital in Gorée recovering from an epidemic fever then raging in Cape Verde which caused temporary fits of delirium. With my moral strength impaired and not in full possession of my mental faculties, I was made to sign this memorial without even reading it. It appears that it tended to blame M. Savigny for his conduct on the raft, for which I personally owe him only praise. It appears also, according to what I have been told, that I have been made to certify that the towrope broke and was not loosened. I declare that my signature at the bottom of this memorial, having been surreptitiously obtained, is null and void."

In the first edition Corréard had referred to the

pressures improperly brought against himself, then also ill in Senegal, by members of the governor's staff at the orders of the governor; but he had not named the principal person, Griffon du Bellay, secretary to Schmaltz, because Griffon had been his companion on the raft. Savigny had met Griffon du Bellay again at Rochefort, to find that the man had been horrified by the implications of Savigny's published narrative. He could understand very well what would happen to anyone who associated himself with that. He had therefore been forced to say that it was nothing to do with him and even to join in the attacks on Savigny. Now, however, he wrote an open letter to Savigny, retracting, regretting that he had ever been forced to act against a man "whose firmness did not a little contribute to saving our lives." He hinted at some of the pressures put upon him, when he added, "I fancied that the account which he [Savigny] had drawn up might render us odious to all our relations and friends." This letter was dated January 7, 1818, for publication in a later edition of the book, and shortly afterwards Griffon du Bellay also found himself without employment from the Ministry of Marine.

Edition by edition, the book grew as confirmatory narratives came in, being added as notes or footnotes. An officer of the frigate, who concealed his identity for obvious reasons, checked the text insofar as it related to matters of seamanship and threw a good deal of authoritative light on the strange maneuverings of M. Richefort, the self-appointed "navigational" expert, which had caused the tragedy. M. Landry, uncle of Bredif, the mining engineer, contributed a substantial narrative by that witness which had been privately written without political motive or any thought of publication or protest. It was uncritical of the governor's actions during the evacuation of the *Medusa*, but the panic, disorder and cowardice which were general were described from a different point of view and with additional detail. The group which Bredif had joined, led by Lieutenant Espiaux, had displayed a courage and determination which served to highlight the lamentable performance by the peak of the command pyramid.

There were some discrepancies with Bredif's narrative of what he saw or believed he saw, first from the already abandoned *Medusa* and then from the desperately overcrowded longboat commanded by the only rescuer, Lieutenant Espiaux. He did not see the towrope connecting the governor's barge with the raft deliberately loosed by the first lieutenant amid cries of "Let's leave them" or "Let's abandon them." He assumed that it had broken in the general confusion. Indeed, Corréard calculated that only about twenty men were close enough and had a sufficiently clear view to swear to that. He was one of them. What Bredif did see was the effect the approach of the overcrowded longboat, in which he was seated, had upon the line of rowing boats which had been roped together to tow the raft. He had written to his sister: "The boats, in order to avoid us, cut the ropes which united them together and made all the sail they could from us. In the midst of this confusion, the rope which towed the raft broke also, and a hundred and fifty men were abandoned in the midst of the ocean, without any hope of relief." There could not have been a more sober and devastating indictment: raft abandoned, longboat abandoned, governor, captain and first lieutenant fleeing for the horizon.

The veterans of the Napoleonic wars, who had conquered all Europe, gritted their teeth when they read that. Then with bitter relish they turned to the footnotes where Savigny and Corréard had grouped together with devastating effect all their firepower against the man fundamentally responsible, their enemy, the minister himself. They asked him how he felt at having confided "seven or eight expeditions to officers who do no more honor to his choice and discernment than the expedition to Senegal has done." Then they listed some of the cases which had become public knowledge.

"Besides the *Medusa*, which was conducted straight upon the Arguin Bank by the Viscount de Chaumareys, Knight of Saint-Louis, of the Legion of Honor, and in the intervals of his campaigns, customs officer at Bellac in Upper Vienne, everybody knows that the *Golo*, bound from Toulon to Pondichéry, nearly perished on the coast by the unskillfulness of the captain, Chevalier Amblard, Knight of Saint-Louis and of the Legion of Honor, who, in order not to lose touch with maritime affairs, had become a salt merchant near Toulon. Neither is the debut of the Viscount de Cheffontaine forgotten who, on leaving Rochefort for the isle of Bourbon, arrived instead at Plymouth without his masts three or four days later. Who does not know that it would be in our power to mention more examples of this kind?"

They quoted from a debate in the chamber of deputies, in which a member had referred memorably to those "shadows of officers" who had been given important commands by favoritism. These men, pointed out Savigny and Corréard, had "had the privilege of losing the vessels and people of the state without it being possible for the law to reach them. It would be difficult to suppose that they intended their own destruction; they have proved well enough that they know how to provide for their own safety.

They could say, 'We did not appoint ourselves; it is not we who are to blame.' "

The public did not know, for the minister had hushed it up, that de Chaumareys had already been punished; but not the man who had appointed him. Some of the émigrés may have felt these comments to be unfair, because, more than twenty years before, the Revolution had had the same distressing effect upon the navy as had the recent return to command of the émigrés.

The venom with which Honorary Colonel Schmaltz was pursued was probably to most people's tastes. They wrote of "his great application to business, the numerous occupations, the diverse enterprises which have agitated his life"; of his outstanding record as "an apothecary in Bengal, a physician in Madagascar, a dealer in small wares and land surveyor in Java, a shopkeeper's clerk in the isle of France and Holland, an engineer in the camp of Batavia, commandant at Guadeloupe, chief of a bureau at Paris" and now, "with the orders of Saint-Louis and the Legion of Honor, the rank of colonel and the command of a colony." There was indeed something extremely odd about the career of Schmaltz; possibly it had involved undercover intelligence work of some kind. As Savigny and Corréard hinted, Schmaltz proved totally ruthless and unscrupulous where his own self-interest was concerned.

The two authors suddenly found that they had acquired a power base. They had written and had published their own book in despair and desperation, as an attempt to lash back at their tormentors. Now, thought Corréard, as they had been so remarkably successful and as there clearly was money in the business, why should they not publish other people's books? He took premises at the Palais Royal and starting with political pamphlets began a new career as a publisher with an established "edge" in the protest market. Above his new bookshop he placed an eye-catching sign: *Au naufrage de la Méduse.*

The appearance of this bookshop in the center of Paris made it a gathering point for the political opposition. By his desire to stifle, if not to harass criticism, M. Du Bouchage, Minister of Marine, had achieved the exact opposite of what he had intended. His opponents in his own government and around the throne could now move against the principle Du Bouchage stood for, not only in the navy but in regard to the army as well. That year, 1818, the law of Gouvion de Saint-Cyr was passed. The entire officers corps was thrown open to all men of merit and experience and was no longer to be the exclusive preserve of the émigrés and the aristocracy. The immediate political battle was over, although there was an aftermath of resentment among the émigrés. And in the same year, 1818, M. Schmaltz was recalled from Senegal and another governor appointed in his place. The minister was defeated, the governor replaced, the captain imprisoned. This had taken two years, but it was not the end of the *Medusa* affair. Far from it.

\*　　\*　　\*

Of course, there were some errors in the book by Savigny and Corréard. They did not have access to official records, to start with. They give the name of one of the three men found still alive in the *Medusa* after nearly two months as "Dales." The court-martial minutes show that it was actually "Dalestre." Like de Chaumareys they made an elementary geographical error in their positioning of a coastal feature, the Saint John River in their case. Unlike de Chaumareys, they did not have a chart at the time. However, unlike de Chaumareys, they had their work checked by an officer of the *Medusa*, who really did know what he was talking about, and they printed his correction verbatim. And, finally, again unlike de Chaumareys, or for that matter, M. Schmaltz, they did not cover up by deleting the mistake but left it as evidence for any ill-wisher to quote.

In expanding their story the two authors did not offer a strictly impartial overall account. Savigny and Corréard did not pretend to be anything but embittered by their experiences. Indeed, they proclaimed their attack. It is all quite honest. In the English translation, their rather mannered and studied tone suggests a "stiff upper lip"—pride that they had behaved well, contempt for those who had not. This is a normal reaction, however much one may deplore it. Toward the end of the thirteen days on the raft, a few of those still alive wrote out their experiences on a board, so that their endurance should not be forgotten. This again points to the fact that they felt pride in what they had done.

However, there were other stories of what happened on the raft of the *Medusa*, which put the terrible events in a different and quite horrible light. These contradictory stories were provided by Midshipman Rang, who had escaped in the captain's barge and had no personal knowledge; he merely picked up the stories from two other raft survivors in Senegal. After he had read the book by Savigny and Corréard, he decided to write a narrative of his own and to include these contradictory, second-hand accounts. His work was not published until more than a century later, however, so that there was no controversy at the time, although there may have been whispers in the background.

The stories he heard covered two quite different periods on the raft: the first was that of the "mutiny," the slaughters which occurred early, probably starting on the second day; the second was that of the "mercy killings," which occurred toward the end on conjectural dates, for by that time the few who were left would hardly be in a position to recall the exact sequence of deaths. There was no question that the latter were deliberate, but what is different, and surprising, about one of Rang's witnesses is that he told the midshipman that the mass slaughters of the "mutiny" were also deliberate; that they had been plotted and sparked by the officers.

This witness was a seaman called Thomas, whom Savigny and Corréard describe as a "pilot" in their list of raft survivors. Rang describes him by a French term which, confusingly, can be translated into English as either "helmsman" or "signalman." In English "pilot" means navigator or a set of sailing directions. At a guess, he was probably a helmsman, certainly not an officer. Rang says he was young and, not having any responsibilities, unbiased. He obtained the seaman's confidence and was so startled by his version that he asked Thomas to write it all down for him, briefly. The point being attacked was a passage in Savigny's report reading: "We were not strong enough to prevent them from getting drunk as much as they liked." Other than this, Thomas tells of events in much the same way as Savigny, Corréard and Coudein, although he sometimes differs in his sequences, which could be important.

Thomas's note read: At the beginning of the night,

the officers gathered apart and held a small council. When this was over, some of the men belonging to their group set a barrel of wine in the middle of the raft, then, having smashed it open, left it to be plundered. All the soldiers rushed to it and most of them drank so much they lost their senses. From that moment, the greatest disorder reigned on board the raft; drunken soldiers gathered about on every side, some demanding their hammocks, asking the way to the main deck or the battery deck; others screamed that they were lost and threw themselves into the water. Then, some, having grasped hatchets or knives, wanted to cut the ropes and drown everyone. The officers, fearing they might succeed, rushed on them sword in hand and slaughtered a great number. They were deaf to the cries for mercy coming from these unfortunate men, forty of whom were killed.''

Coudein's official report is only slightly different, in stating that the officers were attacked. He wrote: "They wanted to cut the ropes that bound the raft together, so as to put an end to their lives; but as they feared the officers might prevent them from doing so, they decided to throw us overboard first. A faithful servant came and warned us. The officers, the second surgeon, some passengers, several craftsmen and myself, anxious to save our miserable lives, decided to prevent this abominable action. We armed ourselves with guns and each watched over a different part of the raft where the most essential ropes were located.''

It is highly unlikely that the officers were so foolish as to intend to get the soldiers drunk; this would be a very dangerous proceeding with any soldiers anywhere, let alone men from a low-grade cosmopolitan French battalion standing on a raft abandoned somewhere off the coast of West Africa. What Savigny says is that a wine ration was organized on the first night, but that the breaking open of the barrel and the indiscriminate drinking occurred on the second night, as a result of the men's growing sense of despair and loss of hope. The long-term interest of Thomas's grumbles, however, is merely the fact that they occurred, that different groups among the survivors were blaming each other during the period immediately following the rescue.

It is essential to distinguish the "mercy killings" from the "mutiny." Thomas told Rang, and he was probably right, that they were not so merciful as all that. He described the dispatching of the canteen manageress. "A soldier having been slaughtered and thrown overboard, they said to his wife, the only woman on the raft, "Since your husband has gone into the sea you must join him there," and they forced her overboard."

The other raft survivor to whom Rang talked was Lavillette, whose testimony gives the impression of an organized system of destruction, of groups of men deliberately set against other men, so that the overall numbers on the raft would be rapidly reduced. The ex-sergeant was fever-ridden when this interview took place, but certainly group fought group. And he was to provide that telling vignette of the kissing and prayers to God that took place after every killing and of how, eventually, in revulsion, the guns were thrown overboard. Rang did not know what he was doing in recording these strange tales, some spoken by a man in delirium, others the grumbling confidences of a seaman to an officer. But his motive was exactly that of Savigny: to note as accurately as possible some very strange events which seemed then to defy rational explanation—but do not do so now.

For the story of the raft of the *Medusa* did not end with the downfall of de Chaumareys and Schmaltz in 1817 and 1818, nor with the publication in 1821 of a definitive, illustrated edition of the book by Savigny and Corréard, *Naufrage de la Frégate la Méduse faisant partie de l'expédition du Sénégal en 1816*. There was a great deal more still to come.

\*         \*         \*

In 1820, another eyewitness of the shipwreck returned to France and in 1824 published a personal narrative which included the sufferings of those who trekked through the Sahara. This book was *La Chaumière Africaine* by Madame Dard, which went into English translation three years later. Madame Dard was the former Mademoiselle Charlotte Picard. Her change of name was the result of a strange love affair which had arisen out of the most appalling tragedy.

The ill-luck which had dogged the family as a direct result of the stranding of the frigate and the loss of her father's fortune and all their possessions had continued. M. Picard's outspokenness had not been forgotten and eventually the family was reduced to poverty and then decimated by illness. His young wife was the first to die. Then the children began to sicken and it was then that M. Dard, the director of the French schools in Senegal, visited them frequently in order to help. The little girl, Laura, did not recover, and in August 1819, M. Picard was also stricken. His illness was worsened by a terrible mental depression and a great foreboding of the evil that was to come to his family. War between the Moors and the Negroes had driven them from the cotton plantation into which they had put so much labor and they were now all poor refugees dressed in rags and tatters.

On his deathbed Charlotte's father asked her to promise that she would look after the children, for only then could he rest in peace. He reminded her of their obligations to M. Dard and his other friends who had helped. He said that he forgave his enemies the evils they had made him and his family endure. He and his eldest daughter were obviously very close and the death of her father made the girl desolate. She contemplated suicide in order to follow her father to the grave. Even after her friends had dissuaded her, she was inconsolable, unable to attend the funeral. Then, although the other children were ill, she felt that she must see her father's last resting place, which was beside his wife on the island of Safal where their plantation had been. Leaving the children to her sister Caroline, she made a lonely pilgrimage. The plantation was a wreck, weeds everywhere, the cotton plants withered, the fields of millet, maize and beans rooted up by cattle, the house plundered: a scene of solitude and desolation.

When she could bring herself to search for her father's grave, she found it beautiful, surrounded by shrubs whose branches overhung and seemed to protect it. The utter quiet was broken only by the sounds of birds or the occasional rustle of foliage by the wind. She fell to her knees and remained still for a long time. When she got up, her resolution was made. As if speaking to her father, she promised to give all her care to the tiny children, her stepbrothers and sisters, who were now orphans; and she also promised to make known the misfortunes which had driven him to the tomb.

The day after her return from the island, M. Dard called to say that he would take upon himself the charge of providing for the whole family until he could get them on board a ship for France. Madame Thomas, in whose house they were then living, took her aside and told her in confidence that there was more in this offer than appeared. M. Dard wished to marry her but would not ask until her grief had lessened.

This revelation was not at all unwelcome to the girl, who was very conscious of the family's fall into poverty. In some circles, poverty is regarded as a disgrace if not an actual crime. And in France, especially, a girl's family is expected to contribute handsomely. She recalled her father's words: "M. Dard is an estimable youth. His attachment for us has never diminished in spite of our wretchedness. I am sure he prefers virtue in a wife above all other riches." The young man's career was not bound up exclusively with the colony. He could find employment in France.

The last days in Senegal were distressing, as the young children died one after the other. Gustavus was old enough to go to school, and when his little brother Charles asked where he was (for he had had to be buried immediately), M. Dard tried to postpone the blow by saying that he was at school. Then the boy asked for a hat, so that he could go to the school and see if Gustavus was really there. Charles died also toward the end of 1819.

When in November 1820 the time came to sail for France, all that remained of the original family of nine were the eldest daughter Charlotte, now married to M. Dard, her sister Caroline who remained behind in Senegal and married M. Richard, an agricultural botanist, and the young cousin Alphonse Fleury. After two months in Paris they went to the home of M. Dard on the Côte d'Or, where the bereaved girl found new relations and friends to help her forget her loss. But she did not forget. She settled down to write her book.

# 16

# "Hideous Spectacle...
# Beautiful Picture"
## (The experience as art,
## 1817—1824)

The picture was somber, reddish-brown—and enormous. Ragged clouds poured in a molten sky past the reeling mast of the castaways' raft, sixteen feet above the bottom of the canvas on the Salon wall. From the foam on the left, where it fretted against the damp timbers, to the cadaver on the right, sprawled in the sea with one shrunken leg caught by a beam, was a distance of twenty-three feet. The sheer length and height of the painting seemed to immerse the excited crowd of viewers in the waves, involving them against their will.

"Why, you already feel as though you had one foot in the water!" thought artist Eugène Delacroix. To this young man the scheme of the picture before him was not new. He had posed for one of the emaciated figures slumped exhausted and barely conscious at the moment of rescue. But the effect of the completed work came as a shock to him.

Other figures on that gigantic canvas were more authentic. That man whose left arm with open fingers is thrust out toward the rescue ship as he turns to his companions . . . Is that Corréard, you know, the engineer fellow? Savigny, the surgeon, must be there, too. Perhaps that one by the mast, one of those still upright, not overwhelmed by suffering or despair.

Conjectures flew freely, for although the catalogues in the hands of the viewers described the item merely as a "scene of shipwreck" by Théodore Géricault, everyone knew what raft that was and had heard of the horrors which had taken place upon it. Everyone in Paris was aware also of the political scandal that was threatening the monarchy and the government as a direct result of what might, in other circumstances, have been just another shipwreck among thousands.

So intense was the interest in this one picture that the work of painters famous already, such as Ingres, was eclipsed. That artist's sensuously delicate *Grande Odalisque* was on this, its first showing, largely ignored by the public and censured by the critics.

Ingres himself was critical of that "shipwreck scene" by Géricault. He declared that he wanted no part of such paintings, those "pictures of the dissecting room which show man as a corpse, which show only the ugly, the hideous!" This outburst was caused by nothing so simple as jealousy at the success of a young rival or even an inability to comprehend what we can now appreciate as a startling new approach to art. It proved to be a widespread reaction to the shock effect of the great canvas.

A reviewer took the same line. "All is hideous and passive—not a trait of heroism or grandeur upon which the soul and eye can for one moment repose—nothing to indicate life and sensibility—nothing honorable to humanity. This picture is truly said to be a work to rejoice and glut the sight of vultures."

\*　　　\*　　　\*

Because he had a rich father who supported his artistic ambitions, Géricault could paint what he pleased. He could also study when and where he wished. He had spent more time at the Louvre, standing before the old masters such as Titian and Rubens, than in the formal discipline of the studio. In the year of the wreck of the *Medusa*—1816—he had been in Rome, had stood before Michelangelo's *Last Judgment* and "trembled" at the energy and power of that work. In the year of the book of the *Medusa*, Savigny and Corréard's *Naufrage de la Frégate la Méduse faisant partie de l'expédition du Sénégal en 1816*, the young artist was back in Paris. That was late in 1817, when the two authors were preparing their book for the press and Géricault was moving in the same artistic and political circles at Montmartre as they were. Whether they met by chance or whether Géricault had already decided upon his subject and deliberately sought them out is not known.

Much about the artist is still a mystery. His personal life at this time was kept intensely secret within his family, for he was in the midst of a difficult, stormy love affair with the wife of a relative. The girl, Alexandrine-Modeste, was six years older than the young man and married to one of his uncles. The visit to Italy may have been an attempt to break off that painful relationship. After Géricault's return to Paris in 1817 the girl became pregnant and the following year bore his child.

Géricault was then about twenty-six, "fairly tall and of elegant appearance," noted another young artist in his circle. "His face expressed vivacity and energy, but it also showed great gentleness. I noticed then, as I often did since, that he blushed at the slightest emotion."

The young man was in a turmoil, not only in his personal life, but also artistically. A painter for only seven years, he was still searching for a complete style of his own, an adequate means to express the imperative demand within him to astound the world with some tremendous statement on canvas. The next Paris Salon, to be held in 1819—in less than two years—would be his opportunity.

Thus far, he was regarded as a promising gentleman-artist with a flair for outdoor action pictures which could be bold, even grand. He had exhibited two at a previous Salon, a *Mounted Chasseur* and a *Cuirassier*. There was another side to his talent. He could hint at terrible and dramatic events by the use of a few quietly pathetic human figures isolated from their context. Lately, he had explored the possibilities of painting a recent event, the assassination of a notable politician, but had abandoned the subject when it was shown that the affair had been merely a murder for gain. He belonged to no "school" of art and because he was financially independent did not have to.

The Paris tradition was, broadly, small-scale chocolate-box easel paintings which could be produced by a private individual or giant "king-size" propaganda pieces, heavily subsidized by the government. Previously such "subjects honorable for their national character" had been sponsored by Napoleon; in fact, these were "command" battle pictures, public relations art. Under the monarchy, the subjects were different but the intentions and the methods were the same. The forthcoming Paris Salon was designed to demonstrate the overwhelming might of French talent, flourishing as never before under the Bourbons, to be shown most spectacularly by the vast number of gigantic "set-piece" canvases, over one hundred, which no other nation could match.

It was this national stream of enormous action painting which Géricault was now about to join, but he was made free of sponsorship by his father's support. While other and better-known painters were delving into the legends of ancient Greece and Rome or studying anew the lives of the saints in the hope of an inspiration which might produce a work salable in the new climate, Géricault was reading the newspapers.

No one knows when he decided that the raft would be his subject. Probably he began work on the *Medusa* theme early in 1818. In this, the research stage, he collected "a veritable dossier crammed with authentic proofs and documents." This was not in order to produce a painting accurate in detail but to immerse himself in the story. To depict the experience, he first had to understand it, if possible, as thoroughly as those who had actually suffered, so that when he finally stood before the blank canvas it should seem that he painted as a witness.

There were many stages to undergo before that situation could be created. In all, they occupied a period of about ten months. First, he listened to Savigny and Corréard and absorbed their story. Then he got the designer of the raft, the ship's carpenter of the *Medusa*, to make him first a plan and then a scale model, until finally he had the physical nature of the raft fixed in his subconscious mind.

He visited hospitals to see for himself how the sick and the dying looked and smelled. He borrowed the severed limbs of corpses, and sometimes entire corpses, and took them to his studio, to sketch them; but he was to use few of those drawings. What he was doing was to surround himself with objects which would impress the truth of the experience upon his own soul. He went to the beach at Le Havre, not so much to observe seascapes and marine skies (not at all like the tropic seas where his subject was set) as to sense the sea.

And while this emotional side of his nature was absorbing the facts, the other, technical side was considering where to stop the action. What, really, could be considered the most effective scene of the entire shipwreck story? Had there been a moment which, if caught, would sum up in one split second for all eternity the story of the *Medusa?*

One might think first that the fatal moment was the loosing of the towrope. That was, and is so— but only when presented in scenario form. There is no record, in the form of a preliminary sketch, to suggest that Géricault ever considered this.

What then? The mutiny on the raft? Yes, indeed, this idea did attract Géricault. He made sketches of veritable cascades of crowded, tumbling bodies; he produced one without cascades, a viciously vivid close-up of a struggle with naked steel. But perhaps canni-balism? This also Géricault tried out, and horrifyingly effective it is, with men eating men like crouched carnivorous apes, and the dead half in the water and the damned crying to heaven. In the end he did not use it. In fact, he eliminated all outright traces of cannibalism and employed other means, both more subtle and more powerful, to indicate that aspect of the tragedy.

The scene finally chosen, and the way in which it was to be presented, has a power beyond all these. It is the first sighting of the *Argus*, when the brig's crew did not see the raft but passed on in the distance unaware. The castaways are done for. Only two men can wave, only one can point, two more can pull themselves to their knees. The rest are mostly beyond hope or fear, slumped unaware, as blindly ignorant of the moment as is the crew of the *Argus*. There is only a hint of cannibalism, of what has led up to this moment of false hope. When he outlined this scene, the definitive draft for the final work which was to be done on a gigantic canvas, Géricault was still not quite finished. He altered three things, to oppress the spectator. He raised the horizon high up the picture, he reduced the *Argus* in size to a distant speck and he cut out the waves which had been in the foreground, between the raft and the spectator. Now the raft drifts less alone on that rough and ragged sea. Marine painters were to criticize this part of his composition. What Géricault had really done by this alteration was to zoom in on the scene, so that we can no longer stand back and look at the raft freely adrift. We are on those soiled and sodden timbers.

These preliminary work stages had taken the artist ten months. The painting of the canvas took eight months. It was finished in July 1819, just in time for the opening of the Salon on August 25. The artist had never done anything like it before and he was never to do anything like it again. The concentration required was terrible not only in intensity but also in duration. Géricault hired a large studio and shut himself up for those eight months, shaving his head so that he would not be tempted to go out into the streets.

As the picture grew it acquired an extraordinary aspect. It was as if a frieze of statues was appearing on the canvas. The castaways grouped on the raft were painted individually from models. A few were professional, such as the Negro who was to pose as the peak of a pyramid of human bodies, a contorted group which must be fused with the raft at the bottom and the sea and the sky above. Some were friends. Savigny and Corréard visited the studio to pose for Géricault as themselves.

Few visitors were allowed, but the young artist Montfort was one of them. He wrote: "I was impressed, first of all, by the intensity with which he worked, and also by the quiet and reflection which he needed. He generally started work as soon as there was enough light and continued without interruption until nightfall. What forced him to work in this way was usually the size of the piece which, started in the morning, had to be finished the same day. . . . I was vividly impressed by the care with which Géricault worked. Being still quite young (I was only seventeen), I had trouble keeping still for several hours on end, without getting up and, accidentally, making a little noise with my chair. In the midst of the absolute silence which reigned in the studio, I would sense that this slight noise had disturbed Géricault. . . . I would see him smile at me with a slight expression of reproach. He assured me that the noise of a mouse was enough to stop him from working.

"When evening came Géricault abandoned his palette and took advantage of the last rays of light to contemplate his work. Usually, he was very little satisfied, but on some days he thought he had found the proper way of modeling. The following day he would confess that he was not on the right track and would have to make a fresh effort.

"Once, he had gone [to the Louvre] to see the *Sabines* and the *Leonidas*. He came back discouraged. What he was doing seemed clumsy to him. Referring to the young warriors in the *Leonidas*, he said to me, 'Ah well! Those are tremendous figures!' And he averted his eyes from his own picture."

This was just the depression and self-doubt of the artist, which may be essential to ensure flexibility and responsiveness during the actual process of creation. Visiting painters had no such doubts. In that small studio the impact of the huge figures did seem tremendous, even terrifying. The painter Delacroix always remembered his first visit. "The impression it gave me was so strong that as I left the studio I broke into a run, and kept running like a fool all the way back to the rue de la Planche where I lived then, at the far end of the faubourg Saint-Germain."

The composition changed organically, grew on the canvas, became more terrifying. Yet it was artifice. In order to weld his figures together, and they were already somber, Géricault had to link them by darkness as if they were on a blanket of shadows with only the edges or contours highlighted. The only black sufficiently intense to achieve this darkness was bitumen, which is chemically unstable. Over the years, this was to cause the decay of the painting, so that it can no longer be seen as it was originally.

So far, Géricault had seen his canvas only in his own studio, in one particular type of lighting. When the work was finished and the painting had been moved to the Théâtre Italien, where all the entries for the Salon were being assembled, Géricault was shaken. He saw now that he had raised the peak of his pyramid of human bodies without sufficiently strengthening the base. Hurriedly, he added two figures to the raft at the bottom of the picture, using some of the many ideas and studies which he had worked on and discarded earlier.

Eighteen months of continuous work was now over and it had finished the artist. Géricault was mentally and physically drained, dazed, utterly incapable of valid judgment or further emotional effort. In this state, he made a serious and damaging mistake. The officials of the Salon had been impressed. They paid him the great compliment of allowing the painter to choose for himself where on the walls of the Salon the "scene of shipwreck" should be hung. And Géricault made a monumental error. He selected a prominent position, but high up—actually above a tall doorway. Nothing could have been more calculated to defeat the entire effect of the canvas. The raft needed to be hung lower down so that the viewer would feel that he could virtually walk onto it, actually enter the scene.

As the vast canvas was lifted higher and higher to his chosen place on the wall above the doorway, Géricault was angered and dismayed. He had the strong impression that as it rose, it lost impact. Perhaps that was just because he had failed, because it was a poor painting. His judgment blurred and wearily incapable of decision, he left matters too late. By the time he had convinced himself that he had made a mistake, nothing could be done to change the position of the canvas before the opening of the Salon. That was to be on August 25. Three days later the king himself would visit the exhibition and be introduced to some of the artists.

*       *       *

The critics were divided. They were more than divided, they were puzzled. Even when hung at the wrong height and in the wrong place, the painting still had emotional impact. But what did it *mean?*

Unable to examine the work closely, the reviewers often contradicted each other on matters of fact as well as opinion. The man from *La Gazette de France* condemned it outright as "a work for the delight of vultures," while his colleague writing for the *Revue Encyclopédique* complained that the painting could hardly represent the raft of the *Medusa* as the really convincing details, such as half-devoured portions of human bodies, were nowhere to be seen.

There was a glut of gratuitous advice. It would have

been better if M. Géricault had shown the castaways fighting each other to eat a corpse, wrote the man on the *Revue*. Others advised the artist to moderate his enthusiasm and to study carefully the draughtsmanship of Girodet and David. They assumed that he had dashed off the work in a weekend or so and pointed out that the young man would do better when he became an old man and could devote more time to a subject.

There was much praise, too, most of it exclamatory: "My heart trembled!" . . . "I shudder while I admire!" . . . "What movement, what verve!"

A few expressed mixed feelings with a deliberate objectivity, actually seeking to understand. An aristocrat, Count O'Mahony, who on religious and political grounds should have condemned the work outright, wrote instead: "On a raft which is about to be engulfed by a wave, the painter has assembled the most revolting aspects of despair, rage, hunger, death and putrefaction, and he has expressed them with an abundance of verve, a truth of touch, a boldness of handling and of color which multiply their effect a hundredfold. All must die, there is no chance of salvation, since none of them raises his arms toward Him whom the winds and seas obey. . . . For as they have forgotten God, so they have also forgotten one another. . . . Each sees only his own death and laments only for his own life. . . . Is it possible that suffering should not have joined two souls, two brothers, a father and his son? What a hideous spectacle, but what a beautiful picture!"

The cause of the confusion was in the preconceived ideas of the critics, who failed to fathom its politics. The subject was clearly the infamous raft of the *Medusa*. Therefore it was an antigovernment painting. While one set of critics sought to defend the government by attacking the painting, others attacked the government by praising it. Almost invariably, the views of the art critics coincided with the politics of the paper for which they were writing. Count O'Mahony was an honorable exception. The basic assumption common to them all was that because of his subject matter and because of his friends, especially Savigny and Corréard, Théodore Géricault must be a politically "committed" artist.

Nevertheless, in their clumsy attempts to unlock the meaning of that "shipwreck scene," some stumbled perilously near the truth. While O'Mahony had looked for belief in God and failed to find it, others scanned the various grouped figures for those ideas and emotions usually expressed by Napoleon's painters, such as David, in their depiction of the battlefields of Marengo, Austerlitz, Jena and so on, short of Waterloo. Not surprisingly, they failed. They concluded that Géricault's picture showed nothing except a spectacle of "men jostled between life and death." That troubled them. The truth was that the painting had no message in the political sense.

But as this amazing fact was grasped by hardly anyone in France, the expected visit of the king to the Salon on August 28 was awaited with relish. How would the monarch react to a quite scandalously antiroyalist, antigovernment picture and what, if anything, would he have to say to the young man who had painted it?

Painfully, because he suffered from gout, Louis XVIII limped around the great exhibition, from painting to painting, being introduced to the artists. When he came to Géricault's painting he stayed studying it for a long time and, according to the official *Moniteur Universel*, said a pleasant word to M. Géricault which combined encouragement with judgment. It was reported unofficially that his comment was, "Monsieur Géricault, vous venez de faire un naufrage qui n'en est pas un pour vous!"

"You've made a shipwreck which isn't for you!"

This could mean that Géricault had not offended the government by his choice of subject and need not expect retaliatory action. Or it could have been a really perceptive comment: that the painting compelled the viewer to share an experience which was not to his liking.

The public acclaim and the public criticism, the cautiously favorable reception of his work in official circles did not break Géricault's black despair. He was exhausted, drained. He felt he must go abroad, go to the Orient, have exotic adventures to wash himself clean of the *Medusa*. The country he went to, however, was England; and there there was no escape from the raft. He must still suffer with those suffering men.

An enlarged, revised edition of the book by Savigny and Corréard had already been translated and published in London during 1818 as *Narrative of a Voyage to Senegal in 1816*. It had proved much to the taste of a public then peculiarly fascinated by the sea and also by the records of great maritime disasters. England did not match France in private patronage or bureaucratic subsidies but had found its own solution to the problem of feeding the creative artist: the box office exhibition. Mr. William Bullock, owner of the Egyptian Hall in Piccadilly, arranged to show "Monsieur Jerricault's Great Picture" in 1820. Fifty thousand people are claimed to have seen it and both men profited financially.

Being ignorant of any political implications, the English reviewers judged the painting purely as a work of art. "A tremendous picture of human suffering . . . one of the finest specimens of the French school ever brought to this country" was the judgment in the *Literary Gazette*. That he had not imitated David was here a point in Géricault's favor. He was praised for breaking free of that "cold, pedantic school."

The critic of the *Globe*, reacting to the vainglory of Napoleon's propaganda painters, stressed both the problems and the achievement. "Monsieur Jerricault has selected for his first great historical effort a subject of the utmost difficulty, and with singular absence of the national vanity ascribed to his countrymen, one which it would be well for the naval character of France to have blotted from her maritime annals. The story of the *Medusa* records a narrative of the most criminal ignorance, pusillanimity and individual suffering, which has no parallel in modern history. . . . The artist, however, has selected the subject on account of its difficulties, and he has triumphed over many in the completion of his design. In the first place, to embody and concentrate the interest of this appalling subject, he has selected the time when the ruin on the raft may be said to be complete, and when the wretched survivors were first raised from their state of despair, by the appearance of the vessel that rescued them from their perilous situation. The personification of horror which his grouping exhibits baffles description; there is one figure of an old man, who still retains at his feet the dead body of his son, that is full of appalling expression. It is the very countenance of Ugolino's despair, which Reynolds portrayed with an effect finely forcible indeed, though without the haughty distinction which Michelangelo gave the Italian Nobleman."

To be mentioned in the same paragraph as Michelangelo, before whose *Last Judgment* he had "trembled," must have made the young painter breathless with the realization of what he had achieved.

After London came Dublin. The press ignored Géricault's painting although the *Medusa* as a subject was an oddly popular topic. The sensation of the day there was an exhibition of a series of *Medusa* paintings totaling ten thousand square feet of canvas. In an inventive and novel anticipation of cinema technique the spectators were seated, a full orchestra played appropriate "mood music," and the pictures moved to portray the story of the wreck scene by scene.

Géricault returned to France in 1821, was seriously ill in 1822 and died in 1824, only thirty-three years old. He had never recovered from the black despair which had afflicted him at the end of the exhausting one and a half year's work on his monumental canvas. In his last days, wasting away, he bitterly condemned the uselessness of his short life. He had not produced even so much as five good paintings to justify his life and to be remembered by. He seemed now to dismiss even the *Medusa* painting as a vignette, an achievement of little real worth. But it tormented him and his mind always returned to his memories of the canvas. Confined to a sickbed now, all he could study was a small copy of the original work. Again and again he examined this, anxiously searching for any defects, and finding them, but also clearly asking for contradiction from his friends. His only hope of immortality lay on the raft.

In the year of Géricault's death, the painting was put up for auction. A rich Englishman was among the bidders as were a group of French businessmen who planned to divide the painting into a number of small, more easily salable scenes. The prospects were that the canvas would go abroad to foreigners or be cut to bits by Frenchmen. It was the king and the court who stepped in, bought the picture for the nation and had it hung in the Louvre where it is today.

Géricault's self-doubt and despair proved unjustified. Out of more than 1,300 paintings, 208 sculptures, 157 engravings and 27 architectural designs submitted to the Paris Salon of 1819, few are now remembered. The painting by Théodore Géricault is the great exception. It is regarded as a key work in the history of art, ending one tradition and marking the start of another. Everything to do with it, including preliminary sketches, is regarded as important. The most recent exhibitions of Géricault's work were held in 1971 and 1972 at Los Angeles, Detroit and Philadelphia. The life and work of the artist were the subject of a masterly study by Professor Lorenz Eitner published on both sides of the Atlantic in 1972 under the title *Géricault's Raft of the Medusa*. One hundred and fifty years after the death of the painter, his work still lives, as relevant now as it was then.

It might be thought that the actual ship, the real raft, the personal witness of the survivors might be forgotten, overshadowed by what one great artist had made out of their experiences. That is not true either. What Géricault achieved with oils and brushes and canvas, Savigny and Corréard attained in their writings, based on firsthand observations. Those experiences, so closely and accurately noted, have achieved a different type of immortality. The story of the *Medusa* was not relegated merely to stirring accounts of adventures and survival at sea, to be read casually in front of a winter fire. It was to be increasingly studied in the middle of the twentieth century, as it was realized how much the two authors still had to say to modern man. The story of the *Medusa* did not

end with the court-martial of de Chaumareys or with
the excitement of the Paris Salon of 1819. It has continued to the present day.

# 17

# Repetition in the South Atlantic
## (*The rafts of the* Rio Azul, *June 29 to July 14, 1941*)

Géricault's painting should have been the end of the *Medusa* affair, a terrible moment of time stilled for eternity on canvas. But it was not. Artists and writers went back to the subject again and again, fascinated —or inspired—by some aspect of what they felt was a unique experience which still held some monumental message for mankind.

When T. E. Lawrence wanted to describe the hardships of a desert journey in Arabia, he invoked the thirst image of those suffering men on the raft. When Hans Werner Henze wished to raise a political storm in the modish manner of the 1960s he went back to the raft for his subject. His audience disapproved of his politics, and *Das Floss der Medusa* was hissed off the stage.

The word "Medusa" had gone into the universal language of thinkers as a kind of shorthand, vivid and unmistakable because never again could there be such a unique sequence of pure horror.

Writers on disasters at sea inevitably included the story of the *Medusa* and almost invariably agreed that the events were unique. Common to them all was the horrified assumption that the tragedy of the *Medusa* must—must—represent a special set of circumstances. Yet what is really interesting is how universal it actually is; the fact that we can still learn from it lessons applicable to ourselves.

The unfortunate Corréard is forgotten, but Surgeon Savigny is still remembered and quoted, precisely because he was a surgeon—a naval doctor of experience who was a direct witness of the events he describes.

Nor was he merely a technical witness who collaborated in a popular book. That book is still regarded as important, but its medical aspects were enlarged upon by Savigny in a paper which he submitted to the Faculty of Medicine in 1818 and had published the same year.* Some 150 years later a German student of the subject, Professor Dr. Hans Schadewald, wrote another paper in which he discussed Savigny's testimony in the light of much recent, practical experience.†

Professor Eitner, the art historian, following recent French verdicts, believed that Savigny and Corréard were far from being impartial chroniclers, because they desired to incriminate the frigate's captain while attempting to minimize or explain their own part in the "atrocities" which occurred on the raft.

Professor Schadewald, the student of survival at sea, took the opposite view. He regarded Savigny's technical paper as admirably objective, even surprisingly so, and he rejected any attempt to turn the subject into "art." This medical professor considered the tragedy too horrible to be "warmed up again in any kind of artistic manner" and that justice could be done only through a commonsense and scientific objectivity. He stressed that the raft did

*Observations sur les Effects de la faim et de la soif éprouvés après le naufrage de la frégate du Roi la Méduse en 1816.

†Patho-physiologische und psychologische Beobachtungen des Schiffsarztes Jean-Baptiste-Henri Savigny beim Schiffbruch der Fregatte "La Meduse."

hold a message and that it could not be repeated sufficiently often. It was what Savigny himself had concluded as a result of his experiences: "Moral strength is of greater importance for survival than physical strength." This, of course, was to deny the validity—except as a personal statement—of Géricault's painting. And it is not accepted by some modern French historians who conclude that, on the raft, the officers sacrificed the others to save themselves.

The observations and actions of Savigny and his companions are still being debated, sometimes with bitterness, more than 150 years after the event. And everything centers on this question: Was the sequence of events on the raft truly unique or are there more modern duplicates and parallels?

Although my own father was a naval surgeon (in the British navy), I can claim no medical knowledge. It was therefore all the more important in tracking down evidence to limit myself to witnesses who did have the requisite technical background. Yet as a professional assessor of eyewitness evidence, I had to note that Savigny's narrative was necessarily defective in one respect. Because he could not have been in two places at once, his perspective was essentially that of the sufferer looking out—not that of the objective observer surveying the whole scene from an outside vantage point. I felt that some French historians were being unfair in not allowing for, let alone criticizing him for, this involvement.

Therefore I sought first for a "control" which would point out that conduct on the *Medusa*'s raft which really was strange, although not necessarily unique. It seemed an exacting if not impossible requirement. The circumstances would have to be almost exactly the same. The place would have to be off the coast of West Africa, the time of the year would have to be July, the period spent adrift before being found would have to be about two weeks, hope of rescue should have been glimpsed and then dashed at least once and somewhere there had to be a medical witness.

The story I eventually chose is relatively unknown. I found the evidence in my own files, dating back fifteen years to a time when I had been studying the technical problems of survival at sea.

The raft of the *Medusa* had drifted off the coast of West Africa for thirteen days from July 5 to 17, 1816, after which time only fifteen men were still alive, five of whom died shortly after.

The two rafts of the *Rio Azul* had drifted off the coast of West Africa for sixteen days from June 29 to July 14, 1941, after which time only eleven men were alive, one of whom died at the moment of rescue and another a few days later.

The similarities were startling, but the discrepancies would be even more telling.

The *Rio Azul*, four thousand tons gross, carrying a cargo of "Pepel" iron ore from West Africa, was in convoy until 1800 hours on June 28, 1941, when she received a signal ordering the convoy to disperse. The following day at 1740 hours, alone in the South Atlantic, she was torpedoed.

The torpedoes struck her on the port side below the bridge, breaking the ship in two. The port lifeboat was smashed by the explosion. The falls of the starboard lifeboat went over the side and there was no slack which could be paid off. Both lifeboats were therefore useless and the only hope of the crew of forty-four men lay in the rafts which she carried on deck. There was no time to launch these. In less than sixty seconds after the explosion, the bow and stern cocked up in the air and sank. The crew jumped overboard.

Two rafts floated clear of the wreckage, one of them damaged. They were crudely constructed and consisted of a platform of planks laid on and lashed to metal drums. Most of the supplies they carried, together with the signal flares and other distress signals, had been torn away or destroyed. The damaged raft had lost the drums which would normally have supported one end, so it floated in a lopsided manner, the planks sloping toward the water. Any man clinging to this would likely roll off.

There was a large number of men in the water, some swimming and the nonswimmers clinging to the wreckage. The swimmers gradually made their way toward the rafts and tried to help others to reach them. While this was going on, a large enemy U-boat surfaced about three hundred yards away from the rafts.

The survivors reported her as being in excellent condition. From her general appearance and the fact that her paint was new, they concluded that she had come fairly recently from the shipyards. They counted two guns, one forward and one aft of the conning tower, but were unable to estimate their caliber. The U-boat commander hailed them, saying he would try to have some assistance sent to them. He did not, however, offer to leave them any supplies. The submarine then departed, leaving the rafts with some men on them to drift with the currents—for there were no paddles or oars—and an undetermined number of men clinging to the wreckage or trying to swim.

By nightfall eighteen men had reached the rafts. They huddled there, very cramped and uncomfortable, their sodden clothes clinging to them. The most senior of the survivors were the third mate, the senior radio operator, the chief steward (an old man of sixty-nine) and the bo'sun. Three seamen, two greasers, a fireman and a trimmer had arrived at the rafts, as well as an apprentice, a cabin boy, a deck boy and a galley boy. Of the trained gunners carried by all merchant ships to man the defensive armament, three had survived—two of them were soldiers, men of the Maritime Regiment, R.A., and one was a navy gunner of the D.E.M.S. organization.

As they sat there shivering they could hear out in the darkness the sound of shouting. The cries died away gradually and no more men reached the rafts. At dawn the next morning they were alone on the sea. A number of men who at nightfall had been seen clinging to the wreckage, but too far away to be either rescued or identified, were no longer there.

The eighteen men on the rafts then set about checking what supplies were left and collecting what they could from the litter of floating wreckage in which they were drifting. The sun, with a blazing and pitiless intensity, began to burn the moisture out of them.

Lashed to one of the rafts they found a container holding 1¾ gallons of fresh water. Among eighteen men exposed to the sky for every hour of every day for an unknown number of days to come, this quantity was minute. As a measure for rationing the water they used the brass stopper of a paraffin can. It held the equivalent of about three tablespoonsful. They decided that this would have to be the ration of water for each man each day.

From the drifting litter in the sea they salvaged what treasures they could. Cigarettes and tobacco were picked up—but no matches. Three objects of more vital use were found—one tin holding about ten tablespoonsful of molasses, one tin of egg substitute and one tin of cocoa. Apart from this, there was nothing to eat. They rationed these items also. The method of issue was to moisten a stick and then insert it into a tin, so that a little of the molasses, egg substitute or cocoa stuck to it.

Once only was there a shower. This occurred one night. They hurriedly spread out a tarpaulin and succeeded in catching ½ gallon of rain water. During the entire time they were adrift they had no more to drink and eat than this—a total of 2¼ gallons of water and the contents of the three tins. When men are exposed to the direct blaze of the sun they lose five times more moisture by evaporation than they would under some form of overhead protection. Literally, these men were sucked dry of moisture. At the same time they starved, suffering the headaches and stomach cramps that go with it. During daylight their exposed arms and legs were flayed by the scorching sun.

On the fourth day they saw a ship. Probably a tramp steamer, it was hull down on the horizon with only its masts, bridge and funnel visible. The rafts floated low in the water. Certainly they would not be seen from that distance away. The bo'sun, who had assumed much of the leadership, had foreseen this possibility. As a substitute for the lost flares and distress signals, he had hit upon the idea of employing the seemingly useless tobacco tins as heliographs. Flashed in the sun, their light would carry for miles. Under his leadership, they had also constructed a rough flagpole, with an improvised flag attached, which could be held up and so increase by many miles the distance from which they could be seen.

Excited and hopeful, they waved their flag and flashed the tobacco tins at the vessel on the horizon.

But she passed steadily on her way and at length sank out of sight, their sudden hope burned out into a reaction of lethargic despair.

There was no ease on the rafts, for they were very cramped. As day succeeded day, this became a torment which could only be alleviated by going into the sea. All of them bathed at intervals to stretch their limbs, with the single exception of the elderly chief steward. Otherwise they kept as still as possible, lying down for long periods in order to conserve their energy, which continued to ebb away. They were continually thirsty but found that there was slight relief to be gained by splashing each other with seawater, which they did from time to time.

The temptation to drink seawater was always present. Some of the men succumbed to this, and the unanimous opinion of those who survived was that the practice was harmful. Some of the men also began to drink their own urine. About the effects of this, opinion was divided.

They slept fitfully and nervously, falling off into a sleep which was usually filled with fantastic dreams. Often they saw visions of fresh, clear water.

When not asleep, no one was unduly despondent and prayers were said regularly every day. They were all surprised to find that the craving for food and water did not increase to an unendurable extent. Indeed, it was less than they expected. This was in fact the first sure sign of approaching death.

Less and less were they aware that their arms and legs were cruelly burned by sun and salt water and covered with sores, that they were cramped and thirsty and hungry. As life ebbed they became dull and apathetic, not fully conscious of their condition.

On the thirteenth day adrift, which was July 11, the radio officer died. He was the first. He was followed the next day by the chief steward, the oldest man among them.

On the fifteenth day, one of the gunners went mad. He was one of those who had drunk his own urine. He dived off the raft into the water and was unable to get back. The same day, two others died quietly from exhaustion. These were the trimmer and the cabin boy. Their bodies were pushed overboard during the night and although they were not weighted, by morning they had disappeared. It was assumed that they were eaten by sharks and possibly it was this which first attracted the sharks to the rafts.

By July 14, the third mate also had become mentally deranged. He died very early that morning. During the day it was noticed that one of the seamen had died also. The bodies were pushed overboard. With deaths now taking place in rapid succession, it is clear that even the toughest of the survivors had not long to live. At this point, another ship was sighted and use was made again of the bo'sun's tobacco tins as a heliograph.

This time—by the narrowest of margins and unknown to the survivors—the device worked. The ship, which was actually on escort duty, turned away from the vessels she was protecting to investigate what could have been merely the sun flickering on distant wave tops.

Within the next few minutes, while actually being rescued, the eighth man—the fireman—died. Even the toughest of the survivors admitted that if their hopes of rescue had again been dashed, three or four days more would have been their limit. Sheer disappointment and loss of hope would have finished them off.

They owed their lives, some probably by a matter of hours, to three men: an alert young signalman, an approachable captain and the bo'sun who had devised the method of signaling. His death, ten days after being rescued, was a tragic piece of irony.

The remaining nine men were landed at Scapa Flow a few weeks later and although their wounds and sores took long to heal, they all eventually recovered. Like the survivors of the *Medusa*, they were almost destitute.

This time the medical witness was not among the feeble specters on the raft. Instead he was the doctor of the rescue ship, the man who treated the survivors, who saw them as they surely could not have seen themselves.

When the armed merchant cruiser *Espérance Bay* left Freetown in Sierra Leone, six hundred miles south of Senegal, as escort for a convoy headed north up the coast of West Africa, her captain was a retired naval commander, Geoffrey Holden. He was "one in a thousand," a captain who was approachable, to whom the crew were intensely loyal. Five or six days out of Freetown a new and inexperienced signalman was coming down from the bridge when he noticed something flashing in the water at some distance from the convoy.

It is no small thing for a young seaman to beard the captain of a warship on his own bridge, particularly when he only thinks he has seen something and none of the regular lookouts have reported it. He hesitated a moment. He knew that this captain was not given to biting people's heads off, but it was with some trepidation that he went back to the bridge where Captain Holden stood with his officers. Holden listened, complimented him for drawing his attention to what he thought he might have seen, remarked that it would perhaps be appropriate to warm through the engines. The *Espérance Bay* increased speed and began to turn away from the ships she was protecting.

Holden would have to justify his action if the momentary flashing proved to have some innocent cause or even been a trick of the light on a wave. But when the convoy had fallen a few miles astern, two objects were sighted, floating low in the water.

They were rafts. It was realized with chilling apprehension by all aboard that they could only be from the previous convoy, which had been dispersed by U-boat attack in this area more than two weeks before. If there were men on them, then they had been exposed without shade or cover of any kind to the broiling sun of the South Atlantic for at least fifteen days.

There were men on them still. Eleven blackened travesties of human beings were stretched out on the bare planks. They were all alive at that moment, for they twitched feebly. Around them in the deep water patiently undulated the bodies of the sharks—nearly one shark in the water to every man on the rafts.

With care and great difficulty the utterly exhausted men were helped aboard. One man, alive when on the raft, was dead by the time he had been taken below to the sick bay. It was impossible to say at what precise moment he had died, so close to death were they all.

They were a difficult problem for Doctor C.* because, apart from severe sunburn and saltwater burns on their arms and legs, their vitality had almost flickered out from intense deprivation of fluid and food. A light diet of egg custards and light food was given to them but they had to be encouraged to eat; the craving for food had gone. They hardly knew what was happening to them. They did not know that, while on the rafts, a school of sharks had been keeping them com-

*The doctor, who was in private practice in Portsmouth when interviewed, wished to remain anonymous.

pany a few feet away. Their injuries, burns that would normally have made a man writhe in agony, now caused them hardly any pain. They had gone beyond that. It was hard to bring them back.

One man, their leader, sank fast into a coma. This was the bo'sun, who had saved all their lives by making reflectors out of tobacco tins. He was suffering from kidney failure. If he had been in normal health, it would have been terrible, for this is one of the most agonizing ways of dying that can be imagined. But the bo'sun felt no pain. So far toward death had he sunk already that now he merely became more and more drowsy; after ten days he died.

From the others, as they slowly gained in strength, the doctor bit by bit pieced together their story. The crew of the *Espérance Bay* were intensely curious about what had happened to them, but in the men's shocked and exhausted state, they could not be disturbed by casual visitors. So the doctor put down on paper what he learned from them and had it typed and sold to the crew. The proceeds were given to the nine destitute survivors. It is from this document, amplified by the doctor, that the story of the British rafts has been told.

Tens of thousands of such reports were made and exhaustively studied during and after the Second World War. The curiously conservative sailors were informed that their standard forms of lifesaving apparatus were virtually useless, simply because no one had bothered to find out what the survival problems really were. For instance, the Royal Navy's regulation life raft stood condemned on every count. Only 10 percent of these rafts ever got into the water at all and most of the men on them died anyway. Flotation was all very well, but it was far from being enough. Battle casualties amounted to one-third of the total war losses; two-thirds died by drowning or by exposure of the unprotected body to biting wind and cold or to burning sun and heat. (Report of the Talbot Committee, 1946.)

At the same time the Americans were also studying the problem from their own bitter experiences. They produced a chart showing the expectation of life for men in the sea, using life jackets or rafts. This varied with temperature, but in average conditions survivors had lasted less than sixty minutes.

To quote from an article I wrote in 1958: "The result of these detailed studies of survivors' reports was to show that there was not one problem—but three. The first was to devise lifesaving equipment which could actually be launched, even in adverse conditions. The second was to ensure that this equipment kept the survivors insulated from the three killers: the sea, the sun and the wind. The third was to make sure that the survivors could be located and rescued."

The answer which had by then been newly arrived at and was just being introduced was based on the aircraft dinghy, which had had a good war record, unlike life jackets, life rafts and lifeboats. The new type of life raft was a light inflatable dinghy with an overhead cover called an "Arctic tent" which could be completely closed by flaps at both ends. Like most good inventions, it was more than a century old. The first inflatable life raft was invented by Lieutenant Halkett, R.N., and tested by him in the Bay of Biscay under winter conditions in 1844. The Admiralty turned down the idea but similar craft were used for Arctic exploration in the 1840s and 1850s.

The emphasis was on North Atlantic conditions—cold wind and cold water—rather than on those of the South Atlantic, where the sun may be a torment and survival time is likely to be a matter of days or weeks rather than hours or minutes. Nevertheless, the use of the tent as overhead protection against the sun in the tropics is nowadays regarded as critical for survival, to prevent dehydration. Here also a modern innovation had been "invented" more than a century earlier, for in their last days on the raft the survivors of the *Medusa* had indeed erected a tent as a sun cover, fashioning it out of their useless sail. Had they thought to do so earlier, more of them might have lasted until the moment of rescue. Nevertheless, it took 140 years and two world wars before Ministries relearned that lesson.

The basic difference between the improvised raft of the *Medusa* and the unofficial nonregulation rafts of the *Rio Azul* was that the former lacked flotations. Wooden ships are generally less likely to sink than iron or steel ships, which is why they carried few boats, but in the last resort every sailor knew that he could always make a raft out of the materials on hand, buoying them up with empty casks, for solid wood floats low in the water. It is to the eternal discredit of de Chaumareys and Schmaltz that they made a quick, botched job of the raft. Consequently, we must regard the immersion to their waists in salt water as an adverse, agonizing factor for the survivors of the French ship which was not duplicated in the case of the *Rio Azul*, although one raft was missing half its oil drums.

Some experiences were clearly common to the survivors of both vessels—the drinking of seawater and urine, the relief obtained by bathing, the habit of formal prayer. The sharks also exhibited standard reactions—a small group took station near the floating objects but did not attempt to attack the men. Even mullet do this in hot weather in the English Channel, so it may have been a matter of shade and temperature combined, perhaps, with the mass of the rafts which for small fish are protection and for large fish an ambush position. While the British seem not to have thought of the sea under them as a source of food, containing liquid, the French did try to catch fish, although unsuccessfully. The French also showed initiative in erecting a tent.

*      *      *

It was a French doctor, Alain Bombard, who in 1952 set out to prove that with only a little equipment it was possible to subsist for many months in the South Atlantic on a diet of seawater, plankton and fish. His introduction to the problem the previous year had been in its cold water aspect, the delivery to the hospital where he worked of forty-three trawlermen, still wearing their life belts, who had been in the sea off Boulogne in the springtime for a very short period. They were all dead. One answer to this problem was technical and not always convenient—the use of a buoyant, insulating "survival suit" to replace the almost useless and in some designs actually dangerous life jacket.

Bombard's research began in 1951 with the classic case of the *Medusa*'s raft in 1816 and included Bligh's voyage in a boat from the *Bounty* in 1789. He concluded that Savigny was correct in his basic statement that many survivors died from despair and not from any physical cause in comparable conditions of excessive heat rather than excessive cold. The first step was to combat despair with reason in order to prolong life to its physical limit, and then to extend the physical limit by showing how men could live from the sea. Again, it was not necessary for him to invent the basic statement. The work had already been done by 1888 and was described by Prince Albert I of Monaco, an oceanographer, in a report to the Academy of Sciences in Paris. In July and August of that year an oceanographic vessel operating in the South Atlantic had proved that simple nets, lines and harpoons could extract ample food from the ocean, particularly at night. In that part of the ocean, at that time of the year, no castaway should die of starvation, provided that he had this elementary equipment and the will to live.

The third requirement was for liquid to combat thirst. Here Bombard was to make an original contribution by putting forward theories, proving them in the laboratory and then drawing attention to the fact by a practical test in which he drifted like a castaway across the southern part of the North Atlantic roughly on a line opposite West Africa.

The first of his propositions is that the body of a fish contains much fresh water. Catch enough fish and you will not die of thirst. His second proposition was more controversial. It was based on the fact that fish do not always immediately gravitate toward a floating object; it may be three or four days or more before they begin to do so. Without water, a survivor may become irreversibly dehydrated during this initial period. Bombard's solution was to drink seawater at first, before the fish arrived and provided fresh water. It will be recalled that the men of the *Rio Azul*, while having no definite opinion on the effects of urine drinking, were all agreed that the drinking of seawater had proved harmful. This is indeed the consensus of opinion of centuries.

Bombard, being a doctor, knew that better than most. Drunk in great quantities it inflames the kidneys and this causes death (as in the case of the bo'sun).

The doctor decided to drink seawater but to limit his intake to a daily 1½ pints, because this amount contained the salt which the human body actually requires in that period. Further, he decided to limit the drinking of seawater to the first five days, the critical period when there might be no fish to catch. There was an element of risk, but the doctor was confident that he would survive. There was strident opposition, mainly from old mariners turned bureaucrats whose ancient expertise was being derided (to their minds) by a layman.

The craft which Bombard used was an inflatable dinghy, which provided insulation from the sea only (not from the wind or the sun). For sixty-five days he drifted in the north equatorial current, living on fish which he caught and plankton scooped up with a net. Plankton consists of both vegetable and animal life in almost microscopic forms—fish, lobsters, prawns, all these in their early stages are part of the great fields of plankton in the sea. Although accused of being a charlatan, Bombard made his point unforgettably to practical people.

The two most spectacular examples of genuine castaways following Bombard's example were both from the South Pacific. They were the survival of the Robertson family after 38 days in 1972 and the endurance for 117 days of Maurice and Marilyn Bailey in 1973. These people fished for their food and, further, put up overhead cover to protect themselves from the extremes of cold and heat.

The only real scientific objections to Bombard's own demonstration of his theories seem twofold. First, he was a doctor and knew exactly what he was doing. An ordinary man might not be so confident in his ability to judge just how much seawater was the limit to drink. Second, there stands the awkward fact that there are no ordinary men. Each individual, from his fingerprints to his breathing patterns, is different from every other individual.

A much better test is the survival of a group, and better still is the survival of different groups at widely spaced intervals. The differences which occur between them are probably even more important than the similarities in pinpointing vital evidence. An exception appears to be those hallucinations which affected equally the men of the *Rio Azul*, the men on the *Medusa*'s raft and in at least one recorded case, that of M. Bredif, in one boat of the *Medusa* also. Savigny's opinion was that these were not due entirely to the sun and the heat, as hallucinations occurred at night also, and that there must be another factor, probably a lack of certain nutrients in the food, which affected the minerals in the body. Somehow, he thought, the system is put out of gear and so the hallucinations start.

Both diets, the French and the British, certainly were unbalanced. There was a difference which could be important, however. The French flour, water and wine came from the unsavory hold of a nineteenth-century sailing vessel in the tropics and three weeks out of port, while the British molasses, egg substitute, cocoa and water were in twentieth-century tins.

Professor Schadewald put this question: Was there a specific poison present on the raft of the *Medusa?* Before considering this critical point, one must admit the truth of his statement that Savigny's narrative is a "document unique in medical history." This is the main reason why the case of the *Medusa* is still studied even in a century remarkable for its advances in the field of medical knowledge. There was no doctor on the rafts of the *Rio Azul* to give close-up testimony, and the leader who emerged was the bo'sun, who did not long survive rescue. On the raft of the *Medusa,* however, not only was there a ship's doctor but he was the man who emerged as the leader and quickly recovered from his ordeal. We know, therefore, that he had realized from the first the necessity for strict military discipline, careful thought and above all an emotionally hopeful note in the leadership (even if the leaders did not always believe it), because they saw despair as the deadliest danger of all.

The British report does not stress this to the same extent because, comparatively, morale on the British rafts was much higher, indeed, highly satisfactory. The tougher men would not admit defeat. In the face of all the evidence, they were convinced that they could have gone on for another three or four days, even if the *Espérance Bay* had disappointed them as cruelly as the earlier ship. They had already lasted two days longer than the men of the *Medusa* were required and their losses, proportionately, had been much less. They had managed this without resorting to cannibalism, a factor which must have contributed greatly toward the survival of the last fifteen men on the French raft.

Nor had they fought each other, and, although crowded, there is no record of their having become even exceptionally irritated with each other, although some irritation might be expected on medical and nutritional grounds alone. The voyage of the boat from the *Bounty* in 1789 provided a famous case, in which a near-mutiny broke out, almost resulting in a cutlass duel between the emaciated Lieutenant Bligh and one of his equally emaciated officers. Bligh was a bad officer and a worse captain and no doubt morale was well below normal to start with.

This was certainly the case with the *Medusa* and is

a central fact of the whole affair. First, she was wrecked in peacetime, not sunk by an enemy. Second, she was wrecked by bad management. Third, her abandonment was marked by cowardice as well as incompetence on the part of her captain. Fourth, she was carrying a large number of passengers. Fifth, these passengers were not acclimatized to the tropics. And last, these passengers were of mixed origins and included many convicted felons who were virtually slaves. It is a formidable list.

The difference between a peacetime disaster and a wartime tragedy is immense. In peace, one does not expect to be sunk and there is both shock and protest. In war, one is mentally prepared in advance to face the worst; if you're still alive afterwards, you're lucky.

The crew of the *Rio Azul* was a small, homogeneous body of men crossing the South Atlantic with essential war supplies at the height of the U-boats' success in the area. The soldiers aboard were gunners manning the defensive armament and were therefore part of the crew. Their chances to start with were not good. When the ship broke in two, it sank in sixty seconds, which, considering the cargo it was carrying—iron ore— was to be expected. The lifeboats went down with it. That two rafts floated free was blessed good luck. That many men lived to jump overboard and that eighteen of them actually managed to reach the rafts was amazing good fortune.

The *Medusa*, on the other hand, was undertaking a commonplace voyage which, properly conducted, held few hazards. By a series of perverse stupidities the captain deliberately left his convoy behind and when the frigate was completely alone, despite clear warnings, drove her ashore on a well-known sandbank. He then bungled the process of getting her off and shamefully mismanaged the subsequent premature abandonment of a ship which could not sink and was unlikely to break up. Through personal weakness, incompetence and cowardice he deliberately condemned most of the men on the raft to death.

The basic difference in morale between the two groups of castaways may be appreciated. Even so, there were critical differences among the components of the very large group on the *Medusa*'s raft. The soldiers were not defensive gunners; they were passengers, pure victims, unaccustomed to the sea, unaccustomed to the tropics, placed in an unexpected and terribly unfair situation. The sailors were less downcast and resentful because their profession did involve the possibility of shipwreck and no doubt they comprehended that not all captains were immaculate navigators and shiphandlers. The engineering workmen under Corréard represented a third closed group, while the officers themselves formed yet another, with similar backgrounds, mental outlook and training.

The men on the British rafts were crowded, too crowded to lie down until death had created a space. The men on the French raft were more crowded still and, in addition, were standing to their waists in salt water until death lightened the raft and gave them space also.

The British had a water ration only. The French had wine as well as water and some of them got drunk on the wine. The fighting which broke out may in part have been due to the wine and the result was to inflict saber, bayonet, knife and musket-butt wounds on many, as well as to expend energy. It has been suggested that there may have been a poison in the *Medusa*'s water casks (such liquid was often putrid and alive with organisms), but water was drunk in the *Medusa*'s boats without producing anything more than mild hallucination (if in fact it was the cause at all).

On the French raft such symptoms were incomparably more severe. Instead of merely seeing visions of flowing water, men acted on the strength of their delusions. They demanded and fought for nonexistent portions of chicken. One man was found about to cut a slice off Captain Dupont's leg, believing that the leg was a loaf of white bread. Savigny himself pointed out that this state was far from being unknown. It had been described by the French doctor François Boissier de Sauvages in 1763 as usually occurring in the tropics, but had been identified long before that in reports by the early Spanish seamen in southern waters. They had called it Castilian fever and sometimes attributed the state to sunstroke, although others believed it was due to the bad air in the lower decks of their cramped and crowded vessels.

Savigny doubted both these theories on the ground that there was all too much air on the raft and that the severe hallucinations occurred at night. His own conjecture was that the special conditions of the tropics affected the supply of blood to the brain with results not dissimilar to encephalitis or meningitis. Professor Schadewald considered that a poison in, or a deficiency of, the diet was the likely cause.

He observed, however, that only three men—Savigny, Corréard and Dupont—had apparently kept a clear head all the time, for this was partly a matter of will power, and that a group of twenty or so men which included most of the officers had managed to control the rest. The majority, however, had shown some symptoms of insanity which, under the influence of alcohol, hunger, sleeplessness and the general hopelessness of the situation, had produced an extreme state of excitement—a "temper tantrum"—which had resulted in the mutinies and riots.

This was the reading of a German medical specialist. A French historian, writing even more recently, suggested an artificial and sinister interpretation of these same events. In his view the pattern could fit the theme of "survival of the fittest." The officers and their juniors had moved to the center of the raft to reduce the danger of being swept overboard and by climbing onto the barrels had managed to keep dry. They had started the fighting in order to clear people off the raft to obtain more room for themselves, and they had killed people in order to eat them.

It is absurd to take this as being literally true in the sense of selfishly reasoned conduct. The officers went to the center of the raft and when possible placed themselves on the barrels because this was necessary in order to control such a large body of men tightly packed. In the armies of the time, officers of about the rank of major and above were issued a horse because the animal provided them with a mobile eminence on which they could be seen by all and from which their commands would carry more clearly and compel more attention. After twenty years of war, the conduct of the officers on the raft can be seen as no more than a sensible reflex action, and one which was to be expected of officers. That the nominal commander of the raft, the injured Midshipman Coudein, was soon superseded by the older, more experienced and perhaps more forceful Savigny and his friend Corréard, is only to be expected. Exactly the same happened on the British rafts of the *Rio Azul.* It was the experienced bo'sun who assumed most of the leadership rather than the radio officer, theoretically his senior. It is important to note that it was not leadership in the sense of bullying domination but in spreading the gospel of hope and suggesting means by which they could help themselves and perhaps even save themselves; and they were fully justified in the event because they did just that.

The British experience highlighted the extraordinary "temper tantrums" on the *Medusa*'s raft, amounting almost to insanity. Was this just the result of wine, hunger, heat, hopelessness and lack of sleep? Or was there a specific poison present? Or was there another cause altogether?

# 18

# In the Deserts and
# the Mountains
## *(The age of aviation, 1970—73)*

A purely medical explanation appeared reasonable enough until in September 1970, when three airliners were hijacked to the Middle East and hundreds of passengers were kept prisoner for a week inside them after the huge aircraft had been landed in the Jordan desert. The first aircraft to be seized was an American Jumbo Jet, a Boeing 707 of TWA, hijacked over Brussels at the start of a flight to New York with nine crew members and 149 passengers—a group almost identical in numbers to those isolated on the raft of the *Medusa*. In conditions of extreme heat by day (the nights were cold) they occupied a confined and completely covered space and were forced to remain in their cramped seats by armed guards for seven days as a result of no fault of their own. Like the wreck of the *Medusa*, this was a totally unexpected situation, and like those from the *Medusa*, the castaways had been brought together by chance. Instead of unity, there was an infinity of potential divisions.

There was among the castaways a qualified observer who noted what happened and later presented a paper on the subject.* This was Sylvia R. Jacobson,

---

* "Individual and Group Responses to Confinement in a Sky-jacked Plane," *Amer. J. Orthopsychiat.* 43(3), April 1973, and

Associate Professor of Social Welfare at the Florida State University, Tallahassee. When I first read a summary of this report, it seemed that there was a definite sequence to the psychological and physical deterioration which took place and I was amazed to see how closely it appeared to parallel many of the events on the raft of the *Medusa*. There were only slight differences and these were all caused by the varying nature of the outside events which impinged upon the castaway communities. There were no jelly-fish or butterflies in the cabin of the Jumbo, for instance. But there were equivalent incidents to torment on the one hand and to raise hopes, often illusionary, on the other.

The actual moment of the hijacking was not mentally critical. There was an element of stunned disbelief, similar to that experienced by soldiers in their first battle or civilians under air attack for the first time. The impact of what had happened only began to be realized at about the time when, according to the original flight plan, the passengers should have been arriving at their destination, Kennedy Airport, New York. There they were due to meet their relatives and friends. Now, they thought, they might never see them again. Some became very worried and swapped names and addresses with other passengers in the hope that if they were unlucky, news of what had happened to them might still get through. This moment seems to approximate the stranding of the *Medusa*.

The equivalent to the casting off of the raft was the landing of the Jumbo in a remote place in the desert which was garrisoned and controlled by armed

*Schwalbacher Blätter*, 98, *Jahrgang* XXIV, Heft 2, 1.6.73, Wiesbaden. Also personal communications and discussions with the author.

Arabs of the Popular Front for the Liberation of Palestine. That was final. Once on the ground, at the mercy of their captors for an indefinite time, there arose a conflict *among* the passengers. The subdivision of the passengers had already begun during the flight, but then it had been hardly more than latent, less marked than the conflicts and suspicions which had occurred at the time of the *Medusa*'s stranding, for some of these went back three weeks to their original departure from Rochefort. In the Jumbo there was time during the five-hour flight only for the first tentative appearance of this phenomenon.

"Subgroupings began subtly to form," wrote Sylvia Jacobson. "Families clung more closely to their children. Seatmates and those adjacent, hitherto strangers for the most part, dropped normal psychological barriers; in the sudden sense of unity in danger they whispered together in sudden communion, exchanging conjectures, anxieties, fears. The fourteen college students scanned seat-pocket maps, speculating among themselves, trying to foretell destination, evidencing a sense of adventure. Almost at once, they formed and remained a subgroup. A voice hissed harshly that this was as it had been in the Nazi Holocaust: 'People were led helplessly to their deaths, like sheep.' "

Preliminary lines having begun to form during the flight, the first dangerous division occurred almost immediately after landing and sparked the first actual conflict, approximately equivalent to the agitation concerning Lieutenant d'Anglas which preceded the first mutinous riot on the raft of the *Medusa*. Inside the Jumbo, of course, there could be no question of the passengers physically fighting among themselves. They had guns pointed at them. Their rapidly building antagonisms could not be worked off by strength-sapping hand-to-hand fighting but had to take the internally corrosive form of vicious argument, snapped replies and general nagging.

What Sylvia Jacobson called "the first divisive wedge" came with the Arab demand for passports. This revealed the basic fact of their captivity: although all were hostages of a sort, some were in greater danger than others, much greater danger. She heard the Arabs openly declare that the mass skyjack was an effort to impress the world with the plight of the Palestinians, to ransom their imprisoned "brothers," to express their anger at America for supplying fighter planes to Israel and to demonstrate their protracted and intense resentment and hatred of Israel.

The hunt was for people with Israeli passports. It set apart those who held dual passports of two different nations and families in which parents and children held passports of different nations. "With the demand for passports, an apprehension that was never to leave flooded the cabin," noted Sylvia Jacobson. She herself had queried the demand for passports but had been silenced by murmurs of "Sshh—don't make trouble" from other passengers. The next morning this division was deepened when some passengers asked an Arab doctor to let them get their personal medicines from the baggage in the hold. Other passengers who, although traveling on American passports had a second, Israeli passport in their luggage and feared that these might be found during a search of the cases in the hold, became extremely alarmed. "This evoked a fierce, whispered quarrel," noted Sylvia Jacobson. Eventually, those who wanted medicines gave in, but "subgroups existed in uneasy, distrustful proximity to one another."

This initial situation may be thought to parallel the preliminary lines on the raft, with the officers, sailors and engineering workmen broadly on one side and the mass of the soldiers—but by no means all of them yet —on the other. Also paralleled were the fluctuations between hope and anxiety brought about by outside stimuli, which resulted in alternating periods of calm succeeded by violent quarreling.

A visit by Jordanian army officers brought momentary unity and quiet to the cabin, although they could offer little real promise of help apart from an offer to send in food. But when the food actually arrived, it triggered off yet another half-suppressed explosion. Some Jewish parents urged their children to eat and were sharply criticized by other Jewish parents for accepting non-Kosher food. Yet another divisive element had been introduced, cutting across two previous boundaries, that of the dual-passport holders and that of age, for the adolescents continued to be "a definite, almost closed subgroup, immersed in companionship and self-organization for available satisfaction. They continued to evidence a certain sense of adventure." This was similar to the situation just before a war, which may well be enjoyed by the young, who have few ties or responsibilities, while causing nothing but concern to older people and particularly the elderly.

"By noon, however, the mothers of babies had spontaneously become another subgroup, concerned with the practical problems of caring for their infants and themselves. Formula preparation, bottle heating, the improvisation of cribs against the cold night engaged them. While most passengers continued to speculate on their fate, to read, to pray, to doze, half-heartedly to play cards, the mothers, with busy hands, remained purposefully and enviably engaged and united. Along with the stewardesses, women passengers moved to look after the six children who were traveling alone. It seemed as though this, as other life crises of birth through death, called upon the work of women and their hands."

Some loose parallel may be suggested with the officers on the raft, engaged in the intricacies of rationing or stepping a mast, and also perhaps with the Negroes. These latter had originally divided between the small command group and the large mutinous group but had eventually withdrawn from both groups to form their own self-seeking mutinous party which, by suggesting that they could help the mutineers survive in the desert, tried to influence the side with the greatest numbers.

That evening some of the passengers were ordered out of the Jumbo in order to be evacuated to hotels in Amman. The Indians went first, then other nationals, then mothers and their children, then all the remaining women. But first, they had to sign forms which revealed, one way or the other, whether or not they could be considered Jewish. All Jewish women were ordered back into the cabin, together with two non-Jewish women who pleaded not to be separated from their husbands. Subconscious fears of a new Buchenwald rose to the surface and were openly expressed now.

The arrival of the International Red Cross on the third day changed matters. Spirits rose and there was a feeling of general unity among the passengers. "Sight-seeing" visits by armed men of various North African armies had the same effect. The passengers felt as if they were on display, resented it and united to put on a show of indifference. "Divisiveness was subdued," noted Sylvia Jacobson. Then "suddenly, all passengers were ordered off the plane, ostensibly for air." In their absence there was a search of cabin baggage, in which Israeli passports were found. The Arabs suspected that there were others and demanded that these be given up. The airline stewards advised the passengers to comply.

The main lines of division immediately hardened. There were hostile remarks: "If it were not for the Jews, none of us would be in this spot." This antagonism was reciprocated. Passengers who had engaged in curious and apparently friendly conversation with the Arab doctor and the female Arab guards were the targets. They were attacked for "fraternization with the enemy."

The opposite line of natural development—attempts to impose a command setup to carry out agreed measures for organization and survival—failed almost entirely. Tentative beginnings were met with contempt. "Who gave *you* any special right?"

There may have been a Savigny or a bo'sun who saw what had to be done and could think out detailed measures; but, if so, he did not appear. This may have been because a command staff—inexperienced in crises of this nature—already existed in the aircraft. It was composed of the stewards and air hostesses, trained to act as waiters, waitresses and wet nurses, not leaders or organizers. Their traditional role as reassurers of naïve and nervous passengers in this instance boomeranged. The cabin became a "rumor factory." This emphasized the fact that commands and information must emanate from a single dominating point, whether that be a couple of barrels in the center of a raft or from the aircraft captain's cockpit by loudspeaker.

The outbreak of general irritation on the third day, starting with anti-Jewish remarks, was repeated more aggressively on the fifth day. Some non-American passengers began to agree with the anti-Jewish and anti-American sentiments of the Arab guards and became more forceful in doing so. One American, of recent

European origin, said that he despised American customs and values and was only waiting for retirement to leave the place forever. These outbursts were countered and quelled by the aircraft crew and a black American soldier who was among the passengers.

Although this developing conflict could not be physically indulged in and had to be restricted to abuse, there does seem to be a pattern closely similar to that which developed on the raft of the *Medusa*. The first burst of general irritation was marked by a period of angry posturing, with some reluctance to actually fight, followed by single combats between pugnacious individuals or "champions" of both sides, followed—one is tempted to say inevitably—by a general combat between the two sides.

On the fifth day in the desert the passengers found out that the aircraft had been wired for demolition. "The only reactions seemed numbness, apathy, depressed isolation on the part of some, increased tendency among affiliates for relatively idle talk, bolstering of self-defenses in fitful scapegoating and the ongoing bickering around eating." Where the French castaways had fallen into desultory converse on their worst memories of the Napoleonic wars, here there was a certain "gallows humor." "Veterans of Buchenwald scorned the complaints of others. Compared with what they had lived through, this was a 'Hilton Hotel.'"

They were of course perfectly right. However, what one may call "concentration camp superiority" is not new but rather one form of a trait well known in war contexts, exhibited in Normandy in 1944 where it was identified and classified as "D-Day Snobbery" ("If you'd been here on D-Day, you'd have been dug in by now"), familiar also as the theme of earlier British civilian air raid experience ("My bomb was bigger than your bomb"). The attitude can perform a useful service in lending perspective and particularly in introducing "green" personnel to active and dangerous realities; but, undeniably, it can also be irritating.

On the sixth day the confined passengers in the aircraft began to crack emotionally; they lost their perspective. "There was a general sensing of the rapidly spreading deterioration of health and morale. The atmosphere grew more physically and emotionally oppressive. The remaining men were paler; those of military age showed and complained of gastric disturbances; vomitings increased. Babies were irritable; halfhearted attempts at card playing and checkers were abandoned or increased; more sudden sobbing occurred and stopped; more intimate expressions of loss of hope and longing for death by older ones were heard. Grief over guilt toward others in the past emerged with a seeming lack of coherence." On the raft, the younger men could have fought; in the plane, with their emotions held in check by armed guards, their feelings were deflected internally. Instead of saber wounds, they suffered stomach disorders.

The crazy suspicions which showed early on the raft did not become really marked on the aircraft until this same, sixth day. When a guard became ill and was taken off the plane by another Arab guard, even Sylvia Jacobson was alarmed. "Was this a ploy to get the *fedayeen* off the plane before it exploded? When, some half hour later, he was returned we were newly disquieted. Having been ill, was he thought worthless enough to be blown up with us?" There followed what she wrote of as an "access of paranoia," suspicions which a cool look around would have discounted. Whatever move was made, whether by their captors or by a subgroup, was interpreted by the remainder as a plot to kill them. Given a little more confinement there might have been actual killing. Had the cause of their close detention in unbearably hot circumstances been purely natural, rather than the muzzles of Arab guns, there might have been killing already.

The next day, the seventh, was the last. The remaining passengers in all three aircraft were taken to Amman, while the planes were blown up. But the affair was far from being over emotionally. "In subsequent rescue stages and on the long flight westward to America, recriminations were more open and bitter. . . ." Just so had Thomas complained to Rang about Savigny and the other officers.

What now remains of that French historical view which accuses Savigny of deliberately causing antagonisms on the raft in order to get rid of many of the occupants and so let him and his friends have more space and better rations? Does anything remain even of the long-held view that the strange occurrences on the raft of the *Medusa* were unique, unrepeatable? On the contrary, it may now be said that the *Medusa* narrative continues to be relevant in the twentieth century; that the technological differences between an early nineteenth-century wooden sailing ship and the latest jet airliner are utterly irrelevant. The subject is not transportation methods but the study of groups of people under stress. The *Medusa* case, where everything went to extremes, is therefore still the most valuable piece of evidence we have.

Just as the *Medusa* case must be corrected and "controlled" by equivalent incidents, such as that of the *Rio Azul*, so must the experience of the American Boeing 707 be compared to that of the other two skyjacked aircraft—the Swissair DC-8 and the British VC-10. Sylvia Jacobson was told by the Arab guards that conditions were far worse in the other planes. "I learned that the contrary was true. We, on the American plane, had the worst of the three situations. Aboard another plane, greater total cohesiveness was sustained, and a passenger was heard to say, 'Our fear was controlled, our anxieties uncontrolled.'"

Professor Jacobson is still engaged in a comparative study of these illuminating differences. In the interim, she believes that the determining factors may be: (1) the nature and character of the leadership maintained (or not maintained) by each captain, together with the degree of direct contact he had (or did not have) with the passengers; (2) indigenous passenger leadership fluctuations; (3) in a crisis of this sort the greater degree of efficiency and technical competence of one crew over the others; (4) the presence or absence of women (other than female crew) and children; (5) the behavior of the captors and the vulnerability of the captives to their explicit threats, as well as their nationality.

The basic underlying cause of the irritation which leads to subdivision and the breakdown of physical and mental health has yet to be explained. Climate, helplessness, confinement to a limited space are obvious critical factors. It is difficult to decide the order of their importance. But it may be that space is the real key: that the overcrowding of any type of creature, whether human or not, tends to result in a conflict which is resolved only when there is space enough for the survivors to lie down and stretch out.

In all the raft narratives, both French and British, the sense of relief once death had removed a sufficient number of persons to make life bearable is a subconscious theme easily detected. The French, but not the British, hurried on the removal by butchering each other; but then the French were even more crowded and vulnerable to begin with. And, like the passengers of the American Jumbo Jet, they were mostly a miscellaneous collection of individuals brought haphazardly together. The British were the closely knit survivors of a small, organized crew.

If these observations are fundamental, then the *Medusa* may have a lesson even for the conditions of modern urban life. It is possible that high-rise, high-density "tower blocks"—as opposed to a rather crowded but still closely knit community of slum dwellers who may have occupied the site previously—may lead to alienation and rioting, purposeless or with only an apparent purpose.

One basic aspect of the *Medusa's* story, however, yields to modern perspective. The eating of human flesh, condemned as an "atrocity," and used as a political weapon against Savigny and Corréard, is not now seen in the same light. There is no reason to doubt the genuineness of the immediate revulsions at the discovery of how the survivors had really survived, the confusion in people's minds as to whether they were confronting savages or heroes. For once again, an episode of the *Medusa* has repeated itself in modern times, amid the glistening wonders of twentieth-century technology which have changed nothing basic and can again be dismissed as irrelevant.

For a long time the French experience was thought to be unique. Later in the century, it was true, a comparable event resulted from the stranding of the Donner party in a snowbound pass during the covered-wagon days of the American West. That, too, was thought to be exceptional and scandalous. This was largely because the historians of the sea and the historians of the "Wild West" operated in separate compartments, so to each, each event appeared uniquely horrifying.

However, in the early 1970s two instances of community cannibalism occurred and were widely reported, for they were the result of aircraft accidents—one in Canada, one in South America. Like that of the Donner party, they were cold-climate occurrences; thirst was not a factor but food most certainly was. The small group in Canada were faced with the choice: eat human flesh or die. An Eskimo boy resolutely refused to consume human flesh. He died. The German pilot ate from a body killed in the crash. He lived. With air travel now so common, any one of us might tomorrow be faced with this dilemma.

The crash in the Andes took place in October 1972 and was particularly well covered by the media.* It was also especially interesting because, although many of the basic factors were utterly different from those which had acted on the crew and passengers of the *Medusa*, nevertheless certain patterns of behavior were repeated. Consequently, although it is not necessary to tell the whole story in any detail, some aspects need to be considered, particularly those which appeared to transcend physical differences which occurred in spite of the contrast between the climate of the tropics in summer at sea level and the climate at twelve thousand feet in the Andes in winter.

The pilot of the Uruguayan Air Force Fairchild turboprop had taken his machine through a particular pass in the Andes (because it lacked the performance to go over the top), which meant careful navigation to a check point on one side, a large change of course to fly through the pass in the clouds, followed by another large change of course over a navigational "fix" on the far side of the pass. By some mental aberration the final turn of the dogleg was made

---

* Including two documentary books, *Survive!* by Clay Blair, Jr. (Berkley, 1973), and *Alive* by Piers Paul Read (Lippincott, 1974).

much, much too early and instead of flying north on the far side of the mountains he flew north right into them. Just so had de Chaumareys turned when only half the required distance had been covered and sailed right into a sandbank.

However, as the Fairchild was going a good deal faster—about 240 miles an hour faster—than the *Medusa* when it met a solid object, many of the five crewmen and forty passengers were killed instantly or died soon after. After seventy-two days in the mountains in winter, sixteen young men survived. It was almost miraculous.

The composition of the passenger group was extraordinary, a school rugby team and its supporters. It could hardly have been more homogeneous, more different from that of the *Medusa*. They were almost all men: young, tough, physically fit. As it was a Catholic school, they were all Catholics. And as it was an exclusive school, they were all from the upper classes of their nation. Politically, all bar one were "liberal" or left-wing. Four were medical students, one of whom was to play an important part in their protracted endurance and eventual rescue. The "command" structure of the plane did not survive the crash for long; the pilots, pinned to their seats, died of their injuries. It was all up to the students.

They had hope on their side to begin with, for an accurately directed search pattern put one aircraft right over the scene of the crash a day later. The survivors saw it clearly, but they did not know that the pilot had not seen them, for the wrecked machine was painted white and was partly buried by snow.

The first night was the most horrible, spent crammed inside the wreckage with the dead, the dying and those who had been terribly injured but might live if help came soon. The cold was bitter. Wine was passed around and many of the boys took a drink or two. Some, mercifully, went to sleep. Others could not sleep at all. Others again were irrational. One boy kept crying out that he was president of Uruguay; another said he was going out to find a bar and fix himself a Coke. In the intense cold and thin air of the Andes, exactly the same sort of hallucinations which had been common on the raft of the *Medusa* were repeated. Here, there could be no question of tropic heat or of water poisoned by long storage in the hold of a wooden sailing ship. The *Medusa* survivors had drunk wine too, which may have contributed, but the essential similarity seems to be shock—the shock of the crash or of being fatally cast adrift in a raging sea—a sudden and awful change of circumstance which would also disturb a disciplined human system accustomed to a long-standing routine of sleeping and waking, eating, resting and working. Here climate *would* contribute to the existing psychological and physical disturbances of the system, because both climates, although opposites, were *extreme*: cold and thin air which made breathing difficult or suffocating heat and lifeless air impregnated with desert dust which also made breathing difficult. The cause then is really a series of shocks, fundamental disturbances affecting the nervous system and the breathing system, at well as the digestive system.

None of this is really very surprising and certainly it is not alarming. Given time, all systems will adapt to some extent. But, terribly, the crash of the Fairchild did parallel the *Medusa*'s raft in respect of the dangers of restricted space. Originally there were twenty-eight survivors, some injured, who—in order not to die of cold—had to withdraw to the fuselage at night. This wreckage gave a usable space only fifteen feet long for the twenty-eight people. They had to sleep in "stacked" formation, limbs intertwined or draped over someone else. This, plus the cold, led to cramps and the sufferer would move; often he would disturb, or hit, or kick someone in the face or on a wound, involuntarily. There would be a cry of pain, perhaps wild cursings, sometimes blows, occasionally a fight between two individuals which would bring on a melee involving several others. Clay Blair wrote: "As a result of these fights, so much anger and hostility built up during the nights that they instituted a rule that everybody had to shake hands all around every morning." Just so, in his delirium, Lavillette had told of how, on the raft, "after each slaughter, they would kiss, thanking God; after the last one, all the guns were thrown overboard." These clashes occurred in spite of the fact that all the aircraft survivors could in fact lie down, if uncomfortably. On the *Medusa*'s raft, for many days, no one could lie down, or even sit down; they were tightly packed even when all were standing up.

In the Andes, initially, the survivors burned money in order to melt snow for drinking purposes. Paper currency was much more valuable than coinage in these circumstances. Later, they found more efficient ways of melting the snow and there was never a thirst problem. Consequently, hunger dominated all other desires. It was the medical student Roberto Canessa, a determined nineteen-year-old, who rationalized the problem for them. Their situation was long-term. If they were not seen from the air, then they would have to walk out of the Andes. There was no other alternative. And to do that, they would have to wait until the late spring when the snows would melt. Their food supplies would not last nearly so long and even if they did there would not be enough merely to stay alive. They would have to be physically fit at the start of the march out in the spring or they would not make the distance.

He explained exactly what malnutrition was and how they were all showing the symptoms of it. There were now twenty-six left alive, with ten bodies shallowly buried nearby in an improvised cemetery. Another boy pointed out that to eat these bodies would not be wrong because their friends were already dead; it was not as if they were murdering each other to stay alive.

The pattern which followed was exactly that which had been enacted on the raft of the *Medusa*. There was initial reluctance, then a few became involved and as they grew stronger and the abstainers became obviously weaker, one by one all became involved. All bar one, that is—and he died. It was a grimmer version of the argument in the Jumbo concerning non-Kosher food. There were certain taboos which dictated the choice of corpse. The dead wife of a still-living survivor, by mutual agreement, was not consumed; certain dead friends were not eaten.

The survivors never were found, for the search had long been abandoned. Further, their situation was far worse than they had thought because while they believed themselves to be merely in the foothills of the Andes they were in fact in the middle, surrounded by mountain ranges. Nevertheless, in the spring Roberto Canessa, the medical student, and Fernando Parrado, a twenty-two-year-old engineering student, were still fit enough to walk and climb out of the icy mountains into the green foothills and bring help. The fourteen men who were still alive in the plane were rescued by helicopter. The rescuers were stunned by the scene. Pieces of human bodies, particularly feet, lay around. (Feet contained too many bones and too little flesh to be worth eating.) The rescuers thought, What have we saved—heroes or savages?

Just so had the French reacted to the fifteen survivors of the *Medusa*'s raft in 1816.

During my preliminary study for this book, I made a note: "In almost all disasters at sea, historians like to point out, there is some ennobling or moving feature. They decline to give the story of the *Medusa* the status of a tragedy because, they conclude, the victims were largely responsible for what happened to them. *I wonder how true that is?*"

# INDEX

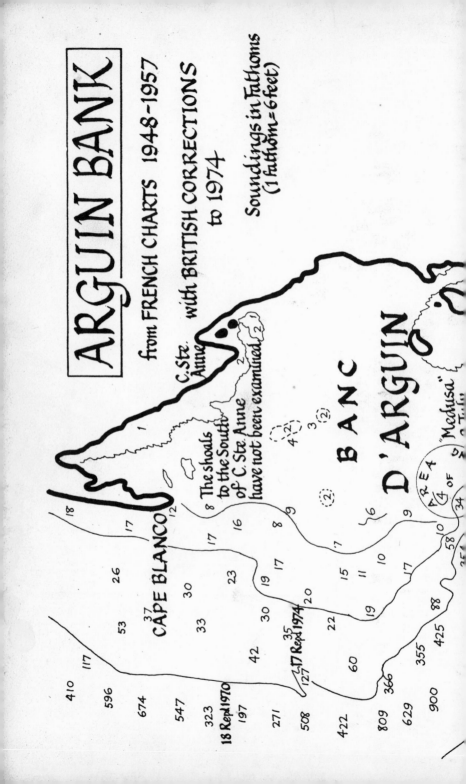

# ARGUIN BANK

from FRENCH CHARTS 1948–1957 with BRITISH CORRECTIONS to 1974

Soundings in Fathoms
(1 fathom = 6 feet)

C. Ste. Anne

The shoals to the South of C. Ste. Anne have not been examined

BANC D'ARGUIN

CAPE BLANCO

"Medusa"

AREA OF